NORMAL LIFE

NORMAL LIFE

Administrative Violence,
Critical Trans Politics, and the
Limits of Law

DEAN SPADE

South End Press
Brooklyn, NY

Cover design by Josh MacPhee/Justseeds.org
Page design and typeset by Josh MacPhee/Justseeds.org

Library of Congress Cataloging-in-Publication Data
Spade, Dean, 1977-
  Normal life : administrative violence, critical trans politics, and the limits of law / Dean Spade.
     p. cm.
  ISBN 978-0-89608-796-5 (pbk.) -- ISBN 978-0-89608-802-3 (ebook)
  1. Transgender people--Legal status, laws, etc.--United States. I. Title.
KF4754.5.S63 2011
342.7308'7–dc23

                                    2011034367

South End Press
Read. Write. Revolt.
PO Box 24773
Brooklyn, NY 11202
www.southendpress.org
southend@southendpress.org

Contents

Preface

In 2002, I opened the doors of the Sylvia Rivera Law Project (SRLP). I had raised enough grant money to rent a desk and a phone at a larger poverty law organization, and had spread the word to other service providers like drug treatment centers, legal aid offices, mental health centers, needle exchanges, and community organizations that I would be providing free legal help to trans people. I never would have guessed the number of people who would call the organization for help or the gravity and complexity of the problems they face.

My first call came from the men's jail in Brooklyn.[1] Jim, a 25-year-old transman, was desperate for help; he was facing a severe threat of rape and already experiencing harassment. Jim is a trans person with an intersex condition.[2] He was raised as a girl, but during adolescence began to identify as male. To his family he remained female-identified, but in the world he identified as male, changing clothes every night when he returned home and trying to avoid contact between his family and everyone else he knew. The stress of living a "double life" was immense, but he knew it was the only way to maintain a relationship with his family, with whom he was very close.

When Jim was nineteen, he was involved in a robbery for which he received a sentence of five years probation. During the second year of that probation period, Jim was arrested for drug possession. He was sentenced to eighteen months of residential drug treatment and sent to a male residential facility. In what was a purportedly therapeutic environment, Jim discussed his intersex condition with his counselor. His confidentiality was broken and soon the entire staff and residential population were aware of Jim's intersex condition and trans history. Jim faced a threat of rape and the staff of the facility refused to help or protect him. Out of fear and self-protection, he ran away from the facility.

I met Jim after he had turned himself in, wanting to deal with his outstanding criminal charges so that he could safely apply to college and get on with his life. Jim was now in a Brooklyn men's jail, again facing a threat of rape. The jail administration's refusal to continue Jim's testosterone treatments had caused him to menstruate; when Jim was strip searched while menstruating, other inmates and staff learned of his status.

Jim and I worked together to convince the judge assigned to his case that Jim could only safely access drug treatment services in an outpatient setting because of the dangers he faced in residential settings. Even when we had convinced the judge of this, we faced the fact that most programs were gender segregated, and would not be safe places for Jim to be known as a trans person with an intersex condition. When I contacted facilities to find a place for Jim, staff at all levels would ask me questions like "Does he pee sitting or standing?" and "Does he have a penis?" indicating to me that Jim would be treated as a novelty and his gender and body characteristics would be a source of gossip. Some facilities said they would not accept Jim because they were not prepared to work with someone like him. Those that did not outright refuse his application indicated their inadequacy to provide him with appropriate treatment. The few lesbian and gay drug treatment programs I identified seemed inappropriate because Jim did not identify as gay and was, in fact, quite unfamiliar with gay and lesbian people and somewhat uncomfortable in queer spaces. Eventually, the judge agreed to let Jim try outpatient treatment on a "zero tolerance" policy where a single relapse would result in jail time. Jim, under enormous stress, engaged in treatment where he was always afraid he might be outed and where his participation in the daily hours of group therapy required hiding his identity. Not surprisingly, Jim relapsed. Now he would be sentenced to prison.

When I went before the judge to request that Jim be placed in a women's prison because of his well-founded fear of sexual assault in men's facilities, the judge's response was, "He can't have it both ways." Once again, Jim's gender and body status and his inability to successfully navigate the gender requirements of the extremely violent systems in which he was entangled—because of his involvement in criminalized activity stemming from his poverty—was considered part of his criminality and a blameworthy status. The judge "threw the book" at Jim, sentencing him to the maximum number of years possible for violating parole and requiring him to serve the time in a men's prison.

Another client I met around the same time was Bianca, a nineteen-year-old transwoman. Bianca came to me for help with a range of issues. First, she wanted to sue her high school. In 1999, Bianca was attending public high school in the Bronx. After struggling with an internal understanding of herself as a woman for several years, Bianca eventually mustered the strength to come out to her peers and teachers. She and another transgender student, a close friend, decided to come out together. They arrived at school one day dressed to reflect their female gender identities. The two students were stopped at the front office and not allowed to enter school. Eventually, they were told to leave and not come back. When their parents called the school to follow up and find out what to do next, their calls were not returned. They were given no referrals to other schools, and no official suspension or expulsion hearings or documents. I met Bianca three years later. She had been unable to obtain legal representation, and when I began investigating the possibility of a lawsuit, I discovered that the statute of limitations had expired. She no longer had a viable legal claim.

When I met Bianca, she was homeless, unemployed, and trying to escape from an abusive relationship. She was afraid to go to the police both because of fear of retaliation from her boyfriend and because she rightly feared the police would not only refuse help, but also humiliate, harass, or hurt her because she was trans. All of her identification (ID) indicated a male name and gender; there would be no way for her to interact with the police without being identified as a trans person. As we searched for places for Bianca to live, we ran up against the fact that all of the homeless shelters insisted on placing her according to birth-assigned gender; Bianca would be the only woman in an all men's facility, and she was afraid of the abuse she could face in such a situation. Women's shelters for domestic violence survivors refused to recognize her as a woman and thus were unwilling to take her in. When Bianca applied for welfare, she was given an assignment to attend a job center as part of participation in a workfare program. When she tried to access the job center, she was brutally harassed outside, and when she finally entered and attempted to use the women's rest room, she was outed and humiliated by staff. Ultimately, she felt too unsafe to return and her benefits were terminated. Bianca's total lack of income also meant that she had no access to the hormone treatments she used to maintain a feminine appearance, which was emotionally necessary and kept her safe from some of the harassment and violence she faced when she was more easily identifiable as a transwoman on the street. Bianca felt her only option for finding income sufficient to pay for the hormones was to engage in criminalized sex work. At this point, she was forced to procure her hormone treatments in underground economies because it would have been cost prohibitive to obtain her medication from a doctor since Medicaid—had she even been given those benefits—would not cover the costs. This put her in further danger of police violence, arrest, and other violence. Additionally, because Bianca was accessing intravenously injected hormones through street economies, she was at greater risk of HIV, hepatitis, and other communicable diseases.

Jim's and Bianca's stories, it turned out, were not unusual. As the calls continued to pour into SRLP, I found there was an enormous number of people facing a series of interlocking problems related to being basically unfathomable to the administrative systems that govern the distribution of life chances: housing, education, health care, identity documentation and records, employment, and public facilities, to name but a few. My clients faced both the conscious bias of transphobia that produces targeted violence as well as numerous administrative catch–22s that render basic life necessities inaccessible. Each client's story demonstrated the inter-weaving of these different types of obstacles. On the bias side, I heard consistent reports of police profiling, police brutality, and false arrest; sexual harassment and assault; beatings and rapes; fir-ings from jobs; evictions; denials and rejections from caseworkers in social service and welfare agencies; rejections from legal services; and family rejection. The impact of each of these situations was exacerbated by the ways gender is an organizing principle of both the economy and the seemingly banal administrative systems that govern everyone's daily life, but have an especially strong presence in the lives of poor people. My clients did not fit into gendered administrative systems, and they paid the price in exclusion, vio-lence, and death. Most had no hope of finding legal employment because of the bias and violences they faced, and therefore turned to a combination of public benefits and criminalized work—often in the sex trade—in order to survive. This meant constant exposure to the criminal punishment system, where they were inevitably locked into gender-segregated facilities that placed them according to birth gender and exposed them to further violence. For immi-grants seeking an adjustment of status that would enable them to live legally in the United States, just one prostitution charge could destroy their eligibility. Even admitting that they had ever engaged in sex work to an immigration lawyer would disqualify them from receiving assistance with the adjustment of status process.

Non-immigrant clients also faced severe documentation problems and specific catch–22s related to identification and health care. Proof of having undergone gender-confirming health care, especially surgery, is required by the majority of ID-issuing agencies in the United States including Departments of Motor Vehicles (DMVs), the Social Security Administration (SSA), and departments issuing birth certificates to change gender on the ID.[3] However, the majority of private health insurers and state Medicaid programs have rules excluding this care from coverage, which means that those who cannot pay for this care out-of-pocket probably cannot get it and thus cannot change the gender on their IDs. In New York, this care is deemed essential for changing gender on birth certificates, though the state simultaneously has a Medicaid program that explicitly excludes this care from coverage. For most trans people, these rules make getting correct ID nearly impossible. Not having appropriate identification creates difficulties and dangers when dealing with employers or the police and other state agents, trying to travel, attempting to cash checks, or entering age-restricted venues: the person's trans identity is exposed every time ID is shown. These barriers make it exceedingly difficult for trans people to gain the economic resources necessary to obtain gender-confirming health care if this is something they want or need. These administrative policies and practices severely constrain access to health care and employment for most trans people.

The stories I heard from my first clients and continued to hear from the trans people I met through my work at SRLP portrayed a set of barriers—both from bias and from the web of inconsistent administrative rules governing gender—that produce significant vulnerability. The impact of these conditions ranges across subpopulations of trans people: even those with class privilege, education, white privilege, US citizenship, physical and mental ability perceived as average or above, and English-language skills experience many of these hurdles. Those with such privileges have many of the same ID problems, often cannot afford health care, experience incidents of physical attack, have their parental rights terminated by courts, are arrested for using bathrooms or barred from gender appropriate bathrooms at work and/or school, are discriminated against in hiring, are discriminated against by insurance companies, and lose family support. Most experience a downward mobility in terms of wealth/income because of their trans identities. However, access to certain privileges that serve in determining the distribution of life chances (e.g., whiteness, perceived ablebodiedness, employment, immigration status) often offer some individuals degrees of buffering from the violences faced by people of color, people with disabilities, immigrants, indigenous people, prisoners, foster youth, and homeless people. The most marginalized trans people experience more extreme vulnerability, in part because more aspects of their lives are directly controlled by legal and administrative systems of domination—prisons, welfare programs, foster care, drug treatment centers, homeless shelters, job training centers—that employ rigid gender binaries. These intersecting vectors of control make obtaining resources especially difficult, restrict access to zones of retreat or safety, and render every loss of a job, family support, or access to an advocate or a health care opportunity more costly. The most marginalized trans populations have the least protection from violence, experience more beatings and rapes, are imprisoned at extremely high rates, and are more likely to be disappeared and killed.

This book looks at the conditions that are shortening trans people's lives and investigates what role law plays in producing those conditions and what role law could or should play in changing them. In the last two decades, the public discourse about trans identities and trans rights has changed significantly. Concern about the exclusion of trans people from gay and lesbian political strategies has heightened. Media coverage of trans issues has increased. Emerging trans political formations have begun institutionalizing by creating new nonprofit organizations and professional associations focused specifically on trans issues, work that also produces new terminology, knowledge, and advocacy tools concerning gender identity and expression. These developments are raising important questions about trans politics. What is the relationship of trans political strategy to the strategies of the lesbian and gay rights work that has garnered so much attention in the last three decades? What role should law reform play in trans political strategy? How will forming nonprofits focused on trans issues impact trans people's lives and trans resistance politics? Who should lead and what forms of leadership should trans politics utilize? What relationship does trans politics have to other political movements and issues? Specifically, how does trans politics interface with anti-racism, feminism, anti-capitalism, anti-imperialism, immigration politics, and disability politics?

In proposing what role law reform should have in trans resistance, this book draws from the insights of Critical Race Theory, women of color feminism, queer theory, and critical disability studies to reveal the mistakes and limitations of white lesbian and gay rights strategies. Critical political and intellectual traditions have generated a vivid picture of the limitations of reform strategies focused on legal equality for movements seeking transformative political change. These traditions have highlighted the ineffectiveness of the discrimination principle as a method of identifying and addressing oppression, and have illustrated that legal declarations of "equality" are often tools for maintaining stratifying social and economic arrangements. Further, these traditions provide ways of understanding the operations of power and control that allow a more accurate identification of the conditions trans people are facing, and the development of more effective strategies for transformation than the liberal legal reform framework permits. Scholars and activists in these traditions such as Ruth Gilmore, Andrea Smith, Angela Davis, Lisa Duggan, Grace Hong, Roderick Ferguson, Chandan Reddy, and Angela Harris[4] describe the operation of key political developments, such as the decreasing bargaining power of workers, the dismantling of welfare programs, the growth of the prison industrial complex (PIC) and immigration enforcement, and the rise of the nonprofit formation, and also identify the complexities involved in practicing resistance politics in an age of cooptation and incorporation. This book examines these questions from a critical trans political perspective, applies the analysis these traditions have developed to the struggles facing trans people, and illustrates the ways trans resistance fits into the larger frameworks being developed in these conversations.

To that end, the chapters that follow raise concerns that have emerged with the institutionalization of the lesbian and gay rights agenda into a law reform-centered strategy. These concerns caution trans scholars and activists to learn from the limitations of that approach. The compromises made in lesbian and gay rights efforts to win formal legal equality gains have come with enormous costs: opportunities for coalition have been missed, large sectors of people affected by homophobia have been alienated, and the actual impact of the "victories" has been so limited as to neutralize their effect on the populations most vulnerable to the worst harms of homophobia. Further, the shifting discourse and strategy of lesbian and gay rights work toward privatization, criminalization, and militarization have caused it to be incorporated into the neoliberal agenda in ways that not only ignore, but also directly disserve and further endanger and marginalize, those most vulnerable to regimes of homophobia and state violence.

This book demands a reconsideration of the assumption that trans politics is the forgotten relative of the lesbian and gay rights strategy, and that its focus should be to seek recognition, inclusion, and incorporation similar to what has been sought by lesbian and gay rights advocates. Instead, I suggest that a more transformative approach exists for trans politics, one that more accurately conceptualizes the conditions trans people face and more directly strategizes change that impacts the well-being of trans people. Such an approach includes law reform work but does not center it, and instead approaches law reform work with the caution urged by the critical traditions to which trans politics is indebted and of which it is a part. It makes demands that exceed what can be won in a legal system that was formed by and exists to perpetuate capitalism, white supremacy, settler colonialism, and heteropatriarchy. It is rooted in a shared imagination of a world without imprisonment, colonialism, immigration enforcement, sexual violence, or wealth disparity. It is sustained by social movement infrastructure that is democratic, non-hierarchical, and centered in healing. This book aims to describe some of what that critical trans politics requires and suggest what models we already have and might expand for practicing critical trans politics.

NOTES

1. These two case studies are adapted from my article, "Compliance Is Gendered: Transgender Survival and Social Welfare," in *Transgender Rights: History, Politics and Law,* eds. Paisley Currah, Shannon Minter, and Richard Juang, (Minneapolis: University of Minnesota Press, 2006), 217–241.

2. "Intersex" is a term used to describe people who have physical conditions that medical professionals assert make them difficult to classify under current medical understandings of what constitutes a "male" or "female" body. Because of these understandings, they are often targets for medical intervention in childhood to make their bodies conform to gender norms. Extensive advocacy has been undertaken to stop these interventions and allow people with intersex conditions to choose whether or not they desire medical intervention that would bring their bodies into greater compliance with gender norms. Jim is a person with an intersex condition who is also transgender, but there is no evidence that people with intersex conditions are more or less likely than others to have a trans identity. For more information, see www.isna.org.

3. I have not included a complete list of current policies in this volume because they change frequently. However, my article "Documenting Gender," *Hastings Law Journal* 59 (2008):731-842, includes descriptions of state and local policies and their requirements as they existed at the time of publication. Advocacy organizations such as the Sylvia Rivera Law Project (www.srlp.org), the National Gay and Lesbian Task Force (www.thetaskforce.org), the National Center for Lesbian Rights (www.nclrights.org) and the National Center for Transgender Equality (www.

nctequality.org) can be contacted to obtain updates about changes to these policies.

4. See, e.g., Ruth Wilson Gilmore, *Golden Gulag: Prisons, Surplus, Crisis, and Opposition in Globalizing California* (Berkeley and Los Angeles: University of California Press, 2007); Angela Y. Davis, *Are Prisons Obsolete?* (New York: Seven Stories Press, 2003); Grace Kyungwon Hong, *The Ruptures of American Capital: Women of Color Feminism and the Culture of Immigrant Labor* (Minneapolis: University of Minnesota Press, 2006); Roderick Ferguson, *Aberrations in Black: Toward a Queer of Color Critique* (Minneapolis: University of Minnesota Press, 2003); Chandan Reddy, *Freedom with Violence: Race, Sexuality and the U.S. State* (Durham, NC: Duke University Press, 2011); Angela P. Harris, "From Stonewall to the Suburbs? Toward a Political Economy of Sexuality," *William and Mary Bill of Rights Journal* 14 (2006): 1539–1582; Lisa Duggan, *The Twilight of Equality? Neoliberalism, Cultural Politics, and the Attack on Democracy* (Boston: Beacon Press: 2004); and Andrea Smith, *Conquest: Sexual Violence and American Indian Genocide* (Cambridge, MA: South End Press, 2005).

Introduction
Rights, Movements,
and Critical Trans Politics

THIS BOOK HAS TWO PRIMARY GOALS. FIRST, IT AIMS TO CHART the current trajectory of trans politics, one that I argue is recapitulating the limits of leftist, lesbian and gay, feminist, and antiracist politics that have centered legal recognition and equality claims. Second, it seeks to elaborate on the possibilities of what I understand as a critical trans politics—that is, a trans politics that demands more than legal recognition and inclusion, seeking instead to transform current logics of state, civil society security, and social equality. In developing this two-fold account of contemporary trans politics I aim to reveal the indispensability of trans organizing and analysis for both leftist thinking and left social movements. Additionally, I aim to address specific sites of intersection where trans activists and organizers can and are finding common cause with some of the most important political agendas of our time: prison abolition, wealth redistribution, and organizing against immigration enforcement. Further, I hope to show how critical trans politics practices resistance. Following the traditions of women of color feminism, this critical approach to resistance refuses to take for granted national stories about social change that actually operate to maintain conditions of suffering and disparity.[1] It questions its own effectiveness, engaging in constant reflection and self-evaluation. And it is about practice and process rather than a point of arrival, resisting hierarchies of truth and reality and instead naming and refusing state violence.[2] Various social movements have had to contend with why legal change in the form of rights has not brought the deep transformation they were seeking, why disparities in life chances have increased during a period when we have seen the elimination of formal segregation and the advent of policies prohibiting discrimination on the basis of sex, race, and disability. Before trans people sign on to what looks good about being recognized by law in ways that seem desireable (e.g., being added to anti-discrimination and hate crime laws), we have to strongly consider why those laws have failed to provide the change that many have hoped for. We need a critical trans politics that perpetually questions its own effectiveness, that refuses to take for granted stories about what counts as change that actually maintain certain structures and categories. We need a critical trans politics that is about practice and process rather than arrival at a singular point of "liberation." To practice this politics we have to tackle some big questions about what law is, what power is, how legal systems are part of the distribution of life chances, and what role changing laws can and cannot have in changing the arrangements that cause such harm to trans people.

Social movements engaged in resistance have given us a very different portrayal of the United States than what is taught in most elementary school classrooms and textbooks. The patriotic narrative delivered at school tells us a few key lies about US law and politics: that the United States is a democracy in which law and policy derive from what a majority of people think is best, that the United States used to be racist and sexist but is now fair and neutral thanks to changes in the law, and that if particular groups experience harm, they can appeal to the law for protection. Social movements have challenged this narrative, identifying the United States as a settler colony and a racial project, founded and built through genocide and enslavement.[3] They have shown that the United States has always had laws that arrange people through categories of indigeneity, race, gender, ability, and national origin to produce populations with different levels of vulnerability to economic exploitation, violence, and poverty. These counter narratives have challenged the notion that violence is a result of private individuals with bad ideas and that the state is where we should look for protection from such violence. Conversely, resistant political theorists and social movements have helped us understand the concept of "state violence," which has been essential for exposing the central harms faced by native people, women, people of color, people with disabilities, and immigrants. They have exposed that state programs and law enforcement are not the arbiters of justice, protection, and safety but are instead sponsors and sites of violence. Additionally, this work has developed the understanding that power is decentralized and that certain practices, ways of knowing, norms, and technologies of power are distributed in myriad ways rather than only from a single person or institution. It has cautioned us against an overly narrow, simplified vision of power that sees power as a possession primarily held by government officials.[4] This perspective eliminates the false notion that we could win the change people need simply by using the electoral process to vote in certain representatives or pass certain laws. It helps us investigate how the norms that produce conditions of disparity and violence emerge from multiple, interwoven locations, and recognize possibilities for resistance as similarly dispersed.

When movement organizers, activists, and intellectuals use various terms that end in "industrial complex," like "military industrial complex" or "prison industrial complex," they are pointing to this kind of multivector analysis of law, power, knowledge, and norms. For example, the term prison industrial complex (PIC) reframes the issue of criminal punishment. It contests the dominant story that tells us that bad individuals need to be exiled to prison to keep others safe. That story casts juried trials as fair and impartial ways of determining who deserves to be punished. Instead, using the term "prison industrial complex" suggests that multiple, connected processes and forces determine how certain populations get labeled as "criminal," how certain behaviors and actions come to be classified as crimes, how racist ideas are mobilized to justify an expansion of imprisonment systems, how various financial interests are implicated in motivating law enforcement expansion, and how criminalization and imprisonment filter through every aspect of how we live and understand ourselves and the world. Living in a society defined by criminalization and imprisonment shapes how we design and build schools and discipline kids who are perceived to misbehave. It relates to how we frame issues in the news and in entertainment media. It relates to how we run homeless services, agriculture policy, elections, and health care systems. It relates to the availability of finance capital and so much more.[5]

This kind of analysis helps us understand that there is not one source of power, no one person at the top dominating everyone below. Rather, there are regimes of practices and knowledge that coalesce in conditions and arrangements that affect everyone and that make certain populations highly vulnerable to imprisonment. Such an analysis also suggests that there is much work to be done to dismantle the trend of racialized-gendered mass imprisonment—in many locations, not just in legislatures, courts, or police precincts. Understanding how the forces producing imprisonment and criminalization operate at multiple sites and registers ranging from laws and policies to education, health care, social service, media, and even our own self-conceptions helps us both account for the enormity of the significance of imprisonment and understand that addressing it is not simply a matter of appealing to one central source of power or decision-making. Power is not a matter of one dominant individual or institution, but instead manifests in interconnected, contradictory sites where regimes of knowledge and practice circulate and take hold.

This way of understanding the dispersion of power helps us realize that power is not simply about certain individuals being targeted for death or exclusion by a ruler, but instead about the creation of norms that distribute vulnerability and security. When we think about power this way, we undertake a different kind of examination of conditions that concern us, asking different questions. Mitchell Dean describes how this kind of analysis attends to

> the routines of bureaucracy; the technologies of notation, recording, compiling, presenting and transporting of information, the theories, programmes, knowledge and expertise that compose a field to be governed and invest it with purposes and objectives; the ways of seeing and representing embedded in practices of government; and the different agencies with various capacities that the practices of government require, elicit, form and reform. To examine regimes of government is to conduct analysis in the plural: there is already a plurality of regimes of practices in a given territory, each composed from a multiplicity of in principle unlimited and heterogeneous elements bound together by a variety of relations and capable of polymorphous connections with one another. Regimes of practices can be identified whenever there exists a relatively stable field of correlation of visibilities, mentalities, technologies and agencies, such that they constitute a kind of taken-for-granted point of reference for any form of problematization.[6]

This kind of analysis can be seen in the work of those using "industrial complex" terms to describe and resist the forces of militarization and criminal punishment that pervade US society. It can also be seen in the work that has been done for disability justice. Critical disability studies and the disability rights and disability justice movements have shown us how regimes of knowledge and practices in every area of life establish norms of "healthy" bodies and minds, and consign those who are perceived to fall outside those norms to abandonment and imprisonment. Policies and practices rooted in eugenics have attempted (and continue to attempt) to eliminate the existence of people who fall outside those norms. Native scholars and activists have shown how white European cultural norms determine everything from what property is to what gender and family structure should look like, and how every instance of the imposition of these norms have been used in the service of the genocide of indigenous people. In these locations and many others, we can see how the circulation of norms creates an idea that undergirds conditions of violence, exploitation, and poverty that social movements have resisted—the idea that the national population (constructed as those who meet racial, gender, sexual, ability, national origin, and other norms) must be protected from those "others" (those outside of such norms) who are portrayed again and again in new iterations at various historical moments as "threats" or "drains." This operation of norms is central to producing the idea of the national body as ever-threatened and to justifying the exclusion of certain populations from programs that distribute wealth and life chances (white schools, Social Security benefits, land and housing distribution programs) and the targeting of these same populations for imprisonment and violence (including criminal punishment, immigration enforcement, racist drug laws, sterilization, and medical experimentation). Even though norms are incorporated into various spaces and institutions inconsistently and applied arbitrarily, they still achieve the overall purpose of producing security for some populations and vulnerability for others. Many social movements have produced analyses of how various groups are harmed by the promotion of a national identity centered in norms about race, bodies, health, gender, and reproduction. These constructs often operate in the background and are presumed as "neutral" features of various administrative systems. The existence and operation of such administrative norms is therefore less visible than those moments when people are fired or killed or excluded explicitly because of their race or body type or gender, yet they sometimes produce more significant harm because they structure the entire context of life. I am going to return again and again in the chapters that follow to key examples, such as the dismantling of welfare programs and the expansion of criminal and immigration enforcement, that are central to contemporary politics and help illustrate how life chances are distributed through racialized-gendered systems of meaning and control, often in the form of programs that attest to be race- and gender-neutral and merely administrative.

Throughout this book, I use the term "subjection" to talk about the workings of systems of meaning and control such as racism, ableism, sexism, homophobia, transphobia, and xenophobia. I use "subjection" because it indicates that power relations impact how we know ourselves as subjects through these systems of meaning and control—the ways we understand our own bodies, the things we believe about ourselves and our relationships with other people and with institutions, and the ways we imagine change and transformation. I use "subjection" rather than "oppression" because "oppression" brings to mind the notion that one set of people are dominating another set of people, that one set of people "have power" and another set are denied it. As I will argue in more detail in Chapter 3, the operations of power are more complicated than that. If we seek to imagine transformation, if we want to alleviate harm, redistribute wealth and life chances, and build participatory and accountable resistance formations, our strategies need to be careful not to oversimplify how power operates. Thinking about power only as top/down, oppressor/oppressed, dominator/dominated can cause us to miss opportunities for intervention and to pick targets for change that are not the most strategic. The term "subjection" captures how the systems of meaning and control that concern us permeate our lives, our ways of knowing about the world, and our ways of imagining transformation.

For example, racism does not only occur in moments when individual people of color are excluded from employment opportunities by individual white people. Racism also occurs when media perpetuate stereotypes about people of color. Racism determines policy discussions about everything from health care to agriculture to national security. Racism shapes how individuals and communities see ourselves and understand our relationships to one another. Racism determines what schools will be well funded and which communities will be sited for toxic industry. Racism shapes how things like beauty, reason, intelligence, and enterprise are culturally defined. Racism determines who will be arrested, what public benefits programs will be cut, and what behaviors will be considered criminal. Racism does not just flow from the top down but rather permeates the entire field of action. The invention of racial categories—the "racialization" of peoples—was essential to establishing the interests in land and labor that founded the United States.[7] The continued maintenance and reinvention of racial categories and new sites of racialization have been essential to the distribution of wealth and life chances. Similarly, the shifting understandings of gender, ability, and migration—and the meanings attached to different populations through those shifts—determine who lives, for how long, and under what conditions. They also frame all discussions of what resisting harmful arrangements can look like. "Subjection" is a term that tries to capture that complexity and the significance of how thoroughly our ways of living, thinking, and knowing ourselves and the world are imbued with the meanings and distributions wrought through these various categories of identity, and how multifaceted the relations of these categories are to one another.

This way of thinking about how systems of meaning and control operate helps us acknowledge how important constant self-reflection is and how essential participatory movements that center the leadership of people facing the most direct harms from systems of subjection are. This way of thinking about power and control can also help us spot traps of co-optation and incorporation that our resistance projects face. This book looks at how legal reform itself sometimes operates as one such trap.

While this book is about how power works, it is also about resistance. It is about the strategies emerging from a population often identified by its failure to meet norms associated with gender. This text proposes a politics rooted in questioning how those norms come to be and how they impact—and extinguish—the lives of trans people. It also considers how norms like these become part of the resistance itself, and proposes a trans politics that tirelessly interrogates processes of normalization by analyzing their impacts and revising its resistance strategies as it observes their unintended consequences. To do so, this book examines what relationship trans politics has to "individual rights"—the framework most frequently articulated by the demands of many contemporary social movements—and investigates other ways to conceive of law reform tactics in trans resistance that forgo the limitations of demands for individual rights.

The critical analysis built by many resistant social movements illuminates the limitations of a theory of law reform that aims to punish the "few bad apples" supposedly responsible for racism, sexism, ableism, xenophobia, or transphobia. It also helps us understand why, since US law has been structured from its inception to create a racialized-gendered distribution of life chances that perpetuates violence, genocide, land theft, and exploitation, we will not resolve those issues solely by appealing to law. We must also be cautious not to believe what the law says about itself since time and again the law has changed, been declared newly neutral or fair or protective, and then once more failed to transform the conditions of disparity and violence that people were resisting. Given the insights gleaned from social movements that have wrangled with violent legal regimes and with law reform strategies, this book aims to think through how a critical trans politics might conceptualize the role of law reform in our resistance struggles. If we refuse to believe what the law says about itself, if we understand that power does not operate through the domination of a central figure or institution over the masses but is instead diverse, multifaceted, and decentralized, and if we realize that the transformation needed to address the kinds of conditions I described in the Preface will not, and cannot, come through law, how do we engage with legal reform?

I argue that because laws operate as tactics in the distribution of life chances that concern us, we must approach law reform tactically. Meaningful transformation will not occur through pronouncements of equality from various government institutions. Transformative change can only arise through mass mobilization led by populations most directly impacted by the harmful systems that distribute vulnerability and security. Law reform tactics can have a role in mobilization-focused strategies, but law reform must never constitute the sole demand of trans politics. If we seek transformation that is more than symbolic and that reaches those facing the most violent manifestations of transphobia, we must move beyond the politics of recognition and inclusion.

This book places the rise of discourse about trans identities and advocacy for trans recognition in the context of broader political and economic developments—some mainstays of a late 20th-century political economy and other more recent transformations of state and civil society including the emergence of a neoliberal global economy, the War on Terror, the rollback of 1960s and 70s welfare state and civil rights gains, the rise of the nonprofit industrial complex (NPIC), the rapid growth of imprisonment, and the ascendancy of a lesbian and gay rights agenda articulated through liberal notions of privacy and equal opportunity. These political and economic changes must be considered in order to fully understand the conditions shaping trans resistance. In the face of increasing disparities in wealth and life chances domestically and globally, what do promises of "anti-discrimination" or "equal opportunity" actually deliver? What might trans law reformers learn from social movements that have won formal legal protections but whose constituencies remain criminalized and economically marginalized? And how can such critical, historical analysis help reconceptualize the role of law and rights in trans resistance struggles?

Normal Life: Administrative Violence, Critical Trans Politics, and the Limits of Law raises questions about the usefulness of the most commonly articulated legal interventions for transgender rights:

anti-discrimination laws and hate crime laws. It asserts that a different location within the law—the administrative realm—may be the place to look for how law structures and reproduces vulnerability for trans populations. I argue that the anti-discrimination/hate crime law strategy actually misunderstands how power works and what role law has in the functions of power. The anti-discrimination/hate crime law strategy relies on the belief that if we change what the law says about a particular group to make it say "good things" (e.g., creating laws that say you are not allowed to fire someone just because they are trans) and not "bad things" (e.g., eliminating laws that explicitly criminalize people for cross-dressing or having certain kinds of sex) then those people's lives will improve. This approach to law reform relies on an individual rights framework that emphasizes harms caused to individuals by other individuals who kill or fire them because they are members of the group. It seeks remedies that punish individuals who do those harmful things motivated by bias. This analysis misunderstands how power functions and can lead to approaches to law reform that actually expand the reach of violent and harmful systems. In order to properly understand power and transphobic harm, we need to shift our focus from the individual rights framing of discrimination and "hate violence" and think more broadly about how gender categories are enforced on all people in ways that have particularly dangerous outcomes for trans people. Such a shift requires us to examine how administrative norms or regularities create structured insecurity and (mal)distribute life chances across populations. This attention to the distribution of life chances acknowledges that even when laws are changed to say different things about a targeted group, that group may still experience disproportionate poverty as well as lack of access to health care, housing, and education. Those law reforms do nothing to prevent violences like criminalization and immigration enforcement. Legal systems that have official rules of nondiscrimination still operate in ways that disadvantage whole populations—and this is not due solely, or even primarily, to individual bias.

I argue for a model of thinking about power and law that expands our analysis to examine systems that administer life chances through purportedly "neutral" criteria, understanding that those systems are often locations where racist, sexist, homophobic, ableist, xenophobic, and transphobic outcomes are produced. Through this lens, we look more at impact than intent. We look more at what legal regimes do rather than what they say about what they do. We look at how vulnerability is distributed across populations, not just among individuals. This allows us to shape resistance strategies that have a better chance at actually addressing the conditions that concern us, rather than just changing the window-dressing that attends them.

While there are a number of critical paradigms for evaluating legal equality, this book emerges out of the space opened by Critical Race Theory's comprehension of the paradox of rights: rights mediate emergent social groups, and rights claims often serve as the resistance framework of such groups, yet declarations of universal rights often actually mask and perpetuate the structured conditions of harm and disparity faced by those groups. Critical Race Theory is an intellectual movement that emerged in the late 1980s that studies and seeks to transform the relationship between race and the structures of contemporary society, including the law.

Key thinkers in the Critial Race Theory field such as Derek Bell, Kimberlé Crenshaw, and Cheryl Harris have made arguments that have rocked legal scholarship at its roots. They have critiqued the law reforms of the civil rights movement, suggesting that those reforms did not sufficiently alter conditions facing people of color, and arguing that racism is inherent in US law. Derek Bell's "interest-convergence" theory asserts that "[t]he interest of blacks in achieving racial equality will be accommodated only when it converges with the interests of whites."[8] This argument suggests that those interested in ending white supremacy must look critically at purported legal victories, recognizing that they are often merely adjustments that maintain systems of control and maldistribution. Cheryl Harris's article "Whiteness as Property" exposed how US property law is rooted in racialized property statuses that attend chattel slavery, genocide, and land theft, and how US law has continued to produce whiteness as a form of property at the expense of people of color.[9] Kimberlé Crenshaw's theory of "intersectionality" has significantly influenced scholarship and social movements far outside of law schools.[10] Her work argues that people who experience multiple vectors of subjection, for example racism and sexism, face unique harms not captured by racial justice movements that use male experience as the norm or feminist movements that use white women's experience as the norm. These works, and other key interventions made by critical race theorists, have inspired critical scholars in law and many other fields to examine the operations of law and racialization from new perspectives.

Normal Life draws from the insights of Critical Race Theory and also modifies and reworks these insights for the specificities of a critical trans analysis. Critical Race Theory has identified the barriers that dominant legal models of intentional discrimination—with their focus on punishing individual discriminators—have created to solve subordination. It has also drawn attention to the distributive functions of law, providing solutions that avoid the liberal pitfall of individualizing conceptions of both oppressors and victims. *Normal Life* takes up this approach and expands its analysis further into the domain of administrative law in order to illustrate how modes of administrative governance produce what we come to think of as natural or pre-existing identities. This book argues that rather than looking to the typical areas of "equality law" such as anti-discrimination law or hate crime law to inquire about and intervene in harm facing targeted and vulnerable populations, we should look at the administrative governance that typically comes from state agencies like departments of Health, Motor Vehicles, Corrections, Child Welfare, and Education, and federal agencies like the Customs and Border Protection, U.S. Immigration and Customs Enforcement (ICE), the Bureau of Indian Affairs, the Bureau of Prisons, the Food and Drug Administration, and the Environmental Protection Administration. Rather than understanding administrative systems merely as responsible for sorting and managing what "naturally" exists, I argue that administrative systems that classify people actually invent and produce meaning for the categories they administer, and that those categories manage both the population and the distribution of security and vulnerability. Such an analysis allows us to reframe trans politics in terms of the distribution of life chances and brings us to new and different questions about why trans people suffer from economic marginalization, criminalization, and deportation, and what can be done about it.

Normal Life asks us to redirect attention away from recognition-and-inclusion-focused law reforms that are often assumed to be the natural legal reform targets of trans resistance, perhaps because they have been the targets of gay and lesbian legal reform. Rather than a focus on changing the law in ways that are supposed to declare the equality and worth of trans people's lives but in fact prove to have little impact on the daily lives of the people they purportedly protect, a distributive analysis suggests a focus on laws and policies that produce systemic norms and regularities that make trans people's lives administratively impossible. I will specifically discuss three areas of law and policy that have a very significant impact on trans people's lives: rules that govern gender classification on ID, rules that govern sex-segregation of key institutions (shelters, group homes, jails, prisons, bathrooms), and rules that govern access to gender-confirming health care for trans people.[11] This book reconceptualizes the role of law reform in trans resistance strategies, arguing against a focus on what the law says about trans people and for a focus on intervening in the law and policy venues that most directly impact the survival of trans people as part of a broader trans politics whose demands are not limited to formal legal equality. By exposing the limits of formal legal equality and examining the conditions facing trans communities, this book brings us to the larger question of whether legal recognition and inclusion are felicitous goals for trans politics. It suggests that such goals undermine the disruptive potential of trans resistance and also threaten to divide potential alliances among trans people, such as cross-race, cross-class, and cross-ability alliances, as they have in lesbian and gay politics. Legal equality goals threaten to provide nothing more than adjustments to the window-dressing of neoliberal violence that ultimately disserve and further marginalize the most vulnerable trans populations. As an alternative, the book proposes a politics based upon the so-called "impossible" worldview of trans political existence. Such a politics builds from the space created by the insistence of government agencies, social service providers, media, and many nontrans activists and nonprofiteers that the existence of trans people is impossible and/or that our issues are not politically viable. *Normal Life* suggests these challenges are potential starting points for a trans politics that openly opposes liberal and neoliberal agendas and finds solidarity with other struggles articulated by the forgotten, the inconceivable, the spectacularized, and the unimaginable. Finding overlap and inspiration in the analysis and resistance articulated through women of color feminism, disability justice politics, prison abolition, and other struggles against colonialism, criminalization, immigration enforcement, and capitalism has far more to offer trans people. Developing this framework for our resistance will also contribute trans understandings of the necessary analytical, strategic, and tactical tools and models to other emerging formations that are struggling to formulate resistance to neoliberalism in these complex and difficult times.

Chapter One, "Trans Law and Politics on a Neoliberal Landscape," introduces the central concern of this book: what does or could trans politics mean in the current political context and how should we understand strategies for trans legal reform in these times? To begin that inquiry, I describe the set of trends organized under the term "neoliberalism," including policy changes like privatization, trade liberalization, labor and environmental deregulation, the elimination of health and welfare programs, increased immigration enforcement, and the expansion of imprisonment. These forces, together, have contributed to an overall upward distribution of wealth and drastically decreased life chances for poor people.[12] The hallmarks of neoliberalism are co-optation and incorporation, meaning that the words and ideas of resistance movements are frequently recast to produce results that disserve the initial purposes for which they were deployed, and instead become legitimizing tools for white supremacist, capitalist, patriarchal, ableist political agendas.[13] These trends have had significant impacts on social movements in the United States, harming their constituents and undermining the effectiveness of their resistance. In the last three decades we have seen a massive growth in imprisonment, a dismantling of our social safety nets, decreasing job security, a rollback of 1960s civil rights gains, and the advent of the War on Drugs and the War on Terror, both of which shifted massive public resources toward racist surveillance and increased criminalization of poor people and people of color.[14] At the same time, the ability of social movements to respond to these changes has been hampered by the drastic consolidation of the corporate media, wealthy philanthropists' control over movement agendas through the nonprofitization of activism, the abandonment of essential poverty alleviation programs and social services by local, state, and federal governments, and the targeted dismantling of the most important movements of the 1960s and 1970s by the Federal Bureau of Investigation (FBI).[15]

In the context of these trends, activists and scholars have observed that many social movements have become more conservative, abandoning goals of radical redistribution and taking up agendas that fit more closely with neoliberal ideas.[16] Lesbian and gay rights work has received a great deal of critique on this front as it has drifted toward a legal rights agenda (anti-discrimination protections, marriage rights, and military inclusion) that provides little redress for the growing numbers of people confronting reduced life chances in the face of an increasing wealth divide, growing criminalization and immigration enforcement, and endless war. As trans activism has emerged more visibly, and trans populations have increasingly described experiences of economic marginalization and criminalization, an important set of questions has emerged. Should trans activism follow the strategies, deemed "successful" by some, of the lesbian and gay legal reform agenda? For which trans people would such strategies win gains and for whom might they worsen conditions? This book argues that we must depart from the models created by most well-funded lesbian and gay rights nonprofits, and proposes an approach aimed at producing resistance that will actually address the criminalization, poverty, and violence that trans people face every day.

Chapter Two, "What's Wrong with Rights?," examines the most common legal interventions taken up in the struggle for trans rights thus far: gender identity–inclusive anti-discrimination and hate crime laws. These strategies have been marketed by the most well-funded lesbian and gay legal reform organizations as the benchmarks of trans equality and the key aims of the trans component of the emergent "LGBT" politics. Chapter Two analyzes the limitations of these two reforms, examining why the campaigns that have been deemed successful in these areas have not sufficiently improved the lives of trans people. Anti-discrimination laws have failed to address the legal issues that create the greatest vulnerabilities for trans people: criminalization, immigration enforcement, lack of access to ID that reflects the current gender, placement in sex-segregated facilities (bathrooms, shelters, residential treatment programs), and exclusions of gender-confirming health care for trans people from Medicaid, private insurance policies, and various health care programs for people in state custody. Further, anti-discrimination laws (if/where they are in place) are generally not enforced for any of the groups covered by them. Courts have made it very hard to prevail in cases attempting to enforce anti-discrimination laws, and discrimination on the basis of race, disability, and sex, for example, are still commonplace despite being officially illegal. As critiques of deterrence models of criminal punishment have shown elsewhere, hate crime laws do nothing to prevent violence against transgender people but instead focus on mobilizing resources for criminal punishment systems' response to such violence. Because trans people are frequent targets of criminal punishment systems and face severe violence at the hands of police and in prisons every day, investment in such a system for solving safety issues actually stands to increase harm and violence.

To get at the limitations of these strategies, this chapter introduces core concepts from Critical Race Theory that explain why rights frameworks that focus on individual discrimination through the "perpetrator perspective" fail and how they obscure structural racism. Using these tools, this chapter illustrates how the US legal system's conceptualization of racism, particularly the discrimination principle's reliance on individualism, simultaneously hides and preserves conditions of subjection. Further, it suggests that focusing on trans experiences not addressed by the discrimination/hate crime paradigm can lead us to a more robust vision of what structural disparity is, what the law's role in producing it really looks like, and what role law reform might have in addressing it.

Chapter Three, "Rethinking Transphobia and Power—Beyond a Rights Framework," introduces an alternative way of thinking about power and systems of meaning and control that departs from traditional legal frameworks of discrimination and equality, and reflects the marginalization being described by trans people. Having analyzed the limitations of what the discrimination doctrine allows us to recognize as subjection (intentional, individual discrimination), and having examined how the shift toward such a limited "formal legal equality" approach is part of a neoliberal abandonment of the broad redistribution demands of prior social movements, we now uncover a framework for thinking about law and power that better understands the harm facing trans populations. This chapter explains key concepts from critical disability studies, Critical Race

Theory, women of color feminism, and from the work of Michel
Foucault to describe a way of thinking about power based in an
analysis of the distribution of life chances. These interventions
provide an entry point into thinking about subjection and
control beyond the realm of intentional, individual bias or
violence, and instead interrogates empty declarations of "equal
opportunity" and "equality" promoted in US law. Using these
conceptual tools, we examine the complex vectors leading to high
rates of unemployment,[17] homelessness,[18] and imprisonment for
trans people, and trace how the administration of life chances
through traditional gender categories produces trans vulnerability
to premature death.[19] Focusing on key administrative barriers to
trans survival, especially access to ID, placement in sex-segregated
facilities, and access to health care, this chapter argues that the
best opportunities for legal intervention to combat transphobia
are different from what is imagined by the legal equality model.
The conceptual tools introduced in this chapter allow us to think
in terms of populations and the allocation of resources and life
chances, and redirect our attention from discrimination-focused
law reforms toward the administrative apparatuses in law that
mobilize race, gender, and ability classifications to promote and
maximize certain forms of life and ways of being. This analysis
allows a critical approach to the role of legal reform in trans
resistance, generating a different way to think about law reform
work on the whole.

Chapter Four, "Administrating Gender," applies this analysis
to three specific areas of law where the administration of gender
norms causes trans people the most trouble: identification, sex
segregation, and access to health care. A brief summary of the
current state of the law in these realms in the United States reveals the inconsistency of laws and policies in this area between
different states and even between different agencies within any
given state. These inconsistencies expose how gender is already
an unstable category in US law. This instability, when combined
with the rigidity of administrative gender enforcement, produces

myriad catch–22s that generate insecurity and violence in the lives of trans people, especially in the context of the War on Terror in which inconsistencies in identifying information have become a more significant obstacle to most basic and essential administrative processes. This chapter illustrates how anti-discrimination and hate crime laws fail to target the most urgent legal problems of trans populations. It further conceptualizes how the administrative focus of areas like poverty law, immigration law, and disability law are the proper targets of trans law reform interventions. Administrative systems often appear "neutral," especially when discrimination has been framed as a problem of individuals with bad intentions who need to be prohibited from their bad acts by law. This chapter reveals how systems like public benefits and housing programs, work eligibility verification programs, criminal and immigration enforcements systems, and health care programs that purport to distribute life chances through neutral and standard criteria are in fact sites of significant harm. Rather than imagining law or government as the protector of trans people from bashers or discriminators, we see that the very administrative systems that determine what populations the law exists to promote and protect are the greatest sources of danger and violence for trans people. Viewing trans marginalization through an examination of law's administrative functions rather than a focus on whether law declares certain groups equal opens a space for imagining a trans resistance law reform agenda that centralizes race, indigeneity, poverty, immigration, and disability analysis. With this understanding, we can focus less on what the law says about itself and the rights of individuals and more on what impact various legal regimes have on distressed populations.

Chapter Five, "Law Reform and Movement Building," considers the broader question of how to place law reform projects within trans movement building. The most well-funded lesbian and gay rights organizations have been criticized for focusing on law reform goals, with critics arguing that such focus yields only formal legal equality gains that do not reach the most vulnerable targets of homophobia.[20] I argue that there is a place for law reform projects within effective trans resistance, but law reform should not be the central demand of trans resistance. Instead, I suggest four specific roles for law reform projects. First, they can be tools for helping trans people survive in order that they might participate in and lead grassroots organizing work. Because trans people face enormous vulnerability and violence in a variety of legal systems, law reform and individual legal assistance (deportation, eviction, and criminal defense, for example) are vital tools for trans movement organizations in order to support the members they seek to organize. Second, because of the enormous role of harmful administrative and legal apparatuses in trans people's lives, legal help can be an excellent point of politicization for trans people, turning individual experiences of harm into a shared understanding of collective struggle. Often those who come for legal help on a particular issue, if they are invited into membership to do broader work, will learn about experiences different from their own, grow solidarity analysis, and deepen and expand their political understanding and commitment to resistance. Third, law reform campaigns can produce opportunities for organizing that develop new leaders. Finally, law reform strategies can be part of campaigns that aim to expose contradictions in systems of control, sometimes shifting paradigms with that exposure.

All four of these roles point to an organizing theory of change focused on mass mobilization that raises demands that exceed what can be accomplished in the narrow realm of contemporary litigation and policy reform. Demands that are emerging in trans communities, like prison abolition, the elimination of poverty, access to full health care, and an end to immigration enforcement cannot be conceptualized or won within the realm of US law. For this reason, centralizing law reform demands and the leadership of lawyers only stands to limit the horizons of trans political interventions—and puts trans resistance work at risk of colluding with a neoliberal agenda and with the white supremacy and settler colonialism that US law is founded upon.

Chapter Five, "Law Reform and Movement Building," also introduces the Four Pillars of Social Justice Infrastructure, a tool developed by the Miami Workers' Center (MWC),[21] which articulates the ways that elite strategies like law reform, while components of social movements, undermine the possibility for mass mobilization that produces transformative change when they are centered. Activists and scholars have observed a shift in movements from mass-based grassroots strategies of the 1960s and 70s to professionalized, funded, nonprofit formations that are dominant today. By "professionalized" I mean to point out that whereas resistance movements have previously been dominated by membership-based grassroots organizations with little staffing, the last few decades have seen an explosion of nonprofits that have changed movement work and expectations to look more like a career track for people with graduate degrees. These new formations are dominated by norms typical of other professions, including unequal pay scales, poor working conditions for people without race, class, and education privilege, and hierarchical decision-making structures. Taking on the institutional norms associated with "professionalism" has decreased the accountability of much movement work. Long term goals of transformative change have been replaced with short term fundraising goals managed by people who get paid to shape the work to match funders' tastes. This chapter suggests ways that trans activists might avoid common traps inherent to this institutionalization. It looks at some of the major concerns with institutionalization, especially nonprofitization, and explores principles, strategies, and models that racial and economic justice–focused trans organizations are developing to address them.

Trans resistance is emerging in a context of neoliberal politics where the choice to struggle for nothing more than incorporation into the neoliberal order is the most obvious option. We can translate the pain of having community members murdered every month into more punishing power for the criminal system that targets us. We can fight to have the state declare us equal through anti-discrimination laws, yet watch as the majority of trans people remain unemployed, incapable of getting ID, kept out of social services and health care, and consigned to prisons that guarantee sexual assault and medical neglect. Abandonment and imprisonment remain the offers of neoliberalism for all but a few trans people, yet law reform strategies beckon us to join the neoliberal order. The paths to equality laid out by the "successful" lesbian and gay rights model to which we are assumed to aspire have little to offer us in terms of concrete change to our life chances; what they offer instead is the legitimization and expansion of systems that are killing us.

Trans people are told by the law, state agencies, private discriminators, and our families that we are impossible people who cannot exist, cannot be seen, cannot be classified, and cannot fit anywhere. We are told by the better-funded lesbian and gay rights groups, as they continually leave us aside, that we are not politically viable; our lives are not a political possibility that can be conceived. Inside this impossibility, I argue, lies our specific political potential—a potential to formulate demands and strategies to meet those demands that exceed the containment of neoliberal politics. A critical trans politics is emerging that refuses empty promises of "equal opportunity" and "safety" underwritten by settler colonialism, racist, sexist, classist, ableist, and xenophobic imprisonment, and ever-growing wealth disparity. This politics aims to center the concerns and leadership of the most vulnerable and to build transformative change through mobilization. It is reconceptualizing the role of law reform in social movements, acknowledging that legal equality demands are a feature of systemic injustice, not a remedy. It is confronting the harms that come to trans people at the hands of violent systems structured through law itself—not by demanding recognition and inclusion in those systems, but by working to dismantle them while simultaneously supporting those most exposed to their harms. This critical trans politics is part of a larger framework of resistance that must grapple with the complex relationships between power, law, and violence, and the obstacles social movements are facing in the context of neoliberalism.

NOTES

1. As Grace Hong has observed, "Women of color feminist practice identifies the state as a site of violence, not resolution, and in so doing, it displaces rights-based struggles. . . . Further, unlike single-axis forms of organizing, such as the mainstream white feminist movement, traditional labor organizing, or race-based movements, women of color feminism's insistence on difference, coalitional politics, and a careful examination of the intersecting processes of race, gender, sexuality, and class, which make singular identifications impossible, displaces a U.S. nationalist subject formation based on homogeneity, equivalence, and identification." Grace Hong, *The Ruptures of American Capital: Women of Color Feminism and the Culture of Immigrant Labor* (Minneapolis: University of Minnesota Press, 2006), xiv. Jodi Melamed has argued, "Women of color feminism's 'theory in the flesh' demands a reckoning with the full materiality of the lives of women of color in a way that gives the lie to the divisions of knowledge and epistemic structures that at once constitute and disavow the links between liberal freedoms and regulatory violence, while insisting—as a political collectivity—on 'something else to be,' on the need to act communally to craft social relations and value forms relatively unbound from those of capitalist globalization." Jodi Melamed, "Rationalizing Violence in the New Racial Capitalism," Critical Ethnic Studies and the Future of Genocide Conference, University of California, Riverside, March 11, 2011, 10.

2. Chela Sandoval, *Methodology of the Oppressed* (Minneapolis: University of Minnesota Press, 2000), 54.

3. Saidiya Hartman's book, *Scenes of Subjection: Terror, Slavery, and Self-Making in Nineteenth Century America* (New York: Oxford Press, 1997), is a particularly useful tool for understanding how the formal end of slavery did not have the liberatory significance for Black people in the United States that national narratives suggest, but instead marked a

transition to new forms of the same relations of subjection. She suggests that the national narrative about "equal rights" is, itself, a feature of this continued subjection. She writes, "the double bind of equality and exclusion distinguishes modern state racism from its antebellum predecessor" and "the wedding of equality and exclusion" is "commonplace . . . in the liberal state." 9–10. Her work "examine[s] the role of rights in facilitating relations of domination. . . . From this vantage point, emancipation appears less the grand event of liberation than a point of transition between modes of servitude and racial subjection." 6.

4.   Foucault critiqued how those theorizing resistance often oversimplify their understanding of the state: "The state . . . does not have this unity, this individuality, this rigorous functionality. . . . the state is no more than a composite reality and a mythicized abstraction." Michel Foucault, "Governmentality," in *The Foucault Effect: Studies in Governmentality*, eds. Graham Burchell, Colin Gordon, and Peter Miller (Chicago: University of Chicago Press, 1991), 103.

5.   Ruth Wilson Gilmore, *Golden Gulag: Prisons, Surplus, Crisis, and Opposition in Globalizing California* (Berkeley and Los Angeles: University of California Press, 2007); Angela Y. Davis, *Are Prisons Obsolete?* (New York: Seven Stories Press, 2003); Loïc Waquant, *Punishing the Poor: The Neoliberal Government of Social Insecurity* (Durham, NC: Duke University Press, 2009); Craig Willse, "Surplus Life: The Neoliberal Making and Managing of Housing Insecurity," PhD dissertation, City University of New York, 2010.

6.   Mitchell Dean, *Governmentality: Power and Rule in Modern Society*. 2nd ed. (London: SAGE Publications, 2010), 37.

7.   Jodi Melamed provided a useful formulation of racialization and commentary on how it has shifted after what Howard Winant has called the World War II racial break in her remarks at the 2011 Critical Ethnic Studies Conference at the University of California, Riverside.

> Racialization is a process that constitutes differential relations of value and valuelessness according to reigning economic-political orders, while appearing to be (and being) a normative system that "merely" sorts human

beings according to categories of difference. In other words, racialization converts the effects of differential value-making into categories of difference that make it possible to order, analyze, organize, and evaluate what emerges out of force relations as the permissible content of other domains of modernity (economy, law, governance). Under white supremacist modernity, the color line was an adequate cultural technology for converting processes of differential value-making into world-ordering systems of knowledge and valued and valueless human forms. It precipitated out of and rationalized agrarian, colonial, and industrial capitalist modes of constituting power, addressing those designated as valueless largely through punitive, negating, disqualifying, exclusionary, and violent, physically coercive measures. In a formally anti-racist liberal capitalist modernity, white supremacist forms of violence continue, but we have an intensification of normative and rationalizing modes of violence, which work by *ascribing* norms of legibility/illegibility and *mandating* punishment, abandonment, or disposability for norm violators. Instead of a color line, official anti-racisms allow for greater flexibility in exercising and prescribing racialized terms of value and valuelessness. Here, it is useful to cite Nikhil Singh's definition of race as "historical repertoires and cultural and signifying systems that stigmatize and depreciate some forms of humanity for the purposes of another's health, development, safety, profit or pleasure." After the racial break, categories of racialized privilege and stigma determined by economic, cultural, and ideological criteria become unevenly detached from phenotype, so that traditionally recognized racial identities—Black, Asian, white, Arab—now occupy both sides of the privilege/stigma divide, which itself is always on the move, precipitating of the material circumstances it rationalizes. Importantly, for official anti-racisms, racialization procedures also confer privilege or stigma in accord with limited repertoires of anti-racist value, so that during various phases, "white liberal," "multicultural American," and "global citizen" emerge as privileged racial subjects, while those without value within the circuits of racialized global capitalism are disqualified as "unpatriotic," "damaged," "criminal," "xenophobic," or "illegal."

Melamed, "Rationalizing Violence in the New Racial Capitalism." 4-5.

8. Derrick A. Bell, Jr., "Brown v. Board of Education and the Interest-Convergence Dilemma," *Harvard Law Review*, 93:(1980): 518.

9. Cheryl I. Harris, "Whiteness as Property," *Harvard Law Review* 106:8 (1993): 1707.

10. Kimberlé Williams Crenshaw, "Mapping the Margins: Intersectionality, Identity Politics and Violence against Women of Color," in *Critical Race Theory: The Key Writings That Formed the Movement*, eds. Kimberlé Williams Crenshaw, Neil Gotanda, Garry Peller, and Kendall Thomas (New York: The New Press, 1996), 357–383.

11. I use the term "gender-confirming health care for trans people" for a few reasons. First, the same programs that exclude coverage of this care or deny this care for trans people often cover it for non-trans people, so the distinction is not about certain kinds of procedures or medications; it is about who is seeking them. That is politically significant because those who oppose coverage and provision of this care often cast it as experimental and medically unnecessary. Second, I use this term to refer to a range of care, avoiding terms like "sex reassignment surgery" that focus on a small part of the total kinds of gender-confirming care that trans people often seek and are denied, which can include mental health care, hormone treatment, and/or various surgical procedures depending on the needs of the individual.

12. Angela P. Harris, "From Stonewall to the Suburbs? Toward a Political Economy of Sexuality," *William and Mary Bill of Rights Journal* 14 (2006): 1539–1582; Lisa Duggan, *The Twilight of Equality? Neoliberalism, Cultural Politics, and the Attack on Democracy* (Boston: Beacon Press, 2004).

13. Anna M. Agathangelou, D. Morgan Bassichis, and Tamara L. Spira, "Intimate Investments: Homonormativity, Global Lockdown, and the Seductions of Empire," *Radical History Review* , no. 100 (Winter 2008): 120–143.

14. Ruth Wilson Gilmore, "Globalisation and US Prison Growth: From Military Keynesianism to Post-Keynesian Militarism," *Race & Class*

40, no. 2–3 (March 1999): 171–188.

15. Dylan Rodríguez, "The Political Logic of the Non-Profit Industrial Complex," in *The Revolution Will Not Be Funded: Beyond the Non-Profit Industrial Complex*, ed. INCITE! Women of Color against Violence (Cambridge, MA: South End Press, 2007), 21–40; and Ruth Wilson Gilmore, "In the Shadow of the Shadow State," in *The Revolution Will Not Be Funded*, 41–52.

16. Harris, "From Stonewall to the Suburbs?"; Dean Spade and Rickke Mananzala, "The Non-Profit Industrial Complex and Trans Resistance," *Sexuality Research and Social Policy: Journal of NSRC* 5, no. 1 (March 2008): 53–71.

17. A 2009 study found that 47 percent of transgender people surveyed had experienced an adverse job outcome, such as being fired, not hired, or denied a promotion, and 97 percent had experienced harassment or mistreatment on the job based on trans identity. National Gay and Lesbian Task Force and National Center for Transgender Equality, "National Transgender Discrimination Survey: Preliminary Findings on Employment and Economic Insecurity," www.thetaskforce.org/reports_and_research/trans_survey_preliminary_findings. December 1, 2009.

18. The same study found that nearly one fifth of respondents (19 percent) reported that they had become homeless due to being transgender.

19. Ruth Wilson Gilmore has defined racism as "the state-sanctioned or extralegal production and exploitation of group-differentiated vulnerability to premature death." Gilmore, *Golden Gulag*, 28. I find this definition useful for thinking about how various systems of meaning and control distribute chances at life and death. Because traditional legal definitions of discrimination focus on finding an individual discriminator who can be proven to have intended to discriminate, harmful conditions that are faced by populations targeted for abandonment and imprisonment cannot be addressed. Thinking about the distribution of vulnerability to premature death across the population allows us to see the significance of administration and let go of the focus on individual wrongdoers and intent.

20. Angela P. Harris, "From Stonewall to the Suburbs?; Lisa Duggan,

The Twilight of Equality?; Priya Kandaswamy, Mattie Eudora Richardson, and Marlon Bailey, "Is Gay Marriage Racist? A Conversation with Marlon M. Bailey, Priya Kandaswamy and Mattie Eudora Richardson," *That's Revolting: Queer Strategies for Resisting Assimilation*, ed. Mattilda Sycamore (New York: Soft Skull Press, 2006), 87–93; Kenyon Farrow, "Is Gay Marriage Anti-Black?" June 2005, http://kenyonfarrow. com/2005/06/14/is-gay-marriage-anti-black/; Chandan Reddy, "Time for Rights? Loving, Gay Marriage and the Limits of Legal Justice," *Fordham Law Journal*, 76 (2008): 2849.

21. The Miami Workers Center "helps working class people build grassroots organizations and develop their leadership capacity through aggressive community organizing campaigns and education programs. The Center also actively builds coalitions and enters alliances to amplify progressive power and win racial, community, social, and economic justice. Through its combined efforts the Center has taken on issues around welfare reform, affordable housing, tenants and voter rights, racial justice, gentrification and economic development, and fair trade. [It] has spoken out against war and empire, greed, racist policies, and discriminatory initiatives against immigrants and gay and lesbian people. The MWC office has become a central site in the growing 'storm' of social justice that is growing in South Florida. It is a locus of community power, individual transformation, alliance building, hope, and inspiration." www.miami-workerscenter.org.

Chapter 1
Trans Law and Politics
on a Neoliberal Landscape

IN ORDER TO EFFECTIVELY CONCEPTUALIZE POLITICAL AND ECO-
nomic marginalization, shortened life spans, and an emergent notion of organized resistance among the set of gender rule-breakers
currently being loosely gathered under a "trans" umbrella, and to
raise questions about the usefulness of law reform strategies in
this resistance, it is important to consider the context in which
these conditions are embedded. The concept of neoliberalism is
a useful tool for describing the context in which emergent forms
of trans resistance are appearing. Scholars and activists have used
the term "neoliberalism" in recent years to describe a range of
interlocking trends in domestic and international politics that
constitute the current political landscape. The term is slippery
and imperfect. Neoliberalism is used to mean lots of different
things by lots of different people, and it is sometimes used to
refer to conditions that we could understand as not new at all,
like state violence toward people of color, US military imperialism, and attacks on poor people. However, I find the term useful because it allows space for critical insight into the range of
practices producing effects at the register of law, policy, economy,
identity, organization, and affect. It helps us look at a set of things
together and understand their interlocking relationships rather
than analyzing them in ways that make us miss key connections.

Neoliberalism has not only shaped the larger social, economic, and political conditions that trans people find themselves in, but has also produced a specific lesbian and gay rights formation that trans politics operates in relation to. The concept of neoliberalism is useful both for raising concerns about the effects of the lesbian and gay rights formation on trans people, and for calling into question the usefulness of the lesbian and gay rights model for trans law reform efforts.

Neoliberalism has been used to conceptually draw together several key trends shaping contemporary policies and practices that have redistributed life chances over the last forty years. These trends include a significant shift in the relationships of workers to owners, producing a decrease in real wages,[1] an increase in contingent labor, and the decline of labor unions; the dismantling of welfare programs; trade liberalization (sometimes called "globalization"); and increasing criminalization and immigration enforcement. Neoliberalism is also associated with the rollback of the gains of the civil rights movement and other social movements of the 1960s and 70s, combined with the mobilization of racist, sexist, and xenophobic images and ideas to bolster these changes. Further, the emotional or affective registers of neoliberalism are attuned to notions of "freedom" and "choice" that obscure systemic inequalities and turn social movements toward goals of inclusion and incorporation and away from demands for redistribution and structural transformation.

At a broad level, the advent of neoliberal politics has resulted in an upward distribution of wealth.[2] Simply put, the rich have gotten richer and the poor have gotten poorer.[3] The real wages of Americans have not increased since the 1970s, and the bargaining power of workers trying to improve the conditions under which they labor has declined significantly. Today fewer workers are part of labor unions, and major law and policy changes have made it harder for workers to organize and utilize tools like labor strikes to increase bargaining power and push demands.[4] More workers have been forced into the contingent labor force, working as "temps" of various kinds without job security or benefits. At the same time, these developments are lauded by proponents of neoliberalism as increased "flexibility" and "choice" in the job market, where workers are portrayed as having more of an entrepreneurial role in their own employment as independent contractors. In reality, workers have lost real compensation, in terms of both wages and benefits. These changes in the relationship between workers and owners, and the reduction in unionization in particular, have resulted in the loss of certain important benefits that were fought for—and won—by organized labor forces in some industries and for some employees. Benefits such as old age pensions and health care that many used to access through their jobs have disappeared as labor has been restructured. During the same period state programs to support poor people, people with disabilities, and old people have also been dismantled. As a result, more and more people have been left without the basic safety nets necessary to ensure their very survival.

At the same time, the already weakened welfare state has been steadily attacked, eliminating entitlement to basic safety nets for the poorest people. The real worth of already inadequate benefits has continuously decreased since the 1970s while the laws and policies governing these programs have simultaneously changed to exclude more and more people from eligibility. Lifetime limits, new provisions excluding immigrants, family caps limiting benefits for new children entering a family, and new regimes of work requirements imposed on those in need of benefits were introduced in the 1990s to "end welfare as we know it."[5] These drastic policy changes have left millions of poor people with less access to basic necessities: these changes have destroyed public housing projects, greatly reduced vital health and social services, and produced a significant increase in the number of people living without shelter.

Globally, the upward distribution of wealth has been aided by trends of trade liberalization combined with coercive rules imposed upon poor/indebted countries by rich/grantor countries.

Both of these elements create rules that reduce the ability of
countries to protect their workers and natural environments from
exploitation and build programs like education and health care
systems that increase the well-being and security of their own
people. Trade agreements like the North American Free Trade
Agreement (NAFTA) and the Free Trade Area of the Americas
Agreement (FTAA) are used by corporations to attack rules that
protect workers or the environment, arguing that such rules are
barriers to "free trade." At the same time, organizations such as the
International Monetary Fund (IMF) and the World Bank place
limitations on what indebted countries can do, forcing them to
focus on producing cash crops in order to make payments on debts
instead of investing money in basic necessities and infrastructure
within the country, or growing sustenance crops to feed their
people. The structures of trade liberalization and coercive debt
allow wealthy countries and corporations to perpetuate resource
extraction against poor countries and their populations, leaving
their people in peril. These conditions drastically impact the life
spans of people in poor countries: deaths from preventable and
treatable disease, hunger, and environmental damage are the direct
result of economic arrangements that divest exploited nations of
control over local human and natural resources.[6] These conditions
also produce increased migration as people flee economic,
political, and environmental disasters seeking safety and a means
of survival. Many of these people risk enormous danger, and even
death, when traveling to rich countries. And when—or if—they
arrive, they then face racism, sexism, xenophobia, homophobia,
transphobia, economic exploitation, and criminalization.[7]

These changes in global economic arrangements, such as the
emergence of "free trade agreements" and debt schemes that replaced prior forms of colonialism with new ways of controlling
countries, have also had significant impacts within the United
States. Domestic job loss has resulted as corporations move their
operations to places with more exploitable and unprotected work-
forces. As more and more working class people feel the effects of

economic restructuring that reduces their earnings and employment security, politicians and the media offer racist and xenophobic scapegoating to exploit this dissatisfaction, preventing the discontent from producing interventions on these economic agendas. As workers in the United States experience the impacts of their declining power, the media and government have shaped messages that channel frustration at these changes into policies of racialized control rather than economic reforms that might benefit those workers.

Sexist, racist, and xenophobic images and ideas have been mobilized in the media and by politicians to transform growing economic loss and dissatisfaction into calls for "law and order."[8] Increasingly, social problems rooted in poverty and the racial wealth divide have been portrayed as issues of "crime," and increased policing and imprisonment have been framed as the solution.[9] The last thirty years has seen a massive growth in structures of law enforcement, both in the criminal punishment and immigration contexts, fueled by the rhetorical devices of the War on Drugs and the War on Terror. Numerous law changes have criminalized behaviors that were previously not criminalized and drastically enhanced sentences for existing crimes. Mandatory minimum sentences for drug violations have severely increased the significance of drug convictions, despite an overall reduction of drug use in the United States during this period.[10] "Three strikes" laws, which create a mandatory extended prison sentence for people convicted of three crimes listed as "serious," have been adopted by almost half the states in the United States, contributing to the drastic growth in imprisonment. Behaviors associated with being poor, such as panhandling, sleeping outdoors, entering public transit without paying the fare, and writing graffiti have also been increasingly criminalized, resulting in many poor and homeless people ending up more entangled in the criminal system.[11] Many cities have taken up "quality of life" policing strategies that target for arrest people in the sex trade, homeless people, youth, people with disabilities, and people of color as part of efforts to make cities comfortable for white gentrifiers.[12] The result of these trends has been a rapid growth of imprisonment such that the United States now imprisons one in 100 people.[13] With only 5 percent of the world's population, the United States now has 25 percent of the world's prisoners. Over 60 percent of US prisoners are people of color; and one in three Black men now experience imprisonment during their lifetimes.[14] Native populations also experience particularly high rates of imprisonment; at a rate of 709 per 100,000, the imprisonment rate for Native populations is second only to the rate of imprisonment for Black people, estimated at 1,815 per 100,000.[15] Women are the fastest growing segment of the imprisoned population. The rate of imprisonment for women has increased at nearly double the rate of men since 1985 and there are now more than eight times as many women locked up in state and federal prisons and local jails as there were in 1980. "War on Drugs" policy changes account for much of this shift—40 percent of criminal convictions leading to incarceration of women in 2000 were for drug crimes.[16] Two-thirds of women imprisoned in the United States are women of color.[17]

Such trends have prompted many commentators to observe that imprisonment of communities of color is an extension of systems of chattel slavery and genocide of indigenous people.[18] Angela Davis has described the historical trajectory that formed the criminal punishment system as a response to the formal abolition of slavery. As she and others have pointed out, the Thirteenth Amendment's abolition of involuntary servitude includes a very important caveat: "except as punishment for crime, whereof the party shall have been duly convicted." As Davis traces, in the years following the abolition of slavery, southern prisons drastically expanded and went from being almost entirely white to primarily imprisoning Black people. New laws were passed—the Black Codes—that made an enormous range of behaviors (e.g., drunkenness and vagrancy) criminal solely if the accused was Black. These legal schemes permitted the newly freed slaves to be recaptured into a new system of forced labor, control, and racial violence. The nature of imprisonment changed during this time, taking on the methods of punishment common to slavery, such as whipping, and implementing the convict leasing system that allowed former slave owners to lease the labor of prisoners who were forced to work under conditions many observers have suggested were even more violent than those of slavery.[19] The contemporary criminal punishment system finds its origins in this racially targeted control and exploitation of people of color, and its continuation of those tactics can be seen in its contemporary operations. As Davis asserts,

> Here we have a penal system that was racist in many respects—discriminatory arrests and sentences, conditions of work, modes of punishment. . . . The persistence of the prison as the main form of punishment, with its racist and sexist dimensions, has created this historical continuity between the nineteenth- and early-twentieth-century convict lease system and the privatized prison business today. While the convict lease system was legally abolished, its structures of exploitation have reemerged in the patterns of privatization, and, more generally, in the wide-ranging corporatization of punishment that has produced a prison industrial complex.

The specific origins of the criminal punishment system in relation to chattel slavery has not limited the targets of that system to Black people. While Black people continue to be the primary targets, other people of color and poor white people are also profoundly impacted by caging and policing, both through the criminal punishment system and the immigration enforcement system. In the last decade, the War on Terror has prompted a massive growth in immigration enforcement, including imprisonment, significant law changes reducing the rights of people imprisoned in immigration facilities,[20] and an overhaul of the administrative systems that govern identification in ways that lock immigrants out of basic services and make them more vulnerable to exploitation. In the last decade law changes at both the state and federal level have made it more difficult to get ID and government benefits. Some of these changes have been fueled by well-publicized campaigns such as the 1994 campaign to pass Proposition 187 in California, a proposed law that aimed to ensure that undocumented immigrants could not use public services such as health care, education, and other social services. The 2005 REAL ID Act, passed by Congress, focused on changing how states issue drivers licenses in order to prevent undocumented immigrants from obtaining ID. Many other law and policy changes that garnered less attention similarly reduced access to key services and ID for undocumented people. During the same period, the federal government has increased its enforcement of immigration laws, imprisoning and deporting more people and creating new programs, like the controversial "Secure Communities" program,[21] that increase the use of state and local criminal justice enforcement resources for targeting immigrants.

Law and policy changes that have increased criminalization and immigration enforcement have been implemented through the utilization of some important reframings. In the wake of the political upheaval of the 1960s and 70s, where strong social justice movements' demands for redistribution and transformation gained visibility and were then systemically attacked and dismantled by the FBI's Counter Intelligence Program (COINTELPRO) and other governmentally orchestrated operations, conservatives regrouped using racist, sexist, and xenophobic scapegoating.[22] Movement organizing and social protest became "crime" and increasingly "terrorism," justifying the imprisonment of political activists from effective organizations and the ongoing surveillance and criminalization of dissent. Additionally, the War on Drugs changed how drug use is perceived, flooding the culture with racist images of dangerous, violent drug users and dealers. Understandings of drug addiction as a health issue, to the extent that they existed, were replaced by the framing of drug abuse as a criminal issue, with punishments for drug possession increasing significantly. The War on Drugs resulted in massive prison expansion to accommodate a growing mass of drug offenders serving increasingly long sentences. New laws like the Americans with Disabilities Act (ADA) of 1990 specifically identified drug users as people to be excluded from protections aimed at eliminating stigma from health impairments.[23] Even though drug abuse declined precipitously in the United States starting in the mid 1970s, confinement of people based on drug convictions in state and federal prisons increased 975 percent between 1982 and 1996.[24] With the advent of the War on Terror in 2001, an enormous range of law and policy changes resulting in locking up immigrants was justified through a new framing of all immigration policy issues as "terrorism prevention." This criminalizing framework extends to the realm of social welfare policies. The notion of people defrauding welfare and Social Security Disability benefits systems was popularized by media "exposés" on the topic, contributing to the racist portrayal of the poor as criminal and supporting policies reducing poverty alleviation programs and enhancing punishment systems. At the same time, law changes dealing with drug use or possession included eliminating eligibility for college financial aid and public housing for people with drug convictions and enhancing the barriers to employment, credit, and social services for communities targeted by increased policing and imprisonment.[25] Fueled by racist, sexist, and xenophobic scapegoating, the last four decades have seen simultaneous slashes to social services and massive growth of state capacities to surveil, police, and imprison, suggesting a disingenuity to the "small government" credos of politicians in power during the past four decades.[26]

This period also saw a major rollback in the law reform gains of the civil rights movement. The dismantling of Jim Crow laws and the implementation of policies aimed at integrating school systems and workplaces to redistribute economic opportunity and leadership had only a brief life before legislatures and courts eliminated them.[27] The civil rights movement succeeded in changing US law to eliminate explicit racial segregation and exclusion laws, but courts responded by creating a new doctrine of "colorblindness" that took the teeth out of these law changes and preserved the racial status quo. One way that this was accomplished was by making affirmative action programs and school desegregation programs illegal because of their race consciousness.[28] Another key tactic was creating a doctrine of anti-discrimination law that makes it almost impossible to prove discrimination.[29] These two elements allow the United States to continue to espouse racial equality as the law of the land while blaming wealth inequalities on populations whose "failure" to thrive under these purportedly equal conditions must be their own fault. This also serves to ensure that the law is an ineffective tool for addressing ongoing racism that results in racially disparate access to wealth, education, housing, health care, and social services. These methods also mirror the general trend in neoliberal politics of denying that unequal conditions exist, portraying any unequal conditions that do exist as natural or neutral, and suggesting that key access/resource issues are a matter of individual "freedom" and "choice." The deep inequality of education between public school systems that falls along race and class lines, courts tell us, is a matter of the choices of parents to move to particular areas and cannot be addressed by courts.[30] Workers are now "free" to move between workplaces, working temporarily and flexibly, without those cumbersome relationships to long-term employers accompanied by things like meaningful rights to organize, pensions, health insurance, and job security. Through these lenses, systemic inequality has become increasingly unspeakable and the long-term myth of meritocracy in the United States, coupled with the renewed rhetoric of "personal responsibility," suggests that those benefiting from the upward distribution are doing so because of their moral fitness, and, respectively, that those on the losing end are blameworthy, lazy, and, of course, dangerous.

The changes in conditions and the ideas undergirding the neoliberal project have also significantly impacted what social movement politics look like in the United States.[31] The conservative turn has been reflected in social movement politics, where the radical projects of the 1960s and 1970s that were targeted for dismantling by the FBI were replaced by a growing nonprofit sector.[32] Emerging nonprofit organizations both filled the gaps left as the government abandoned key social and legal services designed to assist poor populations, and created a new elite sector of law and policy reform funded by wealthy philanthropists. This new sector differs significantly from the more grassroots and mass-based social movements of earlier eras. Its reform projects reflect the neoliberal shift toward the politics of inclusion and incorporation rather than redistribution and deep transformation. The newly expanded nonprofit sector is most concerned with services and policy change. Traditional strategies of mass-based organizing have been underfunded and systematically dismantled, as funders prefer to channel resources toward project-oriented programs with short timelines for quantifiable outcomes. In this context, social justice has become a career track populated by individuals with specialized professional training who rely on business management models to run nonprofits "efficiently." The leadership and decision-making come from these disproportionately white, upper-class paid leaders and donors, which has significantly shifted priorities toward work that stabilizes structural inequality by legitimizing and advancing dominant systems of meaning and control rather than making demands for deeper transformation.

The legal reform work that currently operates under the rubric of lesbian and gay rights (or sometimes LGBT rights) is an example of this shift from a more transformative social movement agenda to an inclusion- and incorporation-focused professionalized nonprofit legal reform project. Countless scholars and activists have critiqued the direction that lesbian and gay rights activism has taken since the incendiary moments of the late 1960s when criminalized gender and sexual outsiders fought back against police harassment and brutality at New York City's Stonewall Inn and San Francisco's Compton's Cafeteria.[33] The activism that arose during that period started as street resistance and unfunded ad hoc organizations, initially taking the form of protests and marches, utilizing strategies that were mirrored across a range of movements, resisting police brutality and militarism, and opposing patriarchal and racist norms and violences. This emerging sexuality/gender-focused resistance was institutionalized in the 1980s into nonprofit structures led by white lawyers and other people with class and education privilege. Critics of these developments have used a variety of terms and concepts to describe the shift, including charges that the focus became assimilation;[34] that the work increasingly marginalized low-income people,[35] people of color,[36] and transgender people;[37] and that the resistance became co-opted by neoliberalism[38] and conservative egalitarianism. Critics have argued that as the gay movement of the 1970s institutionalized into the lesbian and gay rights movement in the 1980s—forming such institutions as Gay and Lesbian Advocates and Defenders (GLAD), the Gay and Lesbian Alliance Against Defamation (GLAAD), the Human Rights Campaign (HRC), Lambda Legal Defense and Education Fund, and the National Gay and Lesbian Task Force (NGLTF)—the focus of the most well-funded, well-publicized work on behalf of queers shifted drastically.[39]

From its roots in bottle-throwing resistance to police brutality and the claiming of queer sexual public space, the focus of lesbian and gay rights work moved toward the more conservative model of equality promoted in US law and culture through the myth of equal opportunity. The thrust of the work of these organizations became the quest for inclusion in and recognition by dominant US institutions rather than questioning and challenging the fundamental inequalities promoted by those institutions. The key agenda items became anti-discrimination laws focused on employment (e.g., the federal Employment Non-Discrimination Act [ENDA], as well as equivalent state statutes), military inclusion, decriminalization of sodomy, hate crime laws, and a range of reforms focused on relationship recognition that increasingly narrowed to focus on the legal recognition of same-sex marriages.

Participatory forms of organizing, such as nonprofessional membership-based grassroots organizations, were replaced by hierarchical, staff-run organizations operated by people with graduate degrees. Broad concerns with policing and punishment, militarism, and wealth distribution taken up by some earlier manifestations of lesbian and gay activism were replaced with a focus on formal legal equality that could produce gains only for people already served by existing social and economic arrangements.[40] For example, choosing to frame equal access to health care through a demand for same-sex marriage rights means fighting for health care access that would only affect people with jobs that include health benefits they can share with a partner, which is an increasingly uncommon privilege.[41] Similarly, addressing the economic marginalization of queer people solely through the lens of anti-discrimination laws that bar discrimination in employment on the basis of sexual orientation—despite the facts that these laws have been ineffective at eradicating discrimination on the basis of race, sex, disability, and national origin, and that most people do not have access to the legal resources needed to enforce these kinds of rights—has been criticized as marking an investment in formal legal equality while ignoring the plight of the most economically marginalized queers. Framing issues related to child custody through a lens of marital recognition, similarly, means ignoring the racist, sexist, and classist operation of the child welfare system and passing up opportunities to form coalitions across populations targeted for family dissolution by that system. Black people, indigenous people, people with disabilities, queer and trans people, prisoners, and poor people face enormous targeting in child welfare systems. Seeking "family recognition" rights through marriage, therefore, means seeking such rights only for queer and trans people who can actually expect to be protected by that institution. Since the availability of marriage does not protect straight people of color, poor people, prisoners, or people with disabilities from having their families torn apart by child welfare systems, it is unlikely to do so for queer poor people, queer people of color, queer prisoners, and queer people with disabilities. The quest for marriage seems to have far fewer benefits, then, for queers whose families are targets of state violence and who have no spousal access to health care or immigration status, and seems to primarily benefit those whose race, class, immigration, and ability privilege would allow them to increase their well-being by incorporation into the government's privileged relationship status. The framing of marriage as the most essential legal need of queer people, and as the method through which queer people can obtain key benefits in many realms, ignores how race, class, ability, indigeneity, and immigration status determine access to those benefits and reduces the gay rights agenda to a project of restoring race, class, ability and immigration status privilege to the most privileged gays and lesbians.

The following chart provides some examples of the framings and demands developed by the most visible and well-resourced lesbian and gay organizations for addressing key problems facing queer and trans communities and compares them to alternative framings offered by queer and trans activists and organizations who center racial and economic justice.[42] Each of these examples makes visible the centering of formal legal equality demands, and the limited potential of those demands to transform the conditions facing highly vulnerable queer and trans people. This chart does not aim to be exhaustive, only to illustrate some of the concerns raised and alternative approaches proposed to the "official" gay and lesbian law reform agenda.

These questions of issue framing and prioritization came to the forefront during the welfare reform debates and subsequent policy changes of the mid-1990s; social justice activists criticized lesbian and gay rights organizations for not resisting the elimination of social welfare programs despite the fact that these policy changes

The Big Problems	*The Official Lesbian & Gay Solutions*	*Critical Queer and Trans Political Approaches*
Queer and trans people, poor people, people of color, and immigrants have minimal access to quality health care	Legalize same-sex marriage to allow people with health benefits from their jobs to share with same-sex partners	Medicaid/Medicare activism; fight for universal health care; fight for transgender health care; protest deadly medical neglect of people in state custody
Violence against queer and trans people	Pass hate crime legislation to increase prison sentences and strengthen local and federal law enforcement; collect statistics on rates of violence; collaborate with local and federal law enforcement to prosecute hate violence and domestic violence	Develop community-based responses to violence that support collective healing and accountability; join with movements addressing root causes of queer and trans premature death: police violence, imprisonment, poverty, lack of health care and housing
Queer and trans people experience violence and discrimination in the military	Eliminate bans on participation of gays and lesbians in US military	Join with movements to oppose racist, sexist, imperialist military actions abroad and at home; demand reduction/elimination of defense budget
Unfair and punitive immigration system	Legalize same-sex marriage to allow same-sex international couples to apply for legal residency for the immigrating spouse	Oppose the use of immigration policy to criminalize people of color, exploit workers, and maintain deadly wealth gap between the US and the Global South; support current prisoners; engage in local and national campaigns against "Secure Communities" and other federal programs that increase racial profiling and deportation

The Big Problems	The Official Lesbian & Gay Solutions	Critical Queer and Trans Political Approaches
Queer and trans families are vulnerable to legal intervention and separation from the state and/or nonqueer and nontrans people	Legalize same-sex marriage to provide a route to "legalize" families with two parents of the same sex; pass laws banning adoption discrimination on the basis of sexual orientation	Join with other people targeted by family law and the child welfare system (poor families, imprisoned parents, native families, families of color, people with disabilities) to fight for community and family self-determination and the rights of people to keep their kids in their families and communities
Institutions fail to recognize family connections outside of heterosexual marriage in contexts like hospital visitation and inheritance	Legalize same-sex marriage to formally recognize same-sex partners in the eyes of the law	Change policies like hospital visitation to recognize a variety of family structures, not just opposite-sex and same-sex couples; abolish inheritance and demand radical redistribution of wealth and an end to poverty

had devastating effects for low-income queers.[43] Similar critiques have been made of the efforts to pass hate crime laws, arguing that the aim of enhancing penalties for assaults perpetrated because of anti-gay animus directs resources to criminal punishment agencies, a move that is deeply misguided and dangerous.[44] Queer activists focused on opposing police brutality and mass incarceration of low-income people and people of color in the United States have argued that hate crime laws do nothing to prevent violence against queer and trans people, much of which happens at the hands of employees of the criminal punishment system, a system to which hate crime laws lend more resources.[45] The shift in focus from police accountability to partnering with the criminal punishment system and aiming for increased penalties represents a significant betrayal of the concerns of low-income queer and trans people and queer and trans people of color, who are frequent targets of police and prisons. This move centers the perspective and experience of white, economically privileged queers who may feel protected by the police and criminal punishment systems. Those who feel protected and are not directly impacted by the violence of imprisonment and policing are less likely to see the urgent need for a fundamental shift away from relying on that system.

Overall, the lesbian and gay rights agenda has shifted toward preserving and promoting the class and race privilege of a small number of elite gay and lesbian professionals while marginalizing or overtly excluding the needs and experiences of people of color, immigrants, people with disabilities, indigenous people, trans people, and poor people. The institutionalization of lesbian and gay rights that started in the 1980s and produced a model of leadership based on educational privilege and a model of change centering elite strategies and law reform facilitated the abandonment of social justice struggles that concern the most vulnerable queer and trans people in favor of the advancement of narrow campaigns to include the most privileged queers in dominant institutions. As the leading lesbian and gay rights organizations emerged, they were (and remain) primarily funded and staffed by white gay people with professional degrees and/or wealth. These organizations operate through hierarchical models of governance, concentrating decision-making power in board members and senior staff who are even more likely to be white, wealthy, and have graduate-level educations.

The gay rights agenda, then, has come to reflect the needs and experiences of those leaders more than the experiences of queer and trans people not present in these elite spaces. The mostly white, educationally privileged paid leaders can imagine themselves fired from a job for being gay or lesbian, harassed on the street (often by an imagined assailant of color),[46] excluded from Boy Scouts, or kept out of military service. They do not imagine themselves as potentially imprisoned, on welfare, homeless, in the juvenile punishment and foster care systems, in danger of deportation, or the target of continuous police harassment. Because such figures shaped and continue to shape the "gay agenda," those issues do not receive the resources they warrant and require. Furthermore, these paid nonprofit leaders come out of graduate schools more than from transformative, grassroots social movements of people facing centuries of state violence. Because of this, they do not possess the critiques of notions such as formal legal equality, assimilation, professionalism and equal rights that are developed through grassroots mobilization work. Even relatively popular feminist critiques of the institution of marriage could not trump the new call for "marriage equality"—meaning access for same-sex couples to the fundamentally unequal institution designed to privilege certain family formations for the purpose of state control.[47]

Where the money for this lesbian and gay rights nonprofit formation comes from, and how it is distributed, is also an area of significant concern. The largest white-founded and white-led organizations doing lesbian and gay rights work have generated much revenue through both foundation grants[48] and sponsorship by corporations such as American Airlines, Budweiser, IBM, and Coors. These partnerships, which include advertising for the corporations, have been criticized by queers concerned about the narrow framework of organizations willing to promote corporations whose labor and environmental practices have been widely critiqued. These partnerships have furthered the ongoing criticism that lesbian and gay rights work has become a "single-issue politics" that ignores vital social justice issues, promoting a political agenda that concerns gays and lesbians experiencing marginalization through a single vector of identity only—sexual orientation. Such a politics excludes queer and trans people who experience homophobia simultaneously with transphobia, poverty, ableism, xenophobia, racism, sexism, criminalization, economic exploitation, and/or other forms of subjection.

Lesbian and gay organizations have also generally followed a model of governance and efficacy based on private sector norms rather than social justice values. The most well-funded organizations have pay scales similar to the private sector, with executive directors often making three to four times the salaries of the lowest paid employees. Pay often correlates to educational privilege, which again means that the greatest share of resources goes to white employees from privileged backgrounds while the least goes to employees of color and people without educational privilege. Furthermore, these organizations for the most part do not provide health benefits that include gender-confirming health care for trans people, despite the fact that this social justice issue is an essential one for trans politics. These organizations also have a record of not prioritizing the development of racial justice within their work. Many have consistently refused direct requests for meaningful anti-oppression training and development work within the organizations. Their refusal to devote resources to the development of internal anti-racist practices reflects the broader marginalization of issues important to people of color in these agendas.

Overall, the most well-funded lesbian and gay rights organizations provide stark examples of the critiques made by activists from across a wide range of social justice movements regarding the shift from the transformative demands of the 1960s and 70s to the narrow focus of the grant-funded "social justice entrepreneurs" of today. Lack of community accountability, elitism, concentration of wealth and resources in the hands of white elites, and exploitative labor practices have become norms within these organizations, creating and maintaining disappointing and dangerous political agendas that fail to support meaningful, widespread resistance to violent institutions in the United States—and sometimes even bolstering them. Through the rise of the nonprofit form, certain logics that support criminalization, militarism, and wealth disparity have penetrated and transformed spaces that were once locations of fomenting resistance to state violence.[49] Increasingly, neoliberalism means that social issues taken up by nonprofits are separated from a broader commitment to social justice; nonprofits take part in producing and maintaining a racialized-gendered maldistribution of life chances while pursuing their "good work."

As trans activism emerges and institutionalizes, there is often an assumption that following the strategies of lesbian and gay rights organizations, with their strong focus on law reforms including hate crime and anti-discrimination laws, is our surest path to success. Yet, the picture of economic marginalization, vulnerability to imprisonment, and other forms of state violence that trans communities are describing suggests that the "successes" of the lesbian and gay rights organizations do not have enough to offer in terms of redistribution of life chances—and that their strategies will in fact further endanger the most marginalized trans populations. If formal legal equality at best opens doors to dominant institutions for those who are already closest to inclusion (i.e., they would be included if it wasn't for this one characteristic), very few stand to benefit. Given the context of neoliberal politics, in which fewer and fewer people have the kind of racial and economic access necessary to obtain what has been cast as "equal opportunity" in the United States, and where populations deemed disposable are abandoned to poverty and imprisoned only to be released to poverty and recaptured again, we face serious questions about how to formulate meaningful transformative demands and tactics. Specifically, because changing laws is too often the assumed method of changing the lives of marginalized people, we have to take into account the ways in which law reform has been both ineffective and co-optive in the context of neoliberalism and the nonprofitization of resistance. We have to carefully consider the limitations of strategies that aim for inclusion into existing economic and political arrangements rather than challenging the terms of those arrangements. We must endeavor to create and practice a critical trans politics that contributes to building a political context for massive redistribution. A critical trans politics imagines and demands an end to prisons, homelessness, landlords, bosses, immigration enforcement, poverty, and wealth. It imagines a world in which people have what they need and govern themselves in ways that value collectivity, interdependence, and difference. Winning those demands and building the world in which they can be realized requires an unyielding commitment to center racial, economic, ability, and gender justice. It also requires thoughtful, reflective strategizing about how to build leadership and mobilization in ways that reflect those commitments. Our demands for redistribution, access, and participation must be reflected in our resistance work every day—they can't be something we come back for later.

NOTES

1.   "The decline in real wages over the past two generations also has made unpaid leave impractical for a large majority of American families. Average hourly earnings were $8.03 in 1970 but fell to $7.39 by 1993, while average weekly earnings fell from $298 to $255 over the same time period. The median income for American families was $300 less in 1986 than in 1975. The purchasing power of the dollar (measured by consumer prices) was $4.15 in 1950 but only $0.69 in 1993. By 1985, it took two incomes to maintain the same standard of living that was possible with one income in the 1950s." Arielle Horman Grill, "The Myth of Unpaid Family Leave: Can the United States Implement a Paid Leave Policy Based on the Swedish Model?" *Comparative Labor Law Journal* 17 (1996): 373, 383–390; citing Patricia Schroeder, "Parental Leave: The Need for a Federal Policy," in *The Parental Leave Crisis: Toward a National Policy*, eds. Edward F. Zigler and Meryl Frank (New Haven, CT: Yale University Press, 1988), 326, 331; and Bureau of the Census, US Department of Commerce, Statistical Abstract of the United States, 114th ed. (Washington, DC: US Department of Commerce, Bureau of the Census, 1994), 396. See also Pew's Economic Mobility Project, "Economic Mobility: Is the American Dream Alive and Well?," 2009. www.economicmobility.org/assets/pdfs/EMP_American_Dream_Key_Findings.pdf; and US Bureau of the Census, *Measuring*

50 Years of Economic Change Using the March Current Population Survey (Washington, DC: US Government Printing Office, 1998).www.census. gov/prod/3/98pubs/p60-203.pdf.

2.   Lisa Duggan, *The Twilight of Equality? Neoliberalism, Cultural Politics, and the Attack on Democracy* (Boston: Beacon Press, 2004).

3.   In 2009, inequality was at the highest level since the US Census began tracking household income in 1967. The top 1 percentile of households took home 23.5 percent of income in 2007, the largest share since 1928. Emily Kaiser, "How American Income Inequality Hit Levels Not Seen Since the Depression." *Huffington Post*, October 22, 2010. http://www.huffingtonpost.com/2010/10/22/income-inequality-america_n_772687.html.

4.   Some important cases and laws that limit the bargaining power of workers include *Labor Board v. MacKay Radio & Telegraph Co.*, 304 US 333, 345 (1938) (finding that "it [was not] an unfair labor practice [under the National Labor Relations Act (NLRA)] to replace the striking employees with others in an effort to carry on the business"); *Emporium Capwell Co. v. Western Addition*, 420 US 50 (1975) (finding that the NLRA does not protect Black workers picketing their employer over issues of employment discrimination, because they are only allowed to bargain through their union); *American Ship Building Co. v. Labor Board*, 380 US 300 (1965)(holding that an employer did not commit an unfair labor practice under either § 8(a)(1) or § 8(a)(3) of the NLRA when it shut down its operations and hired replacement workers after an impasse had been reached in labor negotiations in order to exert economic pressure on the union); *N.L.R.B. v. Local Union No. 1229, IBEW*, 346 US 464, 477–78 (1953) (holding the discharge of workers for distributing handbills critical of the company during a labor dispute was lawful under the NLRA); and See § 8(b)(4)(ii)(B) of the National Labor Relations Act, 61 Stat. 141, as amended, 29 U.S.C. § 158(b)(4). Labor historians also commonly point to the 1981 Air Traffic Controllers strike as a key turning point in US labor history marking the attack on workers' bargaining power. On August 5, 1981, following the workers' refusal to return to work, President Ronald Reagan fired the 11,345 striking air traffic controllers and banned them from federal service for life. Their union, the

Professional Air Traffic Controllers Organization, was decertified from its right to represent workers by the Federal Labor Relations Authority.

5.   This phrase was one of President Bill Clinton's 1992 campaign promises. The law changes he supported have indeed proven to have severely weakened public benefits systems, throwing many people off benefits and into more severe poverty. "Research show[s] that one in five former recipients ultimately became totally disconnected from any means of support: They no longer had welfare, but they didn't have jobs. They hadn't married or moved in with a partner or family, and they weren't getting disability benefits. And so, after a decline in the late 1990s, the number of people living in extreme poverty (with an income less than half the poverty line, or below about $8,500 for a family of three) shot up by more than a third, from 12.6 million in 2000 to 17.1 million in 2008." Peter Edelman and Barbara Ehrenreich, "Why Welfare Reform Fails Its Recession Test," *The Washington Post* (Washington, D.C.), December 8, 2009. http://www.washingtonpost.com/wp-dyn/content/article/2009/12/04/AR2009120402604.html; "According to the think tank Center on Budget and Policy Priorities, federal aid to poor families supported 84 percent of eligible households in 1995, but 10 years later, Temporary Aid for Needy Families [TANF] reached just 40 percent. Serving a shrinking percentage of needy people means the program has 'become less effective over time' at countering extreme poverty, or those living below half the poverty level." Michelle Chen, "It's Time to Restore the Social Safety Net," *Centre Daily Times* (State College, PA), June 23, 2010; "By 2008, the number of children receiving TANF had fallen to only 22 percent of the number of poor children, down from 62 percent under Aid to Families with Dependent Children [AFDC] in 1995. Eligibility criteria in some states is set at subpoverty levels, making many poor children ineligible, and barriers to access have blocked many poor children who are eligible from actually getting assistance. The percentage of eligible families receiving benefits has declined precipitously under TANF, falling from 84 percent in AFDC's last full year in 1995 to 40 percent in 2005, the most recent year for which the federal government has provided estimates of the number of families eligible for but not receiving TANF. TANF benefit levels are grossly inadequate for the

families the program does reach, and have been eroded by inflation or only minimally increased in most states since 1996. In July 2008, TANF benefit amounts were far below the official poverty guideline in every state." Deepak Bhargava et al, *Battered by the Storm: How the Safety Net Is Failing Americans and How to Fix It* (Wahington, DC: Institute for Policy Studies, the Center for Community Change, Jobs with Justice, and Legal Momentum, 2009), www.ips-dc.org/reports/battered-by-the-storm; "Nearly 16 million Americans are living in severe poverty, the McClatchy Washington Bureau reported recently. These are individuals making less than $5,080 a year and families of four bringing in less than $9,903 a year, hardly imaginable in this day and age. That number has been growing rapidly since 2000. And, as a percentage, those living in severe poverty has reached a 32-year high. Even more troubling, the report noted that in any given month only 10 percent of the severe poor received Temporary Assistance for Needy Families and only 36 percent received food stamps." "Tracking Poverty: Continue Survey of Program Effectiveness," *The Sacramento Bee*, March 12, 2007.

6.   Ha-Joon Chang, *Bad Samaritans: The Myth of Free Trade and the Secret History of Capitalism* (London: Bloomsbury Press, 2007); Nirmala Erevelles, "Disability in the New World Order," in *Color of Violence: The INCITE! Anthology*, ed. INCITE! Women of Color Against Violence (Cambridge, MA: South End Press, 2006), 25–31; Silvia Federici, "War, Globalization, and Reproduction," in *There Is an Alternative: Subsistence and Worldwide Resistance to Corporate Globalization*, ed. Veronika Bennholdt-Thomsen, Nicholas Faraclas, and Claudia von Werlhof (London: Zed Books, 2001), 133–145; Vijay Prashad, "Debt," in *Keeping Up with the Dow Joneses: Debt, Prison, Workfare* (Cambridge, MA: South End Press, 2003), 1–68; Naomi Klein, *The Shock Doctrine: The Rise of Disaster Capitalism* (New York: Picador, 2007).

7.   David Bacon, *Illegal People: How Globalization Creates Migration and Criminalizes Immigrants* (Boston: Beacon Press, 2008), 51–82; Jennifer M. Chacón, "Unsecured Borders: Immigration Restrictions, Crime Control, and National Security," *Connecticut Law Review* 39, no. 5 (July 2007): 1827; In the year that NAFTA was implemented, 1994, there was an average of 6,000 people in US immigration prison each day.

By 2001, the number had grown to 20,000 per day. In 2008, there was an average of 33,000 people in immigration prison on a daily basis. Anil Kalhan, "Rethinking Immigration Detention," *Columbia Law Review* 110 (2010): 42, 44.

8.   Duggan, *The Twilight of Equality?*

9.   Loïc Waquant, *Punishing the Poor: The Neoliberal Government of Social Insecurity* (Durham, NC: Duke University Press, 2009).

10.   Ruth Wilson Gilmore, "Globalisation and US Prison Growth: From Military Keynesianism to Post Keynesian Militarism," *Race & Class* 40, no. 2–3 (March 1999): 171–188, 173; Angela Y. Davis, *Are Prisons Obsolete?* (New York: Seven Stories Press, 2003).

11.   Alex Vitale, *City of Disorder: How the Quality of Life Campaign Transformed New York Politics* (New York: NYU Press, 2008).

12.   Vitale, *City of Disorder.*

13.   The PEW Center on the States, *One in 100: Behind Bars in America 2008* (2008), www.pewcenteronthestates.org/uploadedFiles/8015PCTS_Prison08_FINAL_2-1-1_FORWEB.pdf.

14.   Thomas P. Bonczar, Prevalence of Imprisonment in the US Population, 1974–2001, NCJ197976 (Washington, DC: US Department of Justice, Bureau of Justice Statistics, 2003); William J. Sabol and Heather Couture, Prisoners at Midyear 2007, NCJ221944 (Washington, DC: US Department of Justice, Bureau of Justice Statistics, 2008).

15.   Greg Guma, "Native Incarceration Rates are Increasing" (*Toward Freedom*, May 27, 2005), www.towardfreedom.com/home/americas/140-native-incarceration-rates-are-increasing-0302.

16.   American Civil Liberties Union, "Facts about the Over-Incarceration of Women in the United States" (2007), www.aclu.org/womens-rights/facts-about-over-incarceration-women-united-states.

17.   Correctional Association of New York, Women in Prison Project, "Women in Prison Fact Sheet" (March 2002), www.prisonpolicy.org/scans/Fact_Sheets_2002.pdf.

18.   Davis, *Are Prisons Obsolete?*; Andrea Smith, "Heteropatriarchy and the Three Pillars of White Supremacy: Rethinking Women of Color Organizing," in *Color of Violence: The INCITE! Anthology*, ed. INCITE!

Women of Color Against Violence (Cambridge, MA: South End Press, 2006), 66–73.

19. Davis, *Are Prisons Obsolete?*, 29.

20. I intentionally use the term "imprisonment" rather than "detention" and "incarceration" when possible for two reasons. First, I fear that those two terms euphemize the practice of caging people and contribute to how that practice becomes ordinary or a matter of course in American culture. Second, I believe we should analyze the rise in both criminal punishment and immigration enforcement uses of imprisonment as connected concerns and avoid terms that make immigration imprisonment seem more temporary or less violent than it is. While "immigration detention" is often portrayed by immigration enforcement officials as short-term and somehow less concerning because it is officially a part of civil rather than criminal law enforcement, in reality it is marked by the same features as criminal punishment imprisonment: racially disproportionate; characterized by sexual assault and medical neglect; arbitrary and often indefinite in its duration; and distributed at the population level hidden behind a rationalization of individual culpability and individual rights.

21. Secure Communities is a program where participating jurisdictions submit the fingerprints of everyone they arrest to federal databases for an immigration check. As of October 2010, 686 jurisdictions in 33 states were participating. Immigration Policy Center, *Secure Communities: A Fact Sheet* (Washington, DC: Immigration Policy Center, November 4, 2010), www.immigrationpolicy.org/just-facts/secure-communities-fact-sheet. Activists around the country are waging campaigns to stop the jurisdictions they live in from joining the program. See Center for Constitutional Rights, *Tell Governor Cuomo: Stop Secure Communities in New York* (New York: Center for Constitutional Rights), http://www.ccrjustice.org/nyscomm; American Friends Service Committee, *Stop "Secure Communities" in Massachusetts*, (Philadelphia: American Friends Service Committee, February, 2011), afsc.org/event/stop-secure-communities-massachusetts; Lornett Turnbull, "State Won't Agree to National Immigration Program." *Seattle Times* (Nov. 28, 2010), seattletimes.nwsource.com/html/localnews/2013545041_secure29m.html?prmid=obinsite.

22. Gilmore, "Globalisation and US Prison Growth."

23. This was a change from the ADA's predecessor, the Rehabilitation Act, which did not exclude current drug users from the group of people who might claim disability discrimination.

24. Gilmore, "Globalisation and US Prison Growth."

25. Erevelles, "Disability in the New World Order."

26. Wendy Brown, *States of Injury* (Princeton, NJ: Princeton University Press, 1999); Waquant, *Punishing the Poor*.

27. Alan David Freeman, "Legitimizing Racial Discrimination Through Anti-Discrimination Law: A Critical Review of Supreme Court Doctrine," in *Critical Race Studies: The Key Writings That Formed the Movement*, ed. Kimberlé Crenshaw, Neil Gotanda, Garry Peller, and Kendall Thomas (New York: The New Press, 1996), 29–45.

28. See *Parents Involved in Community Schools v. Seattle School District No. 1*, 551 US 701 (2007), where the US Supreme Court refused to allow a school district to assign students to public schools for the sole purpose of achieving racial integration, declining to recognize racial balancing as a compelling state interest; *Milliken v. Bradley*, 418 US 717 (1974), where the US Supreme Court held that busing students across district lines for the purpose of racial integration was only permissible with the existence of evidence showing that the school districts had deliberately promoted segregation; and *Hopwood v. Texas*, 78 F.3d 932 (5th Cir. 1996), where the Fifth Circuit Court of Appeals held that the University of Texas School of Law could not use race as a factor when evaluating applicants.

29. See *Washington v. Davis*, 426 US 229 (1976), where the US Supreme Court ruled against two African American men who alleged that the Washington, DC, police department used racially discriminatory hiring procedures by requiring applicants to take a verbal skills test. The court held that under the Fifth Amendment Equal Protection Clause, "[an] official action will not be held unconstitutional solely because it results in a racially disproportionate impact."

30. *Parents Involved in Community Schools*, 551 US 701; *Milliken*, 418 US 717; Angela P. Harris, "From Stonewall to the Suburbs? Toward a Political Economy of Sexuality," William and Mary Bill of Rights Journal

14 (2006): 1539–1582.

31. Portions of the rest of the text in this chapter are adapted from Dean Spade and Rickke Mananzala, "The Non-Profit Industrial Complex and Trans Resistance," *Sexuality Research and Social Policy: Journal of NSRC* 5, no. 1 (March 2008): 53–71.

32. Dylan Rodríguez, "The Political Logic of the Non-Profit Industrial Complex," in *The Revolution Will Not Be Funded: Beyond the Non-Profit Industrial Complex*, ed. INCITE! Women of Color Against Violence (Cambridge, MA: South End Press, 2007).

33. The Stonewall Rebellion is often understood to be a key incendiary moment for contemporary resistance to sexual and gender norms. The Compton's Cafeteria Riot was far less discussed until Susan Stryker's 2005 documentary, *Screaming Queens: The Riot at Compton's Cafeteria* introduced scholars and activists to the important events that unfolded in 1966 when gender and sexual rule-breakers responded to the constant onslaught of police harassment and violence in San Francisco's Tenderloin neighborhood.

34. Ian Barnard, "Fuck Community, or Why I Support Gay-Bashing," in *States of Rage: Emotional Eruption, Violence, and Social Change*, eds. Renée R. Curry and Terry L. Allison (New York: New York University Press, 1996), 74–88; Cathy J. Cohen, "Punks, Bulldaggers, and Welfare Queens: The Radical Potential of Queer Politics?" *GLQ: A Journal of Lesbian and Gay Studies* 3, no. 4 (1997): 437–465; Mattilda Bernstein Sycamore, ed., *That's Revolting! Queer Strategies for Resisting Assimilation* (Brooklyn, NY: Soft Skull Press, 2004); Ruthann Robson, "Assimilation, Marriage, and Lesbian Liberation" *Temple Law Review* 75 (2002): 709.

35. Richard E. Blum, Barbara Ann Perina, and Joseph Nicholas DeFilippis, "Why Welfare Is a Queer Issue," *NYU Review of Law and Social Change* 26 (2001): 207.

36. Kenyon Farrow, "Is Gay Marriage Anti-Black?" (2004), http://kenyonfarrow.com/2005/06/14/is-gay-marriage-anti-black/; Sycamore, *That's Revolting!*; Darren Lenard Hutchinson, "'Gay Rights' for 'Gay Whites'? Race, Sexual Identity, and Equal Protection Discourse," *Cornell Law Review* 85 (2000): 1358.

37. Shannon P. Minter, "Do Transsexuals Dream of Gay Rights? Getting Real About Transgender Inclusion," *Transgender Rights*, ed. Paisley Currah, Richard M. Juang, and Shannon P. Minter (Minneapolis: University of Minnesota Press, 2006),141–170; Sylvia Rivera,"Queens in Exile, the Forgotten Ones," in *Genderqueer: Voices from Beyond the Sexual Binary*, ed. JoanNestle, Riki Wilchins, and Clare Howell (Los Angeles: Alyson Books, 2002), 67–85); Dean Spade, "Fighting to Win," in *That's Revolting! Queer Strategies for Resisting Assimilation*, ed. Mattilda Bernstein Sycamore (Brooklyn, NY: Soft Skull Press, 2004), 31–38.

38. Harris, *From Stonewall to the Suburbs?*; Duggan, *The Twilight of Equality?*

39. Harris, *From Stonewall to the Suburbs?*; Urvashi Vaid, *Virtual Equality: The Mainstreaming of Gay and Lesbian Liberation* (New York: Random House, 1996).

40. Dean Spade and Craig Willse, "Freedom in a Regulatory State?: Lawrence, Marriage and Biopolitics," *Widener Law Review* 11 (2005): 309.

41. Paula Ettlebrick, "Since When Is Marriage a Path to Liberation?" *Out/Look: National Lesbian & Gay Quarterly* 6 (Fall 1989): 14–16; Spade and Willse, "Freedom in a Regulatory State?"

42. This chart is excerpted from Morgan Bassichis, Alex Lee, and Dean Spade, "Building an Abolitionist Trans Movement with Everything We've Got," in *Captive Genders: Transembodiment and the Prison Industrial Complex,* ed. Nat Smith and Eric A. Stanley (Oakland, CA: AK Press, 2011).

43. Blum, Perina, and DeFilippis, "Why Welfare Is a Queer Issue."

44. Laura Magnani, Harmon L. Wray, and the American Friends Service Committee Criminal Justice Task Force, *Beyond Prisons: A New Interfaith Paradigm for Our Failed Prison System* (Minneapolis: Fortress Press, 2006); Dean Spade, "Methodologies of Trans Resistance," in *Blackwell Companion to LGBT/Q Studies*, eds. George Haggerty and Molly McGarry (London: Blackwell Publishing, 2007), 237–261; Joey L. Mogul, Andrea J. Ritchie, and Kay Whitlock, *Queer (In)Justice* (Boston: Beacon Press, 2011); Katherine Whitlock, *In a Time of Broken Bones: A Call to Dialogue on Hate Violence and the Limitations of Hate Crime Laws*

(Philadelphia: American Friends Service Committee, 2001).

45. Dean Spade and Craig Willse, "Confronting the Limits of Gay Hate Crimes Activism: A Radical Critique," *Chicano-Latino Law Review* 21 (2000): 38.

46. Christina Hanhardt describes how early gay vigilante groups aimed at preventing homophobic bashing often took up such work with racist perceptions of bashers in mind, partnering with police to target men of color, often in gentrifying neighborhoods where white gays and lesbians were displacing people of color. Christina Hanhardt "Butterflies, Whistles, and Fists: Gay Safe Streets Patrols and the 'New Gay Ghetto' 1976–1981," *Radical History Review* 100 (Winter 2008): 61–85.

47. Ruth Colker, "Marriage Mimicry: The Law of Domestic Violence," *William and Mary Law Review* 47 (2006): 1841; Katherine M. Franke, "The Politics of Same-sex Marriage Politics," *Columbia Journal of Gender and Law* 15 (2006): 236.

48. According to a 2000 study, 66 percent of foundation board members are men and 90 percent are white. Christine Ahn, "Democratizing American Philanthropy," in *The Revolution Will Not Be Funded: Beyond the Non-Profit Industrial Complex*, ed. INCITE! Women of Color Against Violence (Cambridge, MA: South End Press, 2007), 63–76.

49. Rodríguez, "The Political Logic of the Non-Profit Industrial Complex."

Chapter 2
What's Wrong with Rights?

*Rights discourse in liberal capitalist culture casts as private po-
tentially political contests about distribution of resources and
about relevant parties to decision making. It converts social
problems into matters of individualized, dehistoricized injury
and entitlement, into matters in which there is no harm if
there is no agent and no tangibly violated subject.*
—*Wendy Brown,* States of Injury

AS THE CONCEPT OF TRANS RIGHTS HAS GAINED MORE CURRENCY
in the last two decades, a seeming consensus has emerged about
which law reforms should be sought to better the lives of trans
people.[1] Advocates of trans equality have primarily pursued two
law reform interventions: anti-discrimination laws that list gender identity and/or expression as a category of nondiscrimination, and hate crime laws that include crimes motivated by the
gender identity and/or expression of the victim as triggering the
application of a jurisdiction's hate crime statute. Organizations
like the National Gay and Lesbian Task Force (NGLTF) have
supported state and local organizations around the country in legislative campaigns to pass such laws. Thirteen states (California,
Colorado, Hawaii, Illinois, Iowa, Maine, Minnesota, New Jersey,
New Mexico, Oregon, Rhode Island, Vermont, Washington) and
the District of Columbia currently have laws that include gender

identity and/or expression as a category of anti-discrimination, and 108 counties and cities have such laws. NGLTF estimates that 39 percent of people in the United States live in a jurisdiction where such laws are on the books.[2] Seven states now have hate crime laws that include gender identity and/or expression.[3] In 2009, a federal law, the Matthew Shepard and James Byrd, Jr. Hate Crimes Prevention Act, added gender identity and/or expression to federal hate crime law. An ongoing battle regarding if and how gender identity and/or expression will be included in the Employment Non-Discrimination Act (ENDA), a federal law that would prohibit discrimination on the basis of sexual orientation, continues to be fought between the conservative national gay and lesbian organization, the Human Rights Campaign (HRC), legislators, and a variety of organizations and activists seeking to push an inclusive bill through Congress. These two legal reforms, anti-discrimination bills and hate crime laws, have come to define the idea of "trans rights" in the United States and are presently the most visible efforts made by nonprofit organizations and activists working under this rubric.

The logic behind this law reform strategy is not mysterious. Proponents argue that passing these laws does a number of important things. First, the passage of anti-discrimination laws can create a basis for legal claims against discriminating employers, housing providers, restaurants, hotels, stores, and the like. Trans people's legal claims when facing exclusion in such contexts have often failed in the past, with courts saying that the exclusion is a legitimate preference on the part of the employer, landlord, or business owner.[4] Laws that make gender identity/expression-based exclusion illegal have the potential to influence courts to punish discriminators and provide certain remedies (e.g., back pay or damages) to injured trans people. There is also a hope that such laws, and their enforcement by courts, would send a preventative message to potential discriminators, letting them know that such exclusions will not be tolerated; these laws would ultimately increase access to jobs, housing, and other necessities for trans people.

Hate crime laws are promoted under a related logic. Proponents point out that trans people have a very high murder rate and are subject to a great deal of violence.[5] In many instances, trans people's lives are so devalued by police and prosecutors that trans murders are not investigated or trans people's murderers are given less punishment than is typical in murder sentencing. Proponents believe that hate crime laws will intervene in these situations, making law enforcement take this violence seriously. There is also a symbolic element to the passage of these laws: a statement that trans lives are meaningful, often described by proponents as an assertion that trans people are human. Additionally, both proponents of anti-discrimination laws and hate crime laws argue that the processes of advocating the passage of such laws, including media advocacy representing the lives and concerns of trans people and meetings with legislators to tell them about trans people's experiences, increases positive trans visibility and advances the struggle for trans equality. The data-collection element of hate crime statutes, through which certain government agencies keep count of crimes that fall into this category, is touted by proponents as a chance to make the quantity and severity of trans people's struggles more visible.

The logic of visibility and inclusion surrounding anti-discrimination and hate crime laws campaigns is very popular, yet there are many troubling limitations to the idea that these two reforms comprise a proper approach to problems trans people face in both criminal and civil law contexts. One concern is whether these laws actually improve the life chances of those who are purportedly protected by them. An examination of categories of identity that have been included in these kinds of laws over the last several decades indicates that these kinds of reforms have not eliminated bias, exclusion, or marginalization. Discrimination and violence against people of color have persisted despite law changes that declared it illegal. The persistent and growing racial wealth divide in the United States suggests that these law changes have not had their promised effects, and that the structure of systemic racism is not addressed by the work of these laws.[6] Similarly, the twenty-year history of the Americans with Disabilities Act (ADA) demonstrates disappointing results. Courts have limited the enforcement potential of this law with narrow interpretations of its impact, and people with disabilities remain economically and politically marginalized by systemic ableism. Similar arguments can be made about the persistence of national origin discrimination, sex discrimination, and other forms of pervasive discrimination despite decades of official prohibitions of such behavior. The persistence of wage gaps, illegal terminations, hostile work environments, hiring/firing disparities, and bias-motivated violence for groups whose struggles have supposedly been addressed by anti-discrimination and hate crime laws invites caution when assuming the effectiveness of these measures.

As I discussed in the introduction, hate crime laws do not have a deterrent effect. They focus on punishment and cannot be argued to actually prevent bias-motivated violence. In addition to their failure to prevent harm, they must be considered in the context of the failures of our legal systems and, specifically, the violence of our criminal punishment system. Anti-discrimination laws are not adequately enforced. Most people who experience discrimination cannot afford to access legal help, so their experiences never make it to court. Additionally, the Supreme Court has severely narrowed the enforceability of these laws over the last thirty years, making it extremely difficult to prove discrimination short of a signed letter from a boss or landlord stating, "I am taking this negative action against you because of your [insert characteristic]." Even in cases that seem as obvious as that, people experiencing discrimination often lose. Proving discriminatory intent has become central, making it almost impossible to win these cases when they are brought to court. These laws also have such narrow scopes that they often do not include action taken by some of the most common discriminators against marginalized people: prison guards, welfare workers, workfare supervisors, immigration officers, child welfare workers, and others who have significant control over the lives of marginalized people in the United States. In a neoliberal era characterized by abandonment (reduction of social safety net and infrastructure, especially in poor and people of color communities) and imprisonment (increased immigration and criminal law enforcement), anti-discrimination laws provide little relief to the most vulnerable people.

In addition to these general problems with law reforms that add gender identity/expression to the list of prohibited character-istics, trans litigants have run into specific challenges when seeking redress from discrimination under these laws. Even in jurisdictions where these laws have been put in place, trans litigants have lost discrimination cases about being denied access to a sex-segregated facility.[7] In the employment context, this often means that even when a worker lives in a jurisdiction where discriminating against trans people is supposedly illegal, denying a trans person access to a bathroom that comports with their gender identity at work is not interpreted as a violation of the law. Of course, given the staggering unemployment of trans populations emerging from conditions of homelessness, lack of family support,[8] violence-related trauma, discrimination by potential employers, effects of unmet health needs, and many other factors,[9] even if the legal interpretations of trans people's bathroom access demands were better it would not scratch the surface of trans poverty.[10] However, these interpretations in employment cases involving bathrooms are particularly dangerous because they can be applied by courts to other high-stakes settings where trans people struggle in systems that rely on sex-segregation. Because trans people frequently face violence and discrimination in the context of sex-segregated spaces like shelters, prisons, and group homes, and because bathroom access is often the most contentious issue between trans workers and their employers, these anti-trans legal interpretations take the teeth out of trans-inclusive laws and are an example of the limita-tions of seeking equality through courts and legislatures.

Critical race theorists have developed analyses about the limi-tations of anti-discrimination law that are useful in understanding the ways these law reforms have and will continue to fail to deliver meaningful change to trans people. Alan Freeman's critique of what he terms the "perpetrator perspective" in discrimination law is particularly helpful in conceptualizing the limits of the common trans rights strategies.[11] Freeman's work looks at laws that prohibit discrimination based on race. He exposes how and why anti-discrimination and hate crime statutes do not achieve their promises of equality and freedom for people targeted by discrimination and violence. Freeman argues that discrimination law misunderstands how racism works, which makes it fail to effectively address it.

Discrimination law primarily conceptualizes the harm of racism through the perpetrator/victim dyad, imagining that the fundamental scene is that of a perpetrator who irrationally hates people on the basis of their race and fires or denies service to or beats or kills the victim based on that hatred. The law's adoption of this conception of racism does several things that make it ineffective at eradicating racism and help it contribute to obscuring the actual operations of racism. First, it individualizes racism. It says that racism is about bad individuals who intentionally make discriminatory choices and must be punished. In this (mis)understanding, structural or systemic racism is rendered invisible. Through this function, the law can only attend to disparities that come from the behavior of a perpetrator who intentionally considered the category that must not be considered (e.g., race, gender, disability) in the decision she was making (e.g., hiring, firing, admission, expulsion). Conditions like living in a district with underfunded schools that "happens to be" 96 percent students of color,[12] or having to take an admissions test that has been proven to predict race better than academic success[13] or any of a number of disparities in life conditions (access to adequate food, health care, employment, housing, clean air and water) that we know stem from and reflect long-term patterns of exclusion and exploitation cannot be understood as "violations" under the discrimination principle, and thus remedies cannot be won. This narrow reading of what constitutes a violation and can be recognized as discrimination serves to naturalize and affirm the status quo of maldistribution. Anti-discrimination law seeks out aberrant individuals with overtly biased intentions.[14] Meanwhile, all the daily disparities in life chances that shape our world along lines of race, class, indigeneity, disability, national origin, sex, and gender remain untouchable and affirmed as non-discriminatory or even as fair.

The perpetrator perspective also obscures the historical context of racism. Discrimination is understood as the act of taking into account the identity that discrimination law forbids us to take into account (e.g., race, sex, disability) when making a decision, and it does not regard whether the decision-maker is favoring or harming a traditionally excluded group. In this way, the discrimination principle has been used to eviscerate affirmative action and desegregation programs.[15] This erroneously conceptualized "colorblindness" undermines the possibility of remedying the severe racial disparities in the United States that are rooted in slavery, genocide, land theft, internment, and immigration exclusion, as well as racially explicit policies that historically and presently exclude people of color from the benefits of wealth-building programs for US citizens like Social Security, land grants, and credit and other homeownership support.[16] The conditions that created and continue to reproduce such immense disparities are made invisible by the perpetrator perspective's insistence that any consideration of the prohibited category is equally damaging. This model pretends the playing field is equal, and thus any loss or gain in opportunity based on the category is harmful and creates inequality, again serving to declare the racial status quo neutral. This justification for systemic racism masquerading as a logic of equal opportunity gives rise to the myth of "reverse racism," a concept that misunderstands racism to suggest parallel meanings when white people lose opportunities or access through programs aiming to ameliorate impacts of racism and when people of color lose opportunities due to racism.

Discrimination law's reliance on the perpetrator perspective also creates the false impression that the previously excluded or marginalized group is now equal, that fairness has been imposed, and the legitimacy of the distribution of life chances restored. This declaration of equality and fairness papers over the inequalities and disparities that constitute business as usual and allows them to continue. Narrowing political resistance strategies to seeking inclusion in anti-discrimination law makes the mistaken assumption that gaining recognition and inclusion in this way will equalize our life chances and allow us to compete in the (assumed fair) system. This often constitutes a forfeiture of other critiques, as if the economic system is fair but for the fact that bad discriminators are sometimes allowed to fire trans people for being trans.[17] Defining the problem of oppression so narrowly that an anti-discrimination law could solve it erases the complexity and breadth of the systemic, life-threatening harm that trans resistance seeks to end. Not surprisingly, the rhetoric accompanying these quests for inclusion often focuses on "deserving workers," otherwiose known as people whose other characteristics (race, ability, education, class) would have entitled them to a good chance in the workforce were it not for the illegitimate exclusion that happened.[18] Using as examples the least marginalized of the marginalized, so to speak, becomes necessary when issues are framed so narrowly that a person who faces intersecting vectors of harm would be unlikely to benefit from anti-discrimination law. This framing permits—and even necessitates—that efforts for inclusion in the discrimination regime rely on rhetoric that affirms the legitimacy and fairness of the status quo. The inclusion focus of anti-discrimination law and hate crime law campaigns relies on a strategy of simile, essentially arguing "we are just like you; we do not deserve this different treatment because of this one characteristic." To make that argument, advocates cling to the imagined norms of the US social body and choose poster people who are symbolic of US standards of normalcy, whose lives are easily framed by sound bites that resound in shared notions of injustice. "Perfect plaintiffs" for these cases are white people with high-level jobs and lawful immigration status. The thorny issues facing undocumented immigrants, people experiencing simultaneous discrimination through, for example, race, disability, and gender identity, or people in low-wage jobs where it is particularly hard to prove discrimination, are not addressed by anti-discrimination law. Laws created from such strategies, not surprisingly, routinely fail to protect people with more complicated relationships to marginality. These people, who face the worst economic vulnerability, are not lifted up as the "deserving workers" that anti-discrimination law advocates rally to protect.

Hate crime laws are an even more direct example of the limitations of the perpetrator perspective's conception of oppression. Hate crime laws frame violence in terms of individual wrongdoers. These laws and their advocates portray violence through a lens that oversimplifies its operation and suggests that the criminal punishment system is the proper way to solve it. The violence targeted by hate crime laws is that of purportedly aberrant individuals who have committed acts of violence motivated by bias. Hate crime law advocacy advances the fallacy that such violence is especially reprehensible in the eyes of an equality-minded state, and thus must be punished with enhanced force. While it is no doubt true that violence of this kind is frequent and devastating, critics of hate crime legislation argue that hate crime laws are not the answer. First, as mentioned above, hate crime laws have no deterrent effect: people do not read law books before committing acts of violence and choose against bias-motivated violence because it carries a harsher sentence. Hate crime laws do not and cannot actually increase the life chances of the people they purportedly protect.

Second, hate crime laws strengthen and legitimize the criminal punishment system, a system that targets the very people these laws are supposedly passed to protect. The criminal punishment system was founded on and constantly reproduces the same biases (racism, sexism, homphobia, transphobia, ableism, xenophobia) that advocates of these laws want to eliminate. This is no small point, given the rapid growth of the US criminal punishment system in the last few decades, and the gender, race, and ability disparities in whom it targets. The United States now imprisons 25 percent of the world's prisoners although it has only 5 percent of the world's population.[19] Imprisonment in the United States has quadrupled since the 1980s and continues to increase despite the fact that violent crime and property crime have declined since the 1990s.[20] The United States has the highest documented rate of imprisonment per capita of any country.[21] A 2008 report declared that the United States now imprisons one in every 100 adults.[22] Significant racial, gender, ability, and national origin disparities exist in this imprisonment. One in nine black men between the ages of 20 and 34 are imprisoned. While men still vastly outnumber women in prisons, the rate of imprisonment for women is growing far faster, largely the result of sentencing changes created as part of the War on Drugs, including the advent of mandatory minimum sentences for drug convictions. An estimated 27 percent of federal prisoners are noncitizens.[23] While accurate estimates of rates of imprisonment for people with disabilities are difficult to obtain, it is clear that the combination of severe medical neglect of prisoners, deinstitutionalization of people with psychiatric disabilities without the provision of adequate community services, and the role of drug use in self-medicating account for high rates.[24]

In a context of mass imprisonment and rapid prison growth targeting traditionally marginalized groups, what does it mean to use criminal punishment–enhancing laws to purportedly address violence against those groups? This point has been especially forcefully made by critics who note the origins of the contemporary lesbian and gay rights formation in anti-police activism of the 1960s and 70s, and who question how current lesbian and gay rights work has come to be aligned with a neoliberal "law and order" approach.[25] Could the veterans of the Stonewall and Compton's Cafeteria uprisings against police violence have guessed that a few decades later LGBT law reformers would be supporting passage of the Matthew Shepard and James Byrd, Jr. Hate Crimes Prevention Act, a law that provides millions of dollars to enhance police and prosecutorial resources? Could they have imagined that the police would be claimed as protectors of queer and trans people against violence, while imprisonment and police brutality were skyrocketing? The neoliberal reframing of discrimination and violence that have drastically shifted and undermined strategies of resistance to economic exploitation and state violence produce this narrow law reform agenda that ignores and colludes in the harm and violence faced every day by queer and trans people struggling against racism, ableism, xenophobia, transphobia, homophobia, and poverty.

These concerns are particularly relevant for trans people given our ongoing struggles with police profiling, harassment, violence, and high rates of both youth and adult imprisonment. Trans populations are disproportionately poor because of employment discrimination, family rejection, and difficulty accessing school, medical care, and social services.[26] These factors increase our rate of participation in criminalized work to survive, which, combined with police profiling, produces high levels of criminalization.[27] Trans people in prisons face severe harassment, medical neglect, and violence in both men's and women's facilities. Violence against trans women in men's prisons is consistently reported by prisoners as well as by researchers, and in court cases, testimony from advocates and formerly imprisoned people reveal trends of forced prostitution, sexual slavery, sexual assault, and other violence. Trans people, like all people locked up in women's prisons, are targets of gender-based violence, including sexual assault and rape, most frequently at the hands of correctional staff. Prisoners housed at women's facilities who are perceived as too masculine by prison staff are often at significantly increased risk of harassment and enhanced punishment, including psychologically damaging isolation, for alleged violations of rules against homosexual

contact. These prisoners also face a greater risk of assault motivated by an adverse reaction to gender nonconformity.[28]

Since the criminal punishment system itself is a significant
source of racialized-gendered violence, increasing its resources
and punishment capacity will not reduce violence against trans
people. When advocates of hate crime laws frame the criminal
punishment systems as a solution to the violence trans people
face, they participate in the false logic that criminal punishment
produces safety, when it is clear that it is actually a site of enormous violence. Criminal punishment cannot be the method we
use to stop transphobia when the criminal punishment system is
the most significant perpetrator of violence against trans people.
Many commentators have used this support of the expansion of
punishment regimes through the advent of hate crime advocacy
as an example of co-optation, where resistance struggles that have
named certain conditions or violences come to be used to prop
up the very arrangements that are harming the people who are
resisting. A new mandate to punish transphobic people is added
to the arsenal of justifications for a system that primarily locks up
and destroys the lives of poor people, people of color, indigenous
people, people with disabilities, and immigrants, and that uses
gender-based sexual violence as one of its daily tools of discipline
against people of all genders.[29]

Much of the thinking behind the need for hate crime and
anti-discrimination legislation, including by advocates who
recognize how limited these interventions are as avenues for
increasing the life chances of trans people, is about the significance
of having our experiences of discrimination and violence named
in law. The belief that being named in this way has a benefit
for the well-being of trans people has to be reexamined with
an understanding that the alleged benefits of such naming
provides even greater opportunity for harmful systems to claim
fairness and equality while continuing to kill us. Hate crime
and anti-discrimination laws declare that punishment systems
and economic arrangements are now nontransphobic, yet these

laws not only fail to eradicate transphobia but also strengthen systems that perpetrate it.

This analysis illuminates how law reform work that merely tinkers with systems to make them look more inclusive while leaving their most violent operations intact must be a concern of many social movements today. For example, prison abolitionists in the United States argue that the project of prison reform, which is usually aimed at reducing certain kinds of violence or unfairness in the prison system, has always functioned to maintain and expand imprisonment.[30] Prison reform efforts aimed at reducing a variety of harms, such as gender and sexual violence, medical neglect and abuse, and overcrowding, to name but a few, have often been made by well-meaning people who wanted to address the horrors of prison life. But these reform efforts have been incorporated into the project of prison expansion, mobilized as rationales for building and filling more and more prisons. Abolitionists caution that a system designed from its inception as a technology of racialized control through exile and punishment will use any rationale necessary to achieve that purpose. A recent example of particular interest to feminism and trans politics is the 2003 National Prison Rape Elimination Act (NPREA). While passed in the name of preventing sexual assault, the NPREA has been used to further enforce and increase penalties against prisoners for consensual sexual activity, including activities such as handholding. Abolitionist activists doing prisoner support work have pointed out that because some of the main tools the act uses are punishment tools, those tools have become just another part of the arsenal used by punishment systems to increase sentences, target prisoners of color and queer and trans prisoners, and expand imprisonment. It is unclear whether the new rules have reduced sexual violence, but it is clear that they have increased punishment.[31] Activists considering using law reform as a tool, then, have to be extraordinarily vigilant to determine if we are actually strengthening and expanding various systems' capacities to harm, or if our work is part of dismantling those capacities.

In both prison and immigration reform contexts, trans activists are raising concerns about the danger of dividing affected populations by mobilizing ideas about who constitutes a "deserving" or "undeserving" subject. Campaigns that focus on immigrants portrayed as "hard-working" (code for those who do not need support like public benefits or housing) and "law-abiding" (code for those not caught up in the criminal punishment system), or that frame immigration issues in terms of family unity relying on heteropatriarchal constructs, further stigmatize those who do not fit the "deserving" frame, and create policies that only benefit a narrow swath of affected people. Similarly, campaigns about imprisonment that only focus on people convicted of nonviolent crimes, "political" prisoners, or people exonerated by the introduction of new evidence, risk refining the system in ways that justify and legitimize the bulk of its continued operation by eliminating its most obvious contradictions. Three concerns about law reform projects permeate many sites of resistance. First, these projects change only what the law says about what a system is doing, but not its actual impact. Second, they refine a system in ways that help it continue to target the most vulnerable people, while only partially or temporarily removing a few of the less vulnerable from its path. And finally, law reform projects often provide rationales and justifications for the expansion of harmful systems.

Alan Freeman's critique of the perpetrator perspective helps us understand how a discrimination-focused law reform strategy that aims to prohibit the consideration of certain categories of identity in the context of certain decisions (who to hire, fire, evict, house, or assault) misconceives how the violences of racism, ableism, xenophobia, transphobia, sexism, and homophobia operate. Freeman's work shows how discrimination law fails to remedy the harms it claims to attend to, and actually can empower systems that maldistribute life chances. Reconceptualizing the theory of power and struggle that underlies such law reforms allows us to turn our attention to other systems in law that produce structured insecurity and shortened life spans for trans people, and consider alternative avenues of intervention.

As I argue in the chapters that follow, examining the operation of legal systems that administer life changes at the population level, such as welfare systems, punishment systems, health care systems, and immigration systems, can expose how law operates to sort people into subpopulations facing different exposures to security and insecurity. Looking at sites of the legal administration of societal norms, we can see how certain populations come to have such pervasive experiences with both abandonment and imprisonment. From that vantage point we can strategize about how to use legal reform tools as part of a broader strategy to dismantle capitalism's murderous structures while we build alternative methods of meeting human needs and organizing political participation. Because of the obvious failures of the most popular contemporary law reform strategies to address harms trans people are facing, trans experience can offer a location from which to consider the broader questions of the neoliberal cooptation of social movements through law reform and the institutionalization of resistance, and from which to reframe the problems of violence and poverty that impact marginalized populations in ways that give us new inroads to intervention.

NOTES

1. I shared an earlier version of some of the text in this chapter in my keynote remarks at the Temple Political & Civil Rights Law Review's 2008 Symposium, Intersections of Transgender Lives and the Law. Those remarks were published as "Keynote Address: Trans Law and Politics on a Neoliberal Landscape," *Temple Political & Civil Rights Law Review* 18 (2009): 353–373.

2. National Gay and Lesbian Task Force, "Jurisdictions with Explicitly Transgender-Inclusive Non-Discrimination Laws" (2008), thetaskforce.org/downloads/reports/fact_sheets/all_jurisdictions_w_pop_8_08.pdf.

3.   National Center for Transgender Equality, "Hate Crimes" (2008), www.nctequality.org/Hate_Crimes.asp.2008.

4.   See *Ulane v. Eastern Airlines*, 742 F.2d 1081 (7th Cir. 1984), where the Seventh Circuit Court of Appeals found that a transwoman who was dismissed from her job as an airline pilot was not protected under the sex discrimination clause of Title VII of the Civil Rights Act of 1964, holding that "Title VII does not protect transsexuals"; and *Oiler v. Winn Dixie, Louisiana Inc.*, No.Civ.A. 00–3114, 2002 WL 31098541 (E.D.La. Sept. 16, 2002), where the US District Court for the Eastern District of Louisiana found that a man who was fired from his job for occasionally cross-dressing outside of work was not protected under Title VII sex discrimination, even though his behavior had nothing to do with his job performance.

5.   Rebecca L. Stotzer, "Gender Identity and Hate Crimes: Violence Against Transgender People in Los Angeles County," *Sexuality Research and Social Policy: Journal of NSRC* 5 (March, 2008), 43-52.

6.   Angela P. Harris, "From Stonewall to the Suburbs? Toward a Political Economy of Sexuality," *William and Mary Bill of Rights Journal* 14 (2006): 1539–1582.

7.   See *Goins v. West Group*, 619 N.W.2d 424 (Minn. App. Ct. 2000), where the Minnesota Supreme Court held that employers may restrict bathroom and locker room access based on birth sex; and *Hispanic Aids Forum v. Estate of Bruno,* 16 Misc.3d 960, 839 N.Y.S.2d 691 (N.Y. Sup., 2007) where a New York Supreme Court judge ruled in favor of a nonprofit organization that was facing eviction based on its failure to comply with a landlord's demands that it disclose the birth-sex of its clients. In *Ettsity v. Utah Transit Authority*, 502 F.3d 1215 (10th Cir. 2007), the Tenth Circuit held that a trans woman bus driver who was fired because she used women's restrooms as needed at various stops on her bus route was not protected by Title VII's prohibition against sex discrimination and gender stereotyping.

8.   A recent survey of 6,450 transgender and gender-nonconforming people in the United States found that 57 percent had experienced significant family rejection. Jamie M. Grant, Lisa A. Mottet, and Justin Tanis, *Injustice at Every Turn: A Report of the National Transgender*

Discrimination Survey, Executive Summary (Washington, DC: National Gay and Lesbian Task Force and National Center for Transgender Equality, 2011), www.thetaskforce.org/downloads/reports/reports/ntds_summary.pdf.

9. The same study found that 19 percent of transgender and gender non-conforming people had been refused medical treatment due to their gender, 28 percent had postponed medical care when they were sick or injured due to discrimination, and 48 percent had postponed care when they were sick or injured because they could not afford it. The study also found that respondents reported a rate of HIV infection over four times the national average, with rates higher among trans people of color. Grant, et al., *Injustice at Every Turn*.

10. The study also confirmed that trans people live in extreme poverty. Respondents were nearly four times more likely to have a household income of less than $10,000/year compared to the general population. National Gay and Lesbian Task Force and National Center for Transgender Equality, "Injustice at Every Turn."

11. Alan David Freeman, "Legitimizing Racial Discrimination Through Anti-Discrimination Law: A Critical Review of Supreme Court Doctrine," in *Critical Race Studies: The Key Writings That Formed the Movement*, ed. Kimberlé Crenshaw, Neil Gotanda, Garry Peller, and Kendall Thomas (New York: The New Press, 1996), 29–45.

12. See *San Antonio Independent School District v. Rodriguez*, 411 US 1 (1973), where the US Supreme Court held that the severe imbalance in a school district's funding of its primary and secondary schools based on the income levels of the residents of each district is not an unconstitutional violation of equal protection rights under the Fourteenth Amendment.

13. David M. White, "The Requirement of Race-Conscious Evaluation of LSAT Scores for Equitable Law School Admission," *Berkeley La Raza Law Journal* 12 (2000–2001): 399; Susan Sturm and Lani Guinier, "The Future of Affirmative Action: Reclaiming the Innovative Ideal," *California Law Review* 84 (July 1996): 953.

14. Freeman, "Legitimizing Racial Discrimination Through Anti-Discrimination Law."

15. *Milliken v. Bradley*, 418 US 717 (1974); *Parents Involved in Community Schools v. Seattle School District No. 1*, 551 US 701 (2007).

16. Mazher Ali, Jeanette Huezo, Brian Miller, Wanjiku Mwangi, and Mike Prokosch, *State of the Dream 2011: Austerity for Whom?* (Boston: United for a Fair Economy, 2011), www.faireconomy.org/files/State_of_the_Dream_2011.pdf.

17. Dan Irving, "Normalized Transgressions: Legitimizing the Transsexual Body as Productive," *Radical History Review 100* (2008) 38-59.

18. Irving, "Normalized Transgressions." Several significant famous trans discrimination cases follow this pattern, with both media and advocates portraying the assimilable characteristics of the trans person in order to emphasize their deserving nature. One example is the highly publicized case of Dian Schroer who won a lawsuit after she lost a job at the Library of Congress when she disclosed her trans identity. *Time* magazine described her as

> an ex-Special Forces colonel. . . . Schroer was a dream candidate, a guy out of a Tom Clancy novel: he had jumped from airplanes, undergone grueling combat training in extreme heat and cold, commanded hundreds of soldiers, helped run Haiti during the U.S. intervention in the '90s—and, since 9/11, he had been intimately involved in secret counterterrorism planning at the highest levels of the Pentagon. He had been selected to organize and run a new, classified antiterror organization, and in that position he had routinely briefed Defense Secretary Donald Rumsfeld. He had also briefed Vice President Cheney more than once. Schroer had been an action hero, but he also had the contacts and intellectual dexterity to make him an ideal congressional analyst.

Schroer's public persona as a patriot and terrorist-fighter was used by advocates to promote the idea of her deservingness in ways that those concerned about the racist, anti-immigrant, imperialist War on Terror might take issue with. Critics have similarly pointed out dynamics of deservingness that determine which queer and trans murder victims become icons in the battle for hate crime legislation. White victims tend to be publicly remembered (e.g., Harvey Milk, Brandon Teena, Matthew Shepard), their lives memorialized in films and movies (*Milk, Boys Don't Cry, Larabee*), and laws named after them (Matthew Shepard Local Law Enforcement Enhancement Act). The names of these white victims and the struggles for healing and justice on the part of their friends and family are in greater circulation than victims of color through media and non-profit channels even though people of color lose their lives at higher rates. Sanesha Stewart, Amanda Milan, Marsha P. Johnson, Duanna Johnson, and Ruby Ordeñana are just a few of the trans women of color whose murders have been mourned by local communities but mostly ignored by media, large nonprofits, and lawmakers.

19. Roy Walmsley, "World Prison Population List," 7th ed., (London: International Centre for Prison Studies, 2005).

20. US Department of Justice, "Key Crime and Justice Facts at a Glance" (2009), www.ojp.usdoj.gov/bjs/glance.htm.

21. Walmsley, "World Prison Population List."

22. The PEW Center on the States, *One in 100: Behind Bars in America 2008* (2008), www.pewcenteronthestates.org/uploadedFiles/8015PCTS_Prison08_FINAL_2-1-1_FORWEB.pdf.

23. Government Accounting Office, "Information on Criminal Aliens Incarcerated in Federal and State Prisons and Local Jails," congressional briefing, March 25, 2005, http://gao.gov/new.items/d05337r.pdf.

24. Lauraet Magnani and Harmon L.Wray, *Beyond Prisons: A New Interfaith Paradigm for Our Failed Prison System*, a report by the American Friends Service Committee, Criminal Justice Task Force (Minneapolis: Fortress Press, 2006).

25. Anna M. Agathangelou, D. Morgan Bassichis, and Tamara L. Spira, "Intimate Investments: Homonormativity, Global Lockdown, and the Seductions of Empire," *Radical History Review* no. 100 (Winter 2008): 120–143; Morgan Bassichis, Alex Lee, and Dean Spade, "Building an Abolitionist Trans Movement with Everything We're Got," in *Captive Genders*, ed. Nat Smith and Eric A. Stanley (Oakland, CA: AK Press, 2011); Magnani and Wray, *Beyond Prisons*.

26. Dean Spade, "Documenting Gender," *Hastings Law Journal* 59 (2008):731; Chris Daley and Shannon Minter, *Trans Realities: A Legal Needs Assessment of San Fransisco's Transgender Communities* (San Francisco: Transgender Law Center, 2003).

27. Joey L. Mogul, Andrea J. Ritchie, and Kay Whitlock, *Queer (In) Justice* (Boston: Beacon Press, 2011).

28. D. Morgan Bassichis, *"It's War in Here": A Report on the Treatment of Transgender & Intersex People in New York State Men's Prisons* (New York: Sylvia Rivera Law Project, 2007), http://srlp.org/files/warinhere. pdf; Alexander L. Lee, *Gendered Crime & Punishment: Strategies to Protect Transgender, Gender Variant & Intersex People in America's Prisons* (pts 1 & 2), GIC TIP J. (Summer 2004), GIC TIP J. (Fall 2004); Christopher D. Man and John P. Cronan, "Forecasting Sexual Abuse in Prison: The Prison Subculture of Masculinity as a Backdrop for 'Deliberate Indifference,'" *Journal of Criminal Law and Criminology* 92 (2002):127; Alex Coolman, Lamar Glover, and Kara Gotsch, *Still in Danger: The Ongoing Threat of Sexual Violence Against Transgender Prisoners* (Los Angeles: Stop Prisoner Rape and the ACLU National Prison Project, 2005), www.justdetention. org/pdf/stillindanger.pdf; Janet Baus and Dan Hunt, *Cruel and Unusual* (New York: Reid Productions, 2006).

29. Morgan Bassichis, Alex Lee, and Dean Spade, "Building an Abolitionist Trans Movement with Everything We're Got," in *Captive Genders: Transembodiment and the Prison Industrial Complex,* ed. Nat Smith and Eric A. Stanley (Oakland, CA: AK Press, 2011); Agathangelou, Bassichis, and Spira, "Intimate Investments"; Dean Spade and Craig Willse, "Confronting the Limits of Gay Hate Crimes Activism: A Radical Critique," *Chicano-Latino Law Review* 21 (2000): 38; Sarah Lamble, "Retelling Racialized Violence, Remaking White Innocence: The Politics of Interlocking Oppressions in Transgender Day of Remembrance," *Sexuality Research and Social Policy* 5 (March 2008): 24–42.

30. Angela Y. Davis, *Are Prisons Obsolete?* (New York: Seven Stories Press, 2003).

31. Gabriel Arkles's work has exposed how rules that purport to protect prisoners from sexual violence are frequently used to punish consensual sexual or friendship relationships, prohibit masturbation, and target

queer and gender non-conforming prisoners. The existence of such rules can also increase risks of sexual behavior and create opportunities for blackmail and abuse by corrections officers. See letter from Chase Strangio and Z Gabriel Arkles to Attorney General Eric Holder, May 10, 2010, page 9, http://srlp.org/files/SRLP%20PREA%20comment%20Docket%20no%20OAG-131.pdf; Gabriel Arkles, *Transgender Communities and the Prison Industrial Complex*, lecture, Northeastern University School of Law, February 2010. Arkles's lecture offers as an example of this type of problematic policy-making, Idaho's Prison Rape Elimination Provision (Control No. 325.02.01.001, 2004), www.idoc.idaho.gov/policy/int3250201001.pdf, which includes a prohibition on "male" prisoners having a "feminine or effeminate hairstyle." Email from Gabriel Arkles, February 21, 2011 (on file with the author). Further controversy has emerged around the NPREA since the Department of Justice proposed national standards "for the detection, prevention, reduction, and punishment of prison rape, as mandated by" the NPREA, which exclude immigration facilities. See National Juvenile Defender Center & the Equity Project, Transgender Law Center, Lambda Legal Education and Defense Fund, National Center for Lesbian Rights, American Civil Liberties Union, Sylvia Rivera Law Project, National Center for Transgender Equality, "Protecting Lesbian, Gay, Bisexual, Transgender, Intersex, and Gender Nonconforming people from Sexual Abuse and Harassment in Correctional Settings," Comments Submitted in Response to Docket No. OAG-131; AG Order No. 3244-2011 National Standards to Prevent, Detect, and Respond to Prison Rape, April 4, 2011, 47–48 (on file with the author); Human Rights Watch, ACLU Washington Legislative Office, Immigration Equality, Just Detention International, National Immigrant Justice Center, National Immigration Forum, Physicians for Human Rights, Prison Fellowship, Southern Center for Human Rights, Texas Civil Rights Project, Women's Refugee Commission, "US: Immigration Facilities Should Apply Prison Rape Elimination Act Protections: Letter to US President Barack Obama" (February 15, 2011), http://www.hrw.org/es/news/2011/02/15/us-immigration-facilities-should-apply-prison-rape-elimination-act-protections.

Chapter 3
Rethinking Transphobia and Power—
Beyond a Rights Framework

HAVING LOOKED AT THE LIMITS OF A VICTIM-PERPETRATOR MOD-el, we can now ask what models of power we should use to think more accurately about trans people's experiences of violence, poverty, and shortened lifespans and to inform our resistance. If the passage of laws declaring the hateful, intentional acts of individual perpetrators punishable does not improve the lives of trans people and bolsters the very systems that target us, what should we seek instead? A central argument of this book is that the standard law reform strategies most often employed to remedy the problems faced by trans people fundamentally misunderstand the nature of power and control and the role of law in both. Simply put, they just will not work. In fact, they can even make things worse. To address the violence and marginalization that shortens trans lives, we have to re-conceptualize how those conditions are produced and examine what kinds of resistance will actually alter them. Merely declaring transphobic violence and exclusion illegal is an ineffective use of law reform; other law strategies may be of some use if employed as a small part of a broader trans struggle that articulates demands that far exceed legal reform.

To more fully understand the harms facing trans people that I described in the Preface, and to strategize resistance to them, we need to break out of the narrow narrative that the current law reform framework tells about how power works. Systems of meaning and control that maldistribute life chances, such as racism, ableism, transphobia, xenophobia, and sexism, among others, operate in ways more complicated, diverse, and structural than the perpetrator/victim model allows. Since we want and need to understand why certain people fare poorly, do not have what they need to survive, and experience high levels of violence and vulnerability to premature death, we must analyze how power operates beyond the individual discrimination model. Examining other ways that power and control operate allows us to see which vectors are addressed and accounted for by legal equality claims and which are not, and whether legal equality claims produce or reinforce certain systems of meaning and control while purporting to resolve inequality and violence. We can also begin to formulate resistance strategies that engage the sites and methods of violence that concern us. I have adapted a framework for thinking about power, largely from the work of Michel Foucault, that is helpful for understanding the role of law reform strategies in social movements that work for transformation beyond the limits of law.

Three Modes of Power
Perpetrator/Victim Power: Exclusion and Subtraction

The most familiar way of thinking about questions of power within the liberal rights-focused framework that dominates contemporary politics is to examine incidents of intentional, individualized negative action, discrimination, exclusion, and violence. Some examples that are commonly cited in this framework are "whites only" signs at private businesses; individuals fired or not hired because of gender, race, or sexual orientation; and beatings and murders motivated by bias or hatred. This mode of power is most easily recognized in liberal and rights-based frameworks as a violation requiring remediation—usually individualized punishment as per the perpetrator perspective. Another way to think about the functions of this mode is as power operating through "subtraction"—opportunities, property, health, life taken away from individual victims because of the bad ideas put into action by perpetrators.[1]

As I discussed in Chapter Two, thinking about power in terms of repression or subtraction has been inscribed in law (e.g., anti-discrimination laws and hate crime laws). This model has generated a number of critiques because it fails to account for many of the problems that face groups on the losing end of systems of distribution who seem to remain there despite legal prohibitions on these kinds of negative individualized intentional action. As Alan Freeman argues, the perpetrator perspective prevents us from looking at the unequal conditions that entire populations experience because it focuses on the intentional actions of individual discriminators.[2] The discrimination principle tells us that the government can forbid certain acts through law, and that the law will determine the outcomes we want. This relies on an understanding of power as operating through top-down enforcement and posits law as a central location of declarations by the state that determine outcomes.

Foucault challenges the view that power is primarily about repression or subtraction and suggests that it is significantly more complex. He argues that it is a mistake to view power as being "exercised mainly as a means of deduction . . . a subtraction mechanism, a right to appropriate a portion of the wealth, a tax of products, goods and services, labor and blood, levied on subjects." Instead, Foucault argues, "deduction" is not "the major form of power but merely one element among others, working to incite, reinforce, control, monitor, optimize, and organize the forces under it: a power bent on generating forces, making them grow, and ordering them, rather than one dedicated to . . . making them submit."[3] This perspective is useful in tracing how trans populations come into contact with administrative systems that distribute life chances and promote certain ways of life at the expense of others, all while operating under legal regimes that declare universal equality. A more complete analysis of the multidimensional reality of how racism, homophobia, sexism, transphobia, and ableism function necessitates these additional understandings of how power operates. The two additional modes of power and control I want to discuss are what I will call the "disciplinary" mode of power and the "population-management" mode of power.[4] Naming and examining these two modes allows us to see what the perpetrator/victim, individual/intentional model of discrimination cannot conceive about the operation of systems like racism, sexism, ableism, and transphobia, and allows us to begin to understand a broader set of relationships between law, control, distribution, and redistribution. This discussion also demonstrates why law reforms based on an individual/intentional model of discrimination not only do not resolve the harms they purport to, but serve to strengthen systems of maldistribution and control.

Disciplinary Power:
Norms of Good Behavior and Ways of Being

The disciplinary mode of power refers to how racism, transphobia, sexism, ableism, and homophobia operate through norms that produce ideas about types of people and proper ways to be. These norms are enforced through internal and external policing and discipline. Institutional locations such as medicine, the social sciences, and education—where standards of healthfulness, proper behavior, and socialization are established and taught—are key technologies of disciplinary power. In such locations, we learn how to view our bodies, how our actions make us into certain types of people,[5] and how to practice techniques to modify ourselves to better fit the norms.[6] Foucault describes disciplinary power by saying that it "centers on the body, produces individualizing effects, and manipulates the body as a source of forces that have to be rendered both useful and docile."[7] Through disciplinary norms, we are taught how to be a proper man, woman, boy, girl; how to be healthy, chaste, punctual, productive, intelligent, outgoing, or whatever qualities are valued in our context; and how to avoid (or attempt to avoid) being labeled as truant, criminal, mentally ill, backward, promiscuous, lazy, sociopathic, addicted, slow, or whatever qualities or types are discouraged. We learn the archetypes of proper being and the techniques for reforming ourselves toward these ideals. The impossibility of matching the ideal types generates a lifetime of self- and external policing that keep us occupied with our personal reform efforts.

These norms differ across institutions and subcultures and change over time. One often-discussed example, made famous in the work of Michel Foucault, is how understandings about the relationship of sexual behavior to identity have shifted over time. Classifications taken for granted today, like homosexuality and heterosexuality, were inventions of 19th-century European doctors and scientists who became interested in studying sexual acts that had, until then, been seen as criminal infractions but not as manifestations of a deeper nature or way of being. These doctors and scientists developed the notion that people who engaged in or desired to engage in certain sexual acts and/or gender expressions had a particular type of childhood, physiology, and personality.[8] Foucault wrote,

> As defined by the ancient civil or canonical codes, sodomy was a category of forbidden acts; their perpetrator was nothing more than the juridical subject of them. The nineteenth-century homosexual became a personage, a past, a case history, and a childhood, in addition to being a type of life, a life form, and a morphology, with an indiscreet anatomy and possibly a mysterious physiology. Nothing that went into his total composition was unaffected by his sexuality. . . . It was consubstantial with him, less as a habitual sin than as a singular nature. . . . The sodomite had been a temporary aberration; the homosexual was now a species.[9]

The theories of sexology that Foucault describes emerging in the 19th century changed—though they still underlie contemporary "gay brain" and "gay gene" research—and produced a set of entrenched cultural ideas that guide how people see each other and themselves with regard to the significance of sexual desire. The idea posited by those early sexologists that homosexual desires or acts make someone a certain type of person—a homosexual—rather than simply a range of behaviors and desires that anyone could act upon or experience was thoroughly taken up and forms a key premise of today's lesbian and gay politics. Resistance to pathologizing theories about homosexuality did not reject the idea that homosexual acts and desires are a core aspect of identity. Instead, this idea was entrenched as people claimed those identities as their own and invested in a politics focused on declaring those identities as good, natural, acceptable, and healthy. The idea that some people are gay and others straight, and that sexual desire and/or behavior are defining elements of identity, remains present despite differences in valuation, terminology, and causal theories that have attached to these ideas. The range of debates about homosexuality that have occurred since the invention of the category tend to take for granted that it is a category of persons, that sexual desire is central to identity, and that knowing and telling one's sexual desires is essential to knowing and telling the truth of one's self.

Of course, this process has occurred not just in the realm of sexuality. The invention of various categories of proper and improper subjects is a key feature of disciplinary power that pervades society. The creation and maintenance of such categories of people (e.g., the homosexual, the criminal, the welfare dependent mother, the productive citizen, the terrorist) establish guidelines and norms (e.g., punctuality, heterosexuality, monogamy, dietary norms, racial segregation, manners, dress codes). These norms are enforced through institutions that diagnose, evaluate, take formal or informal disciplinary action, or require trainings, as well as through social or internal approval or shaming. Through these operations, we all learn the norms that govern being a proper man or woman, girl or boy, student, worker, manager, parent, member of our racial group, soldier, age-appropriate dresser, dieter, patriot, or member of our subcultural group. These norms and codes of behavior reach into the most minute details of our bodies, thoughts, and behaviors. The labels and categories generated through our disciplined behavior keep us in our places and help us know how to be ourselves properly.

Foucault suggested that as these norms become internalized, self-regulation would come to displace directly coercive means. This might seem to suggest that disciplinary power is somehow "softer" or less violent than other forms of control. But, as anticolonial re-readings of Foucault by theorists such as Gayatri Chakravorty Spivak, Ann Laura Stoler, and Rey Chow[10] have described, corporeal violence and looming threats of violence have accompanied and bolstered these forms of control. Many have taken this concept of discipline to denote a reduction of violence because control often becomes internalized and thus rendered largely invisible. An examination of race, gender, and colonialism, however, reveals that violence does not end with discipline's emergence. Examples of violent manifestations of enforcing these norms come to mind easily. Consider involuntary psychiatric treatment aimed at changing the mental processes and capacities of people whose behavior or expression is deemed outside certain norms. Another example is the forced assimilation of indigenous people in the United States through boarding school programs that forbade young people from speaking indigenous languages or engaging in indigenous cultural practices and forced them to conform to European gender norms, using violence and separation from family and community to enforce European American ways of being.[11] Examples like these are everywhere in culture—violence is a key means of social control, of enforcing gender, race, ability, class, and other norms. These norms shape how we understand ourselves, others, and the world. They permeate every area of life down to the smallest details of how we chew our food or walk or talk, to the broadest systemic standards of how we keep time, measure productivity, and come to identify and understand human life.

Resistance to the disciplinary mode of control has frequently focused on opposing norms that center whiteness, Christianity, heterosexuality, maleness, gender binarism, and standards of health, intelligence, beauty, and reason that produce violent hierarchies of value. These resistance strategies often focus on exposing disciplinary norms as norms, and proposing alternative ways of being as legitimate. When activists form consciousness-raising groups that encourage people to question standards about how they see their own bodies and identities and replace those norms with other ideas that they consider better, they are engaging with the disciplinary mode of power. White feminist activists and intellectuals in the 1970s are a commonly cited example of this type of work, but it was taken up broadly at that time by Puerto Rican, Black Power, lesbian and gay, and women of color groups, among others. Such groups examined white beauty standards, heterosexism, monogamy, hierarchical governance styles, and other norms, and proposed alternatives ranging from natural hairstyles to polyamory to vegetarianism to collective governance structures. When social movements cultivate critiques of media representations of their communities as lazy, criminal, or mentally ill, they are engaging with disciplinary power. Since the advent of the War on Drugs, Black and youth resistance groups have analyzed and critiqued mainstream media representations of Black youth that fuel racist myths and policies. These groups have also made their own media to represent experiences erased by mainstream media. Similar work has been taken up by immigration activists, pointing out the racism and xenophobia that fuels coverage of immigration issues in the media while simultaneously creating media to document the racism, Islamaphobia, and xenophobia that the War on Terror has wrought. Feminist media critique, similarly, is a rich tradition that has sought to document and expose sexist media portrayals and produce alternatives. Entire media-watch organizations have been created in many movements to specifically take up media critique and response work. Resistance at the level of disciplinary power can also be seen in instances when controversies emerge over whether or not something should be treated as a crime, an illness, or just one way of being among many others (e.g., homosexuality, obesity, trans identity, pregnancy, drug use). Those battles are about resistance to particular disciplinary norms and standards, often emerging from medicine, criminology, and sociology, and reflect a desire to re-code the meanings of certain acts or identities.

Disciplinary control is inadequately addressed by law reform–centered strategies for change. Law reform efforts taken up under the banner of anti-discrimination have often failed to alter these norms. Courts have found that forbidding workers to wear braided hairstyles common to Black cultures is not race discrimination,[12] that firing a worker perceived as male by the employer for wearing pearls does not constitute sex discrimination,[13] that refusing to hire workers with accents different than what is considered standard in the United States is not discrimination on the basis of national origin,[14] and that forcing female employees to wear heavy makeup and highly gendered clothing does not amount to sex discrimination.[15] Because law mostly relies on the individualized perpetrator/victim mode of power when determining whether racism, sexism, ableism, or xenophobia constitutes a violation, challenges to disciplinary norms and standards often fail, leaving racist, sexist, ableist, homophobic, xenophobic, and transphobic standards in place.

Population-Management Power: The Distribution of Life Chances

As I suggested earlier, population management is perhaps the mode of power that is least comprehended and addressed through liberal claims to rights and formal legal equality. Foucault describes the difference between this kind of power and other kinds of power, saying, "it is a question not of imposing law on men, but of disposing things: that is to say, of employing tactics rather than laws, and even of using laws themselves as tactics—to arrange things in such a way that, through a certain number of means, such and such ends may be achieved."[16] This decentralized view of law suggests that laws are merely tactics, rather than that law is the most important form of power. It suggests that power is not primarily operating through prohibition or permission but rather through the arrangement and distribution of security and insecurity. This kind of power, which distributes life chances across populations, is what I am calling "population management." This mode includes interventions that impact the population as a whole, usually interventions undertaken through the logic of promoting the health or security of the nation. Broad-based programs—in fact the very programs that constitute the nation itself—such as taxation, military conscription, social welfare programs (Social Security, Medicaid, public assistance), immigration policy and enforcement, criminal punishment systems, the Census, and identity documentation programs (passports, drivers licensing, birth registration) are technologies of this mode of power. These programs operate through purportedly neutral criteria aimed at distributing health and security and ensuring order. They operate in the name of promoting, protecting, and enhancing the life of the national population and, by doing so, produce clear ideas about the characteristics of who the national population is and which "societal others" should be characterized as "drains" or "threats" to that population.[17]

James C. Scott describes how the modern nation-state is created through the advent of population-level modes of governance. Scott shows how the ability to gather standardized data across the population, facilitated by the creation of standardized weights and measures, language, naming practices, land ownership modalities (freehold estate rather than regionally specific schemes of common land-sharing), and other mechanisms creates state-ness itself by facilitating such basic processes as revenue generation, social control, and militarism.[18] Mitchell Dean explores a similar theme in his work on Foucault's theory of governmentality when he writes

> The internal pacification of a territory, the establishment of monopoly over the use of legitimate violence and taxation, the imposition of a common currency, a common set of laws and legal authorities, certain standards of literacy and language, and even stable and continuous time-space systems, are all integral to the process of state formation. The nation-state was historically constructed through the subordination of various arenas of rule to a more or less central authority and the investment of the duty of the exercise of that authority to long-standing, if not permanent, institutions and personnel.[19]

The programs that constitute the nation by pacifying the territory and producing population-wide regimes of authorized, standardized practice produce and require the identification of "othered" populations. In the United States, from its founding, the distinction between the national population and its constitutive others has always been made through a process of gendered racialization. Gendered racialization was the condition of possibility for the theft of land and labor that established the nation. The distinction between the national population marked out for protection and cultivation and those deemed "internal enemies" or "threats" or "drains" continues to operate through racialized-gendered frameworks. The disciplinary mode of power establishes norms for being a proper productive citizen, worker, adult, man, woman, or student that are enforced on individuals while the population-management mode of power mobilizes those standards and meanings to create policies and programs that apply generally. These general policies and programs use classifications and categories to reach their targets rather than operating on the individual level. In the post–civil rights era, when law has purportedly become "color blind" and otherwise equal, explicit

race and gender classifications are rarely written directly into the
design of these programs. In fact, shameful historical examples
such as the enslavement of millions of Africans, the internment
of Japanese and Japanese Americans, de jure racial segregation,
voting restrictions, and the exclusion of certain populations from
trades, to name but a few, are often evoked to demonstrate how
"fair and equal" US law and culture have become in contrast to
how the United States was before, implying that remaining disparities are based on personal shortcomings since equal opportunity now reigns.

Even though explicit racial and gender exclusions are less
frequently written into law, ideas about race and gender are commonly mobilized to support a general policy or program that
may not explicitly target a group on its face, but that still ac-
complishes its racist/sexist purpose. A memorable example is the
way the depiction of "welfare queens"—portrayed as Black single
mothers "cheating" the welfare system—was used to support the
elimination of certain public assistance programs in the 1990s.[20]
Ronald Reagan famously invoked this mythic image to justify
his attacks on welfare programs, relying on falsified and exag-
gerated anecdotes about women defrauding welfare systems.[21]
Another example is how the demonization of Latin American
immigrants is used to justify heightened immigration enforcement.[22] Depictions of immigrants of color today and historically
have suggested that they take jobs needed by white people and/
or citizens, even when research shows that these assertions have
no basis.[23] A third example of the mobilization of racist and sexist images to promote policies that are neutral on their face but
have a racialized-gendered impact is how the mythology of Black
criminality is produced and used to justify a range of War on
Drugs policies, from sentencing enhancements to exclusion from
public housing and higher education. Support for these population-level programs is mobilized by the use of racist and sexist
images that construct ideas of "us" and "them"—a national population that needs protection and constitutive others who are cast

as threats and drains to that population.[24] The campaigns waged to promote Welfare Reform, the War on Drugs, and the War on Terror have relied on and reproduce racialized-gendered images of the national population, drawing from long-existing racist depictions that perpetually posit white people as chaste, intelligent, responsible, independent, and industrious, and people of color as various combinations of promiscuous, dangerous, dependent, lazy, violent, foreign, and unintelligent.

Foucault helps us understand how producing stateness through population-level programs (including taxation, military conscription, social welfare, education, immigration) always entails the mobilization of ideas about what kind of life must be promoted and what kind of life is a threat and must be left out, rooted out, or extinguished. Because these population-level policy programs, even when they do not explicitly name race and gender in their texts, are actually mobilized through racialized-gendered ideas of the nation, and because they produce and reproduce racialization and gendering of populations as they come to exist, it is not surprising that these programs have racialized-gendered impacts. These policies and programs distribute life chances in a way that does not focus on the individual but rather intervenes on swaths of populations through particular characteristics. As a result, policies and programs that purport to be race and gender neutral will have race- and gender-specific detrimental ramifications. Examples include changes to public assistance programs, increases in drug sentencing, or enhancements to immigration enforcement that are crafted in ways that have the greatest impact on women and people of color, particularly women of color. Policies and programs passed through a mobilization of racist and gendered images will also impact some people not specifically targeted during the mobilization of those images. Some white people will also lose welfare benefits or be deported, even though the campaigns to cut benefit programs or increase immigration enforcement were mobilized by racist images and primarily impact people of color. Other characteristics that put people outside the norms of national identity, such as disability, poverty, or trans identity, enhance vulnerability in these systems, so that white people with these traits are more likely to be impacted by racist policy changes, and people of color with these traits will be especially vulnerable. These methods of power and control are impossible to conceive of under the individual/intentional model of discrimination because such scenarios do not involve an individual person being excluded because of race or gender, and in fact can impact some people not belonging to the primarily targeted group. These examples do not demonstrate the kind of nexus between intention and impact that is imagined in the realm of individual/intentional discrimination models, and yet they create enormous population-level disparities in life chances.[25] Courts, the media, and policy makers, operating on definitions of racism and sexism that require individual intent and a one-to-one nexus of intent and impact, can deny that these programs are racist and sexist and declare them neutral and fair, all the while producing and relying on the racialized-gendered images that promote these programs.

The impact of population-level operations of power, in fact, may be much more significant than the impact of individual discrimination. We can see this in the racial wealth divide in the United States. The individual/intentional discrimination model would ask us to believe that resolving racial inequality in the economy might be best achieved by punishing people who discriminate on the basis of race in the workplace or in offering credit, and that eliminating such behaviors would create a racially neutral and fair economy. However, the racial wealth divide in the United States stems from—and is maintained by—population-level interventions that have ensured the accumulation of wealth by a small number of white people and ensured the inability to accumulate wealth for most people of color. The creation of racialized property statuses at the founding of the United States through slavery and land theft from indigenous peoples were key to establishing wealth for white populations and poverty for people of color. Whiteness was established as the status that bestowed the power to own slaves and profit from their labor and be eligible to own property forcibly taken from indigenous people.[26] Even after the official end of slavery in 1865 and following the initial period of European settlement, ongoing programs and policies have ensured continued poverty, land theft, and economic exploitation of people of color.

Major national programs have maintained and exacerbated the racial wealth divide. For example, although people of color were disproportionately impacted by the Great Depression because of their disproportionate poverty, New Deal programs were designed in ways that mostly benefited white workers. For example, the Social Security Act provided a safety net for millions of workers but excluded domestic and agricultural workers who were largely people of color. The 1935 Wagner Act granted white workers the right to collective bargaining through unions, but it also allowed those unions to exclude and discriminate on the basis of race, helping maintain racial barriers to high paying jobs and exacerbating the racial wealth divide. It also excluded domestic and agricultural workers. Another example is the 1944 Servicemen's Readjustment Act, more commonly known as the G.I. Bill, which assisted many white American war veterans to obtain college educations and home and business loans after World War II but was of little use to veterans of color. Black veterans had a much harder time utilizing the G.I. Bill because of racism at colleges, universities, and banks, and because many were unprepared to attend college because they had received such inadequate public education in the segregated school system. The US Department of Veterans Affairs, with its affiliation to the all white American Legion and Veterans of Foreign Wars, exercised its power to deny or grant the claims of Black members of the armed forces. Jim Crow laws, Asian exclusion laws, redlining, taxation laws, allotment schemes, various treaties denying land rights, and many other population-level government interventions produced and maintained the poverty of people of color while home and business loan programs, land grants, education grants and loans, and government benefits programs supported and continue to support white people in accumulating and sustaining wealth.[27]

The ongoing trend away from taxing wealth and toward taxing income from work has continued to build and maintain this wealth into the contemporary period, just as immigration enforcement, mass incarceration, and attacks on workers' rights, public benefits, public transportation, and public education have continued to keep people of color disproportionately in poverty. To limit our inquiry about why the racial wealth divide exists in the United States today to a search for individual racist employers or bankers suggests that besides these "few bad apples," the economy is racially fair or neutral. Such framing is often accompanied by an assertion that people of color are to blame for their disproportionate poverty. It is often accompanied by the observation that some people of color do experience financial upward mobility, which, it is asserted, must mean that racism does not mediate economic participation. This logic relies on the individual/intentional model of racism and functions to obscure the true conditions and operations of power that produce a correlation between wealth, race, and lifespan. It is only when we look at purportedly race-neutral population-level modes of control and distribution that we can understand and account for the racial wealth divide rather than permitting it to be justified through racism.

The myth of legal equality in the United States is supported by the narrative that US laws used to exclude people on the basis of race and gender but now they do not. Supposedly, all is now fair and equal. However, our nation itself was built by the establishment of population-level systems of property and labor regulation that created and utilized racial and gender categories from the beginning. The population-level programs that were mobilized from their inception by explicit race and gender exclusions continue to do the work of distributing security and vulnerability along race and gender lines, just under the auspices of race and gender neutral criteria. The race and gender rhetoric changes as struggles reshape the language and frameworks, but policies and programs used to manage and distribute resources across the population are still mobilized by race and gender, and continue to distribute security and vulnerability across the population through those vectors.[28]

Turning to the example of the history of welfare in the United States also reveals how even as population-level programs become officially race and gender neutral over time, they continue to target harm and violence through vectors of gender and race. The creation of the first income support programs in the United States benefited white widows of soldiers. These programs were created through a campaign that focused on promoting "the well-being of the race" by ensuring that white mothers had the resources to properly raise the nation's future white leaders in moral homes.[29] As additional programs were added, the United States developed a tiered public benefits system where surviving spouses of soldiers and full-time workers receive higher benefits than parents applying for public assistance not linked to such statuses, and disability and survivor benefit payment levels correspond to employment status and pay prior to disability or death. The tiered structure of the programs causes white people to disproportionately receive higher benefits because they have disproportionately higher rates of employment and pay due to structural racism.

Although the laws governing social welfare are no longer explicitly based on race, the fact that the United States has a tiered social welfare system (as compared with many other countries that provide general benefits) creates significant racial and gender disparity in how much support the benefits actually provide. The creation of a tiered social welfare system allows certain programs to be racially coded in ways that make them more stigmatized and more vulnerable to attack. Aid to Families with Dependent Children (AFDC), the program traditionally called "welfare" in the United States, has consistently been the target of racist and gendered attacks by media, academia, and politicians who have fabricated notions of "cultures of dependency" that pathologize benefits recipients. When compared with other government subsidy programs, such as Social Security benefits, farm subsidies, or corporate tax breaks, the political implications of creating tiered benefits systems that sort recipient populations along lines of race, gender, and income are clear. The Clinton-era attack on and dismantling of AFDC was supported by media "exposés" of "cheats" (usually depicted as unmarried Black mothers). The programs most likely to support people of color were attacked and defunded.[30]

Although "welfare reform" harms many white families, it has had a particularly calamitous impact on female-headed families of color that mirror the underlying racialized-gendered structure of the United States public benefits systems and the specific rhetoric mobilized by the campaign. The numerous programs that subsidize middle class and upper class disproportionately white families, and that utilize more government funds than AFDC benefits, were never subjected to similar attacks.[31] The fact that the public assistance systems of the United States were and are tiered from their inception—making AFDC disproportionately relied on by female-headed families of color—combined with years of social science research that portrayed Black families as pathologically matriarchal and that blamed poor people for poverty, created an ideal context for attacks on the program.[32] This story is typical of the operation of population-level interventions that mobilize ideas of a standard, healthy population. The national population is understood to face a risk from marginalized "others" that are portrayed as drains on or threats to the well-being of the nation. Although the early rhetoric used to establish aid to widows in the United States was more explicitly racist, literally asserting that the program was needed to ensure that white widows could "promote the race" by raising their children, the 1990s attack on AFDC also mobilized ideas about a white public that needed protecting from harmful or socially draining others whose existence was cast as a threat to race and gender norms. Both framings (and all that came between and since) are examples of the racialized-gendered articulation of nationhood that is employed to establish broad-based programs that have populations, rather than individuals, as their targets, and that condition the distributions of life chances.

Similar histories can be traced in other security-focused population-level programs in the United States, such as immigration, criminal punishment, education, and health care. Racialized-gendered conceptions of the nation that depend on the construction of a national population in need of protection from poor people, people of color, immigrants, and others cast as internal and external "enemies" are formed at the inception of security-focused population-level programs and continue to undergird and structure such programs, even if explicit exclusions are eliminated. The language of racial and gendered othering has changed over time as formal legal equality has become the mandate of the law, but these programs are still deployed to the same ends. The forces that produce and reproduce these events are complex and multiple. It was not just President Clinton or the people in the 1996 Congress who dismantled welfare: it was a combination of enduring racist and sexist stereotypes, the mobilization of racial and gender norms in academic research and media, internalized understandings of race, gender, and economy held by millions of Americans, and myriad other conditions that produced these changes. Understanding population-management power illuminates the complexity of how race and gender operate as vectors of the distribution of life chances that cannot simply be solved by passing laws declaring that various groups are now "equal."

The rapid growth of the criminal punishment system in the United States is another obvious site of the operation of population-level interventions mobilized by racialized-gendered narratives. The quadrupling of the US prison system in just a few decades was accomplished in large part by the passage of laws that increased sentences for certain charges related to drug use, possession, and sale. Popular support for these changes was built by panic-inducing discourses from politicians and the media about gang warfare and crack cocaine. Exposé-style media stories, an explosion of police/prosecution television shows and movies, and the declaration of the War on Drugs were employed in the portrayal of a threatening proliferation of violence in Black communities. The policies and practices that resulted were responsible for increased policing in poor neighborhoods while providing law enforcement with more tools for surveilling, arresting, and caging poor people and people of color. These policies and practices also increased barriers to survival and political participation for people convicted of drug possession or sale by eliminating their eligibility for public housing, student loans, and, in certain states, voting rights, among other things.[33] While the criminal punishment system declares itself to be about individual accountability for wrongful acts, the implementation of population-level interventions mobilized through racialized-gendered frameworks of "threat" and "drain" resulted in a system that does not target users and sellers of illegal substances, but instead targets people of color (at the population level) for imprisonment. As we saw earlier by looking at Angela Davis's work, these frameworks have mobilized punishment and confinement consistently since the founding of the United States, though the legal mechanisms formally transitioned from chattel slavery to criminal punishment in the late 1880s.

The distinction between the disciplinary mode of power and population-level control is important here. At the level of norms and discipline, we each learn the rules about how to be. We learn what is perceived as "right" or "proper" and "normal" in various ways, and we struggle and strive to meet those standards (even by inventing our own alternative subcultural norms) and to encourage and coerce others (our children, our co-workers, our elected officials) to follow them. In the disciplinary mode, the meeting and not meeting of these norms occurs at the individual level. We might be shamed or excluded for dressing unprofessionally, for failing to meet white cultural norms, for being too large or too small, too loud or too quiet, too compassionate or too violent, or too feminine or too masculine.

At the population level, however, power works differently and individual behavior is not the target of intervention, nor can it prevent vulnerability. Population-level interventions create conditions of control and distribution that impact people regardless of their individual acts. Living in communities impacted by policy decisions that have made schools, health care, housing, and other infrastructure insufficient, that have been zoned for toxic industries, and where high levels of police presence increase the likelihood of being harassed or even arrested for behavior that is just as common elsewhere but not equally surveilled, are all examples of conditions that impact the health and security of populations regardless of the acts of individuals that either comply or fail to comply with various norms. The opposite is also true: people living in communities with a high quality of services, clean air and water, and who are largely exempt from police harassment and criminal enforcement may retain enormous health and security whether or not they violate social norms.

We can see the operation of population-level power if we consider the examples of these two communities. Teenagers and adults who use drugs in these two communities will not experience the same consequences. Teens in the poorer community are more likely to have the police called in by their school (if they are not already there), while teens in wealthy communities are more likely to have behavior problems solved through parental or school discipline, private drug treatment or therapy. People in the wealthy community are more likely to have private spaces away from police surveillance to buy and use drugs, and more likely to get drugs through safer, less criminalized channels like prescriptions from doctors. Parents who neglect their children will not experience the same consequences. The child welfare system disproportionately targets families of color and poor families for intervention.[34] People with psychiatric disabilities will have very different experiences. The ability to pay for private treatment will

make a significant impact, and the likelihood of experiencing police harassment and arrest for behaving in ways that are outside of
norms is far greater for people of color and poor people. Although
narratives about what constitutes a proper citizen, neighbor, man,
woman, student, or worker impact disciplinary codes that we enforce on ourselves and each other are mobilized in the promotion
of certain population-level interventions, they operate differently
in the individual context versus the population-level context.
Being able to understand the overlapping but distinct operation
of these two vectors of power is essential for forming an accurate
analysis of the arrangements and impact of transphobia, racism,
ableism, xenophobia, sexism, and homophobia—and for conceptualizing methods of resistance.

As Alan Freeman's description of the perpetrator perspective
explains, the law's understanding of the function of racism (and,
we can extrapolate, other forms of control and maldistribution)
is extremely narrow: a violation can only be found when the
formula of intentional, individual discrimination is met.[35]
Such a narrow view depends on naturalizing and erasing the
historical and contemporary conditions that lead different
groups to have such starkly dissimilar life chances. As the history
of anti-discrimination and hate crime laws in the United States
illustrates, using the perpetrator perspective to define and address
racism through law only creates formal legal equality on paper. It
does not and cannot create the kind of massive redistribution of
wealth and life chances that would actually address the impacts
of white supremacy. Using a narrow formal legal equality and
discrimination model tends to focus on changing what the law
explicitly says about a given group but does not address the ways
that legal, policy, and institutional practices create conditions
that severely disadvantage certain populations through
the mobilization of racism, sexism, ableism, transphobia,
xenophobia, and homophobia, but without explicitly and/or
individually addressing subjects through those lenses.

Discipline, Population Management, and Trans Vulnerability

Understanding discipline and population management is essential to discerning the causes of the kind of structured insecurity and shortened life spans faced by trans people described in the Preface. The kinds of harm that occur through both of these modes of power are especially difficult to reach through law reform efforts, and understanding these operations of power helps us to understand why, even when certain law reforms are won, conditions do not improve. Both are very important to examine; however, disciplinary gender norms have received far more attention in trans scholarship and activism than population-level interventions. Trans activists and scholars have explored how the medicalization of trans identities forces trans people to conform to rigid disciplinary gender norms in order to access medical technologies if we want or need them; how gender norms motivate employers to pass over trans applicants for hire or to fire trans employees; how gender norms in social services, families, and religious organizations often result in the abandonment or abuse of trans people; and how gender norms are used even within various trans communities to establish norms of transness that we enforce against one another and against ourselves. Analyzing how trans and gender nonconforming vulnerability is produced through population-level interventions is essential and has been explored less.

Thinking about population-management power can help us do a few key things. First, we can analyze the use of gender as an administrative category by institutions of all kinds (e.g., schools, hospitals, DMVs, employers, tax systems, prisons, welfare systems, shelters and group homes, transportation systems). Second, we can formulate understandings of the racialized-gendered nature of key population-level interventions (e.g., prison expansion, the War on Terror and the War on Drugs, the expansion of immigration enforcement, the elimination of welfare entitlements) from the perspective of trans and gender nonconforming experiences. Finally, we can formulate strategies for resistance and transformation that will actually reach and alter the harmful practices that shorten trans lives through the mobilization of race and gender norms at the population level.

Such analysis and action requires a deliberate break from the legal rights focus that has come to be portrayed as the natural and preeminent target of marginalized groups, and has been modeled by lesbian and gay rights reform efforts in recent decades. With the recognition that changing what the law explicitly says about a group does not necessarily remedy the structured insecurity faced by that group comes a larger question about transformations that cannot occur through demands for legal recognition and inclusion. In fact, legal inclusion and recognition demands often reinforce the logics of harmful systems by justifying them, contributing to their illusion of fairness and equality, and by reinforcing the targeting of certain perceived "drains" or "internal enemies," carving the group into "the deserving" and "the undeserving" and then addressing only the issues of the favored sector.

The relationship of lesbian and gay law reform projects to the field of criminal law provides an obvious and useful example. The two major interventions of lesbian and gay law reformers in criminal law have been advocating the decriminalization of sodomy and the passage of sexual orientation–inclusive hate crime laws. The choice of these two targets demonstrates the "what the law says about us" focus of the work. If the aims were to reduce the number of lesbian and gay people in prisons and jails or to reduce the medical neglect, nutritional deprivation, rape, and murder of queer people who are imprisoned, the legal strategy would have been vastly different. It might have focused on supporting people currently imprisoned, joining and creating lawsuits focused on prison conditions, opposing sentencing enhancements for drugs and other criminalized behaviors that are responsible for the bulk of imprisonment for all people (including lesbian and gay people), fighting against police violence, actively resisting prison expansion and criminalization, and joining efforts toward prison abolition. Instead, the goal of the interventions taken up by the most well-resourced lesbian and gay organizations was to merely alter the parts of criminal law that explicitly name lesbian and gay people as criminal solely for behavior associated with homosexuality and to lobby to be added to the list of populations explicitly (but not actually) protected by criminal law. This approach concerns itself exclusively with the explicit and intentional operations of homophobia when written into law, but leaves out a distributionary understanding of criminal punishment that would create ideas for intervention that actually improve the life chances of gay and lesbian people who face criminalization. As I argued in Chapter Two, these strategies risk not only failing to improve the life chances of the people they are supposed to help, but also of strengthening the criminal punishment system by allowing it to appear fair and neutral, casting it as a source of protection from violence rather than a primary perpetrator of violence. In the case of hate crime laws, such strategies even enhance its resources and capacity to punish. Does the end of sodomy criminalization and the addition of sexual orientation to hate crime laws mean that the criminal punishment system is no longer homophobic? Of course not. But producing such a narrow criminal law reform agenda suggests so.

Another danger of such a strategy is that it is produced by and enhances race and class divides among lesbians and gays that correlate to experiences in and views of the criminal punishment system. For those living in white communities not targeted for policing and imprisonment, the criminal punishment system may appear to be a protector and its perceived flaws limited to these narrow, explicit inclusions and exclusions. For those lesbian and gay people who live in fear of police harassment and violence, have faced the loss of family members to imprisonment, or are regularly targeted by the juvenile and adult punishment systems, more explicit homophobic inclusion or exclusion in certain aspects of the criminal law may be a small and possibly insignificant demand. Those populations may crave interventions that do more to reduce or end imprisonment and/or protect prisoners. Even more importantly, people who are part of campaigns to dismantle systems because they see those systems articulate control at the population level are likely to understand how reforms that are solely concerned with how those systems describe themselves are misguided and dangerous. As previously discussed, the demand for hate crime legislation has the danger of building the criminal punishment system by enhancing penalties and resources.[36] For groups organizing to oppose policing and imprisonment, including people of color, people with disabilities, and poor people, such reforms run in opposition to their work.

Similar controversies have emerged in other instances where (usually white-led) lesbian and gay (and sometimes trans) reform organizations have sought inclusion or recognition from systems that feminist, racial justice, and disability justice activists and scholars have identified as key nodes of maldistribution of life chances. The quests for inclusion in US military service and in the institution of marriage have generated these same rifts. For those who know that the US military is a primary force of systematic rape, colonization, land and resource theft, genocide, and other racist and gender-based violence, the notion that a lesbian and gay political stance should focus on military inclusion rather than demilitarization is a grave, divisive mistake. For those who have long articulated opposition to state incentivization and reward for heteropatriarchial sexuality and family structures and punishment for others, the idea that lesbian and gay people should seek marriage recognition rather than aim to abolish marriage and achieve more just methods of distribution is similarly problematic. The history of these controversies and the political choices made during their development relates to the rise of neoliberalism in the wake of the social movements of the 1960s and 1970s discussed in Chapter One.

The early gay politics of the Stonewall era was influenced by and included demands for racial justice, feminism, anti-colonialism, and overall demilitarization that were being raised by many vibrant movements domestically and globally at that time. Critiques of policing, imperialism, social norms, and systemic patriarchy (including marriage) were co-articulated and interwoven by many groups and individuals during that period. As the backlash to those movements rose and "law and order" politics emerged along with nonprofitization, a newly conservatized lesbian and gay politics focused on inclusion and recognition came to dominate public discourse about resistance to homophobia. Formal legal equality in the form of marriage inclusion, sodomy decriminalization, anti-discrimination, military inclusion, and the passage of hate crime laws became its prime targets. The analytical frameworks of the social movements of the 1960s and 1970s, which focused on broad, population-level disparities, was replaced by individual discrimination-based understandings of racism, homophobia, ableism, and sexism, both in law and popular culture. The result, thus far, has been legal reforms that mostly maintain—and often bolster—systems of maldistribution and control in the name of equality, individuality, and even diversity.[37]

As trans politics develops, a similar set of choices arise before us. Inclusion and recognition arguments that coalesce around hate crime and anti-discrimination laws are the seemingly obvious targets for trans law reform, both because they have been modeled by lesbian and gay rights strategies and because there is a broadly believed myth in the United States that such strategies ended racial subordination. However, the limitations of these strategies have been well articulated by women of color feminists, critical disability scholars and activists, and critical race theorists, as well as from many engaged in queer and trans resistance. The understanding of control, distribution, and power that these critical perspectives provide exposes the limitations of currently celebrated yet ineffective law reform strategies and generates a theory of change that de-centers law reform in the quest for transformative change.

We must stop believing that what the law says about itself
is true and that what the law says about us is what matters. Our
goal cannot be to get the law to say "good" instead of "bad" things
about people who are marginalized, criminalized, impoverished,
exploited, and exiled. Law reform and an investment in winning
"rights" has proven to legitimize and shore up the very arrangements
that produce the harm we seek to eradicate. If we curtail and
narrow our vision in ways that make it impossible to imagine a
more just world, that limit our imaginations to what a US legal
system, created to establish and maintain slavery and colonialism
can provide, we will perpetuate rather than deeply transform
the arrangements that concern us. Thinking about population-
management power opens up a space for us to reconsider how
we think about those harmful arrangements, what targets and
methods we take for our interventions, and how to strategize the
change we need.

NOTES

1. Michel Foucault, *History of Sexuality Vol. 1: An Introduction*,
Trans. Robert Hurley (New York: Vintage Books, [1978] 1990), 136.

2. Alan David Freeman, "Legitimizing Racial Discrimination
Through Anti-Discrimination Law: A Critical Review of Supreme
Court Doctrine," in *Critical Race Studies: The Key Writings that Formed
the Movement*, ed. Kimberlé Crenshaw, Neil Gotanda, Garry Peller, and
Kendall Thomas. (New York: The New Press, 1996), 29–45.

3. Michel Foucault, *History of Sexuality*, 136.

4. I am relying on Foucault's theorization of discipline and biopol-
itics. See *History of Sexuality*; Michel Foucault, *Society Must Be Defended:
Lectures at the College de France, 1975–76*, Trans. David Macey (New
York: Picador, 2003); and Michel Foucault, *Security, Territory, Population*
(New York: Picador, 2009).

5. Eva Cherniavsy, discussing Michael Hardt's description of
Foucault's concept of discipline as a way of thinking about civil society,
puts it nicely, writing, "Foucauldian discipline . . . is not an ordering of

natural or given social elements, not a restrictive apparatus, in short, but a productive one that conjures the very identities to be managed." Eva Cherniavsy, "Neocitizenship and Critique," *Social Text* 27 (2009): 1–23; quote p. 10.

6. Foucault, *History of Sexuality*; Foucault, *Society Must Be Defended*, 249.

7. Foucault, *Society Must Be Defended*, 249.

8. Foucault, *History of Sexuality*.

9. Foucault, *History of Sexuality*, 43.

10. See Gayatri Chakravorty Spivak, "Can the Subaltern Speak?" in *Marxism and the Interpretation of Culture*, ed. Cary Nelson and Lawrence Grossberg (Chicago: University of Illinois Press, 1988); Ann Laura Stoler, *Race and the Education of Desire: Foucault's* History of Sexuality *and the Colonial Order of Things* (Durham, NC: Duke University Press, 1995); Ann Laura Stoler, *Carnal Knowledge and Imperial Power: Race and the Intimate in Colonial Rule* (Berkeley, CA: University of California Press, 2002); and Rey Chow, *The Protestant Ethnic and the Spirit of Capitalism* (New York: Columbia University Press, 2002). Scott Lauria Morgensen, in his description of the imposition of binary gender norms on colonized indigenous young people subjected to boarding school programs, argues that the "shifting colonial authority from a brutal right of public execution to the normalization of death in regulatory regimes based on discipline . . . [employed] methods [that] were no less terrorizing." Scott Lauria Morgensen, "Settler Homonationalism: Theorizing Settler Colonialism within Queer Modernities," *GLQ: A Journal of Lesbian and Gay Studies* 16 (2010): 105–131, 116.

11. See Andrea Smith, *Conquest: Sexual Violence and American Indian Genocide* (Cambridge, MA: South End Press, 2005), 35–54; Scott Lauria Morgensen, "Settler Homonationalism," 105–131, 111–116.

12. *Rogers v. American Airlines*, 527 F.Supp. 229 (1981).

13. *Ulane v. Eastern Airlines*, 742 F.2d 1081 (1984).

14. *Fragante v. City and County of Honolulu*, 888 F.2d 591 (1989); *Kahakua v. Friday*, 876 F. 2d 896 (9th Cir. 1989); *Salem v. La Salle High School*, No. 82-01310-BR, C.D.Cal. (March 31, 1983); *Gideon v. Riverside Community College District*, 800 F.2d 1145 (1986); Mari

Matsuda, "Voices of America: Accent, Antidiscrimination Law and Jurisprudence for the Last Reconstruction," *Yale Law Journal* 100 (1991): 1329.

15. *Jespersen v. Harrah's Operating Co., Inc.*, 444 F.3d 1104 (9th Cir. 2006).

16. Michel Foucault, "Governmentality," in *The Foucault Effect: Studies in Governmentality*, ed. Graham Burchell, Colin Gordon, and Peter Miller (Chicago: University of Chicago Press, 1991), 95.

17. Foucault describes racism as the technology that justifies killing those marked as inferior in the context of a power mobilized to promote the life of the population: "What in fact is racism? It is primarily a way of introducing a break into the domain of life that is under power's control: the break between what must live and what must die. [. . .] In a normalizing society, race or racism is the precondition that makes killing acceptable. [. . .] When I say 'killing,' I obviously do not mean simply murder as such but also every form of indirect murder: the fact of exposing someone to death, increasing the risk of death for some people, or, quite simply, political death, expulsion, rejection and so on." Mariana Valverde, "Genealogies of European States: Foucauldian Reflections," *Economy and Society* 36, no. 1 (February 2007): 176; Foucault, *Society Must Be Defended*, 254, 258.

18. James C. Scott, *Seeing Like a State: How Certain Schemes to Improve the Human Condition Have Failed* (New Haven, CT: Yale University Press, 1998). Paisley Currah and Lisa Jean Moore's article, "We Won't Know Who You Are: Contesting Sex Designations in New York City Birth Certificates," explores the significance of birth registration programs to the kind of state making Scott describes and provides a useful analysis of recent efforts by trans activists related to birth registration documents. *Hypatia* 24 (2009): 113–135.

19. Mitchell Dean, *Governmentality: Power and Rule in Modern Society*, 2nd ed. (London: SAGE Publications, 2010), 34.

20. "Gendered racism is a concept that can also help us to understand the intensity of white hostility toward the supposedly ubiquitous and stereotypical 'welfare queen.' She is typically portrayed by the mass media and in everyday discourse as an African-American woman who is living

fraudulently, lazily, and 'royally' off generous welfare benefits provided by taxes paid by overworked European Americans. . . . Gendered racism, like racism more generally, is best viewed not as a thing but as a process. Thinking about racism as a process leads us to ask how and why racism occurs in policy arenas such as welfare. By focusing on gendered racism as a process, one can analyze ways in which negative class-, race-, and gender-based images of impoverished, public assistance-reliant mothers are effectively mobilized by racial state actors and others who contribute to welfare-related discourse. It is important to ask why racial state actors choose to single out women of color in this discourse (or use race-coded terms for such women), given that there are plenty of white women who rely on welfare. It is also revealing to explore the functions that effective mobilization of such images serves for whites and for white racial hegemony more generally." Kenneth J. Neubeck and Noel A. Cazenave, *Welfare Racism: Playing the Race Card Against America's Poor* (New York: Routledge: 2001), 30.

21. "Welfare Queen Becomes Issue in Reagan Campaign," *New York Times*, February 15, 1976, 51; Bridgette Baldwin, "Stratification of the Welfare Poor: Intersections of Gender, Race, & 'Worthiness' in Poverty Discourse and Policy," *The Modern American* 6 (2010): 4.

22. The laws passed in 2010 by the Arizona state legislature that required police to question people they suspect to be undocumented immigrants, that banned education programs aimed at Latinos and Latinas, and that required school systems to fire teachers with native-Spanish speaking accents or who spoke English "incorrectly" were a rare instance where many people in the United States seemed to understand that these purportedly race-neutral laws are actually targeted at Latin@ populations. Of course, many of the people who publicly disapproved of one or more of Arizona's new laws, including President Barack Obama, do not generally oppose the broader immigration system which is and always has been, from its inception, enforced in ways that target people of color, people with disabilities, queer and trans people, and poor people. Many of those who have spoken out against Arizona's new laws have entirely failed, for example, to oppose "Secure Communities," a federal program that, similar to Arizona's controversial law, uses local

law enforcement mechanisms increasingly to surveil immigration status with the goal of increasing deportation. Immigration Policy Center,
Secure Communities: A Fact Sheet (Washington, D.C.: Immigration
Policy Center, November 4, 2010), http://www.immigrationpolicy.org/
just-facts/secure-communities-fact-sheet.

23. Mae M. Ngai describes how anti-Filipino violence in 1920s
California was often fueled by rhetoric about job competition. However,
"that conclusion was not supported by the actual patterns of employment
and racial conflict." In fact, there was often a shortage of white labor in
the area and whites often were not interested in the kinds of jobs Filipinos
were hired to do. Misinformation of this kind, fueled by racism and xenophobia, persists in immigration debates throughout the US history of
immigration enforcement. Mae M. Ngai, *Impossible Subjects: Illegal Aliens
and the Making of Modern America* (Princeton, NJ: Princeton University
Press, 2004), 106.

24. Foucault, *Society Must Be Defended,* 254–256.

25. A well-known legal case that demonstrates how the law's narrow
understanding of oppression prevents it from being able to remedy systemic racism is *San Antonio Independent School District v. Rodriguez,* 411
US 1 (1973). In that case, the Supreme Court considered a Texas school
district's method of school financing that was based on property taxes and
resulted in severe disparity between the resources of the schools in the
white wealthy area and the poor area populated by Black and Latino students. The rich schools, which were 81 percent white, 18 percent Latino
and 1 percent Black, had $594 per pupil per year. The poor schools,
which were 90 percent Latino, 6 percent Black, and 4 percent white, had
$356 per pupil per year. The average assessed property value per pupil in
the rich district was $49,000 while in the poor district it was $5,960. The
Supreme Court refused to make a finding that this method of financing
schools deserved the Court's strict scrutiny because of its class- or race-
based impact.

26. Cheryl I. Harris, "Whiteness as Property," *Harvard Law Review*
106 (1993): 1709; Andrea Smith, "Heteropatriarchy and the Three
Pillars of White Supremacy: Rethinking Women of Color Organizing,"
in *Color of Violence: The INCITE! Anthology,* ed. INCITE! Women of

Color Against Violence (Cambridge, MA: South End Press, 2006).

27. See United for a Fair Economy, *Closing the Racial Wealth Divide Training Manual* (Boston: United for a Fair Economy, 2006).

28. Jodi Melamed's remarks at the 2011 Critical Ethnic Studies Conference at UC Riverside addressed this shift in the rhetoric mobilized by the US to maintain racialized distributions of wealth and life chances. Her formulation reveals how these changes have constrained political discourse in ways that assist resistance politics in being co-opted into narrow rights struggles that cannot deliver transformative change. She argued

> Within a framework that redefined racism as "prejudice" and anti-racism as the extension of equal opportunity, possessive individualism, and cultural citizenship to all, Cold War U.S. racial policy was at once a geopolitics that grafted a nonredistributive anti-racism to a U.S. nationalism itself bearing the agency of transnational capitalism. This grafting was decisive. Cold War racial liberalism compelled a field of racial meanings in which dominant anti-racist discourse have to take U.S. ascendancy for granted and to incorporate the interests of the state into the goals of anti-racism. It restricts the settlement of racialized conflict to liberal political terrains that conceal the material inequalities capitalism generates.

29. Gwendolyn Mink, "The Lady and the Tramp: Gender, Race and the Origins of the American Welfare State," in *Women, the State and Welfare*, ed. Linda Gordon (Madison, WI: University of Wisconsin Press, 1990), 92–122; Lisa Duggan, *The Twilight of Equality? Neoliberalism, Cultural Politics, and the Attack on Democracy* (Boston: Beacon Press: 2004).

30. Mink, "The Lady and the Tramp"; Holloway Sparks, "Queens Teens and Model Mothers: Race, Gender and the Discourse of Welfare Reform," in *Race and the Politics of Welfare Reform*, ed. Sanford F. Schram, Joe Soss, and Richard Fording (Ann Arbor, MI: University of Michigan Press, 2003), 188–189; Duggan, *The Twilight of Equality?*

31. Loïc Waquant draws attention to the absurdity of Clinton-era

attacks on welfare by exposing the much larger subsidies for wealthy families that were kept in place.

> [N]otwithstanding the thundering proclamations of politicians from all sides about the necessity to 'end the era of Big government'—the cheery chorus of Clinton's State of the Union address in 1996—the US government continues to provide many kinds of guarantees and support to corporations as well as to the middle and upper classes, starting, for example, with home ownership assistance: almost half of the $64 billion in fiscal deductions for mortgage interest payments and real estate taxes granted in 1994 by Washington (amounting to nearly three times the budget for public housing) went to the 5 percent of American households earning more than $100,000 that year; and 16 percent of that sum went to the top 1 percent of taxpayers with incomes exceeding $200,000. Over seven in ten families in the top 1 percent received mortgage subsidies (averaging $8,457) as against fewer than 3 percent of the families below the $30,000 mark (for a paltry $486 each). This fiscal subsidy of $64 billion to wealthy home owners dwarfed the national outlay for welfare ($17 billion), food stamps ($25 million), and child nutrition assistance ($7.5 billion).

Loïc Waquant, *Punishing the Poor: The Neoliberal Government of Social Insecurity* (Durham: Duke University Press, 2009), 42.

32. Perhaps the most infamous document in this research trend is the 1965 document, *The Negro Family: The Case for National Action*, usually called the Moynihan report. The report argued that Black family life was a "tangle of pathology . . . capable of perpetuating itself without assistance from the white world" and that "at the heart of the deterioration of the fabric of Negro society is the deterioration of the Negro family." It asserted that economic and political equality for Black people hinged on increasing the prevalence of heterosexual nuclear families in the Black community. It was a key document in establishing the racist, sexist, antipoor idea that welfare receipt is a cause and effect of non-adherence to patriarchal norms of family structure. Daniel Patrick Moynihan, *The Negro*

Family: The Case for National Action (Washington, DC: Office of Policy Planning and Research, US Department of Labor, 1965).

33. Patricia Allard, "Crime, Punishment, and Economic Violence," in *Color of Violence: The INCITE! Anthology*, ed. INCITE! Women of Color Against Violence (Cambridge, MA: South End Press, 2006), 157–163.

34. Dorothy Roberts has extensively documented and analyzed the racial disparities in the child welfare system. "More than a half million children taken from their parents are currently in foster care. African Americans are the most likely of any group to be disrupted in this way by government authorities. Black children make up nearly half the foster care population, although they constitute less than one fifth of the nation's children. In Chicago, 95 percent of children in foster care are Black. Once removed from their homes, Black children remain in foster care longer, are moved more often, receive fewer services, and are less likely to be either returned home or adopted than other children." Dorothy Roberts, *Shattered Bonds: The Color of Child Welfare* (New York: Civitas Books, 2002), vi.

35. Freeman, "Legitimizing Racial Discrimination Through Anti-Discrimination Law," 29–45.

36. The 2009 controversies around the addition of the death penalty to the federal hate crime statute brought these tensions to the surface. The National Coalition of Anti-Violence Projects released a statement critiquing the addition of the death penalty clause specifically, while other groups, such as Communities United Against Violence in San Francisco, the Audre Lorde Project, the American Friends Service Committee, and the Sylvia Rivera Law Project in New York City, had critiqued the hate crime law strategy from the start. The controversy brought attention to the real dangers of trying to ally with the criminal punishment system, given its relentless drive to expand itself by adding more and harsher punishments wherever possible. Rebecca Waggoner-Kloek and Sharon Stapel, "Statement of the National Coalition of Anti-Violence Programs" (2009), www.avp.org/documents/NCAVPShepardAct9.24.09.pdf; Sylvia Rivera Law Project, FIERCE, Queers for Economic Justice, Peter Cicchino Youth Project, and the Audre Lorde Project, "SRLP Announces Non-Support of

the Gender Employment Non-Discrimination Act" (2009), http://srlp. org/genda; and Sylvia Rivera Law Project, "SRLP Opposes the Matthew Shepard and James Byrd, Jr. Hate Crimes Prevention Act" (2009), http:// srlp.org/fedhatecrimelaw.

37. See Avery Gordon and Christopher Newfield, eds., *Mapping Multiculturalism* (Minneapolis: University of Minnesota Press, 2008).

Chapter 4
Administrating Gender

As we shift our understanding of power from a focus on individual/intentional discrimination to a focus on norms that govern population management, different areas of law start to appear as the focal points of harm for vulnerable groups. The aim of getting the law to declare a group equal through anti-discrimination and hate crime legislation recedes and we become interested in the legal systems that distribute security and vulnerability at the population level and sort the population into those whose lives are cultivated and those who are abandoned, imprisoned, or extinguished. In this chapter, we turn toward the realm of administrative law—we look at the administrative agencies that are responsible for the bulk of government activities that impact the distribution of life chances. This is a set of operations of law that, compared to anti-discrimination and hate crime laws, are often ignored when it comes to analyzing the harms of racism, transphobia, ableism, homophobia, and sexism.[1] However, when we shift our understanding of power and examine where and how harm and vulnerability operate and are distributed, it is this area of law that comes to the fore. Critical trans politics requires an analysis of how the administration of gender norms impacts trans people's lives and how administrative systems in general are sites of production and implementation of racism, xenophobia, sexism, transphobia, homophobia, and ableism under the guise of neutrality. This analysis is essential for building resistance strategies that can actually intervene on the most pressing harms trans people face and illuminate how and when law reform is a useful tactic in our work.

Control that operates through population-level interventions is particularly significant to trans politics because of the way trans people struggle with gender categorization in the purportedly banal and innocuous daily administration of programs, policies, and institutions (e.g., homeless shelters, prisons, jails, foster care, juvenile punishment, public benefits, immigration documentation, health insurance, Social Security, driver licensing, and public bathrooms). An understanding of power that looks at the distribution of life chances created by population-level interventions draws our attention to how the categorization of people works as a key method of control. Population-level interventions rely on categorization to sort the population rather than targeting individuals based on behaviors or traits. What characteristics are used for such categorization and how those categories are defined and applied creates vectors of vulnerability and security. Many of the administrative processes that vulnerable people find themselves struggling through are contests about such categorizations. Examples include public benefits hearings where applicants contest denials or terminations based on eligibility criteria, Social Security hearings where applicants contest their categorization as nondisabled, immigration proceedings where applicants contest administrative determinations of their asylum petitions, and, of course, the many contexts in which trans people struggle to change their gender classification with various administrative agencies. Our attention to how life chances are distributed rather than simply to what the law says about marginalized groups exposes how various moments of administrative categorization have lethal consequences.

The history of explicit uses of race and gender categorization in US law and policy to distribute certain types of life chances—and the resistance to and elimination of some of those uses—lead many people to falsely and perilously believe the conversation about racialized and gendered administrative categorization is over. The argument goes that since we got rid of Jim Crow laws, race segregation in the military, the Japanese internment, Asian exclusion laws in immigration, gender and racial exclusion in voting, and other overt uses of gender and race categories in population-level programs, things are now fair and equal. As previous chapters have discussed, the shift away from some of the explicit targeting of women and people of color in the written language of law and policy has merely reorganized those functions of maldistribution. As certain methods of control and distribution have become less politically viable, other methods have replaced them, preserving and producing race and gender disparities in the distribution of life chances. High levels of policing in neighborhoods with concentrations of people of color, the creation of tiered public benefits programs, the design of taxation schemes to tax work instead of wealth, the targeting of immigration enforcement to impact certain immigrants more than others, the structuring of public finance of education, health care, and other key necessities, all function to create and maintain these deadly disparities.[2]

One way to think about these population-level programs is that they are created as care-taking programs. They are invented to address perceived risks to the national population and to distribute resources across the population in ways that aim to address those risks. They are aimed at increasing health, security, and well-being—access to food, transportation, public safety, public health, and the like. Because they mobilize the idea of the population (sometimes "society" or "the nation" or "the people"), they are designed in ways that reflect and amplify contemporary understandings of who is "inside" and who is "outside" of the group whose protection and cultivation is being sought, which means they always include determinations of who deserves protection and who is a threat.[3] Norms regarding race, gender, sexuality,

national origin, ability, and indigeneity always condition and
determine who falls on either side of that line. Population-level
care-taking programs always include population surveillance as
a core function of their work. Mitchell Dean's framing of care-
taking population-level interventions—or to use Foucault's term,
"apparatuses of security"—illustrates the simultaneous and dual
nature of the care-taker/surveillance state:

> These apparatuses of security include the use of standing
> armies, police forces, diplomatic corps, intelligence services
> and spies . . . [but] also include health, education and social
> welfare systems. . . . It thus encompasses those institutions
> and practices concerned to defend, maintain and secure a
> national population and those that secure the economic,
> demographic and social processes that are found to exist
> within that population . . . [centralizing] this concern for
> the population and its optimization (in terms of wealth,
> health, happiness, prosperity, efficiency), and the forms of
> knowledge and technical means appropriate to it.[4]

Standardized, categorized data collection is essential to the
creation of these programs because it allows governments, institutions, and agencies (e.g., the US Census Bureau, the New York
Department of Vital Statistics, the Centers for Disease Control,
the Colorado Department of Motor Vehicles) to have a general
picture of the population: its health, vulnerabilities, needs, and
risks. Importantly, it is this way of thinking about population
that allows such programs to exist at all. James C. Scott's work
shows how gathering information and creating population-level
programs using this information is what defines the modern
nation-state.[5] These programs make decisions about what kinds
of data are relevant to their work, what the government/agency/
institution/organization in each case needs to know in order to
implement programs aimed at cultivating a "healthy" population while guarding against risks of various kinds. These decisions about what constitutes a proper data element/manner of

classification and what does not rarely appear as controversial political decisions because people who find the commonly evoked societal norms used in classification familiar and comfortable tend to take these classification systems as neutral givens in their lives.[6] We are used to filling out forms with certain questions. We rarely question how we came to be asked for those particular pieces of information and not others except in moments when we personally have a hard time figuring out which box to check off. Because certain classifications become common and standard, there is often an implied shared understanding that certain things, like gender, are just necessary information for administering government programs. Scott writes, "Categories that may have begun as the artificial inventions of cadastral surveyors, census takers, judges, or police officers can end by becoming categories that organize people's daily experience precisely because they are embedded in state-created institutions that structure that experience."[7] The terms and categories used in the classification of data gathered by the state do not merely collect information about pre-existing types of things, but rather shape the world into those categories that, ultimately, are taken for granted by most and thus appear ahistorical and apolitical. Indeed, many such categorizations are assumed as basic truths.

However, each type of data collected by the US government and the choices made about what to collect and why have histories of controversy and resistance. The creation of birth registration programs and birth certificates, the creation of the Social Security Administration that included the assignment of a unique number to every eligible resident, the use of various racial categories (and changes to racial categorization) on the US Census, the collection of data about HIV infection and other stigmatized illnesses—all of these have met with controversy both regarding how and why government agencies were collecting certain data and how that data collection might impact particular populations.[8] Each of these data collection projects have been key moments of expanding the reach of the government and defining who are members of the "us" of the nation and who are the "outsiders" who must be abandoned or eliminated. Data collection mechanisms that establish and utilize norms are essential to the type of sorting that population management requires.

For trans politics, an area of great concern is the ubiquity of gender data collection in almost every imaginable government and commercial identity verification system. From birth to death, the "M" and "F" boxes are present on nearly every form we fill out: on the identity documents we show to prove ourselves and in the computer records kept by government agencies, banks, and nonprofit organizations. Additionally, gender classification often governs spaces such as bathrooms, homeless shelters, drug treatment programs, mental health services, and spaces of confinement like psychiatric hospitals, juvenile and adult prisons, and immigration prisons (often called "detention centers" despite the fact that the word "detention" misleadingly denotes a relatively short-term confinement, which is, time and again, not the case for people placed in these facilities). The consequences of misclassification or the inability to be fit into the existing classification system are extremely high, particularly in the kinds of institutions and systems that have emerged and grown to target and control poor people and people of color, such as criminal punishment systems, public benefits systems, and immigration systems. The collection of standardized data and its use for identity surveillance have become even more widely implemented with the advent of the War on Terror, increasing vulnerability for many people whose lives and identities are made illegible or impossible by government classification schemes.

Administrative Gender Classification and Trans Lives

For trans people, administrative gender classification and the problems it creates for those who are difficult to classify or are misclassified is a major vector of violence and diminished life chances and life spans. Trans people's gender classification problems are concentrated in three general realms: identity documentation, sex-segregated facilities, and access to health care. Mitchell Dean's description of Foucault's analysis of government is useful for thinking about the multiple locations of the production of sex classification standards and the incoherence of sex classification systems. Such an analysis

> attend[s] to . . . the routines of bureaucracy; the technologies of notation, recording, compiling, presenting and transporting of information, the theories, programmes, knowledge and expertise that compose a field to be governed and invest it with purposes and objectives; the ways of seeing and representing embedded in practices of government; and the different agencies with various capacities that the practices of government require, elicit, form and reform. To examine regimes of government is to conduct analysis in the plural: there is already a plurality of regimes of practices in a given territory, each composed from a multiplicity of in principle unlimited and heterogeneous elements bound together by a variety of relations and capable of polymorphous connections with one another. Regimes of practices can be identified whenever there exists a relatively stable field of correlation of visibilities, mentalities, technologies and agencies, such that they constitute a kind of taken-for-granted point of reference for any form of problematization.[9]

Using this kind of analytical approach to examine the places where trans people experience extremely harmful interfaces with legal systems helps us see the significance of gender classification practices across a variety of locations of regulation. In the United States, administrative systems have emerged out of and been focused on creation and management of racial and gender categories to establish the nation itself through gendered-racialized property regimes. Racializing and gendering are nation-making activities carried out through the creation of population-level interventions, including administrative systems and norms, that preserve and cultivate the lives of some and expose others to premature death. Looking at particular regimes of practices related to the management of gender that impact trans people in significant ways, we can see this operation of population management at work. At each of these sites, significant consequences occur from gender classification problems, and the areas interact to create complex difficulties with far-reaching, long-term ramifications.

Identity Documents

Identity documentation problems often occur for trans people when an agency, institution, or organization that keeps data about people and/or produces identity documents (e.g., driver's licenses, birth certificates, passports, public benefits cards, immigration documents) has incorrect or outdated information or information that conflicts with that of another agency, institution, or organization. For many trans people, this happens because they cannot change the gender marker on certain essential documents. Many agencies, institutions, and organizations have formal or informal gender reclassification policies that require proof of some kind of medical care. Every government agency and program that tracks gender has its own rule or practice (sometimes dependent on a particular clerk's opinion) of what evidence should be shown to warrant an official change in gender status in its records or on its ID. The policies differ drastically. Some require evidence that the person has undergone a particular surgery; others ask for evidence that the person has had some surgery but do not specify which; and some require a doctor's letter confirming that the person is trans and attesting to the medical authorization for or permanence of their membership in a particular gender category. Others will not allow a change of gender at all. A small set of policies allow a person's self-identification to be proof enough to change their gender classification.[10]

The wide range of policies and practices means that many people, depending on where they live and what kind of medical evidence they can produce, cannot get any records or ID corrected, or can only have their gender changed with some agencies but not with others. So, for example, one person born in New York and living in New York might have a birth certificate she cannot change from "M" to "F" because she has not had genital surgery; a driver's license that correctly reflects "F" because she got a doctor's letter; Social Security records that say "M" because she cannot produce evidence of surgery; a name change order that shows her new feminine name; and a Medicaid card that reads "F" because the agency had no official policy and the clerk felt the name change order and driver's license were sufficient. Another person with the same medical evidence might have a completely different set of documents because she was born in California and currently lives in Massachusetts. Most likely, neither person will have a consistent set of documents that correlates to their current gender. For the many people who feel that neither "M" nor "F" accurately describes their gender, there is no possibility of obtaining records that reflect their self-identities. Gender reclassification policies are particularly problematic because they so frequently include surgical requirements. The vast majority of trans people do not undergo surgery, both because it is prohibitively expensive and because many people do not want or need it. The common misperception that surgery is the hallmark of trans experience is also particularly harmful to populations disproportionately lacking access to medical care, including low-income people, people of color, immigrants, and youth. According to a 2009 study, 80 percent of transgender women and 98 percent of transgender men have not undergone genital surgery.[11] Because it is difficult to include people in prisons, people without secure housing, and other highly vulnerable people with exceptionally poor access to health care in such studies, I would suggest that these numbers may even be higher than the study was able to confirm.

Having identity documents that misidentify gender causes extensive problems. An important consequence of identity documentation discrepancy is that it often serves as a significant barrier to employment. A recent study found that 47 percent of trans and gender nonconforming respondents reported having experienced an adverse job outcome, such as being fired, not hired, or denied a promotion, because of their gender.[12] Another study found that only 58 percent of transgender residents of Washington, DC, were employed in paid positions: 29 percent reported no source of income, and another 31 percent reported annual incomes under $10,000.[13] In yet another study, 64 percent of respondents based in San Francisco reported annual incomes in the range of $0–25,000.[14] Possessing identity documents with incorrect gender markers can identify people as transgender in the hiring process, exposing them to discrimination. People whose identity documents do not match their self-understanding or appearance also face heightened vulnerability in interactions with police and other public officials, when traveling, or even when attempting to do basic things like enter age-barred venues or buy age-barred products, or confirm identity for purposes of cashing a check or using a credit card or a public benefits card. Conflicting identity information can also make it difficult to obtain certain identity documents that are vitally necessary for day-to-day survival. With the advent of the War on Terror, and as security culture continues to increase in the United States, identity verification procedures have expanded and intensified in governmental and commercial sectors. As a result, the barriers created by administrative miscategorization are increasing, especially for people whose immigration status and race subjects them to intensified surveillance.

Sex-Segregated Facilities

Misclassification is also a significant problem because sex segregation is used to structure so many services and institutions. People who have gender markers on records and ID that do not match their identity face major obstacles in accessing public bathrooms, drug treatment programs, homeless shelters, domestic violence shelters, foster care group homes, and hospitals. They also face significant vulnerability to violence in those spaces, especially in institutions that cannot be avoided because of their mandatory nature. Such mandatory institutions, such as jails, prisons, juvenile punishment centers, psychiatric institutions, and immigration facilities also tend to be enormously violent already. For many, the inability to access sex-segregated programs that address addiction and homelessness results in an increased likelihood of ending up in criminal punishment systems. Trans women in need of shelter (a disproportionately large population because of the combination of employment discrimination, housing discrimination, and family rejection) often remain on the streets because they are unfairly rejected from women-only domestic violence programs and they know the homeless shelter system will place them in men's facilities, guaranteeing sexual harassment and possibly assault. Many trans youth become street homeless when they run away from group homes that place them according to their birth-assigned gender, exposing them to violence from residents and staff alike. Trans people in distress often cannot receive the mental health treatment they want or need because their gender identity or expression will be seen as something that needs to be "cured" by the providers or facilities serving them. Trans people are also frequently rejected from drug treatment centers because these facilities are sex-segregated and administrators believe that trans patients will be "disruptive." The gender norms that are adopted by mental health and drug treatment providers frequently result in the exclusion of trans people from these vital services. For those seeking court-mandated drug treatment as an alternative to imprisonment, this can result in increased time in prison or jail. Lack of access to treatment also increases the harms of addiction, including economic marginalization and vulnerability to violence and criminalization. Trans people in prisons and jails report extremely high rates of sexual assault.[15]

The operation of gender classification systems prevents access
to essential services for trans people and sets up conditions of extreme violence in residential and imprisonment facilities. Gender
segregation is a mechanism of management and control in the
facilities and institutions where poor people, people of color, immigrants, and other marginalized people are concentrated and
where gender norms are enforced with extreme violence. Trans
and gender nonconforming people's experiences expose how population-management methods organized by race and gender produce structured harm and insecurity for people targeted by criminalization, immigration enforcement, and economic apartheid.

Health Care Access

Gender classification systems also have a significant impact on
access to health care for trans people. Most state Medicaid policies and most health insurance programs exclude from coverage
gender-confirming health care for trans people. Medicaid provides all of the gender-confirming procedures and medications
that trans people request to nontrans people and only denies them
to those seeking them based on a transgender diagnostic profile.
For example, testosterones and estrogens are frequently prescribed
to nontransgender people for a variety of conditions including
hypogonadism, menopause, late onset of puberty, vulvular atro-
phy, atrophic vaginitis, ovary problems (including lack of ovaries),
intersex conditions, breast cancer or prostate cancer, and osteopo-
rosis prevention. Similarly, the chest surgery that transgender men
often seek—removing breast tissue to create a flat chest—is regularly provided and paid for by Medicaid for nontrans men who
develop the common condition gynecomastia, where breast tissue
grows in what are considered abnormal amounts. Nontransgender
women who are diagnosed with hirsutism—where facial or body
hair grows in what are considered abnormal amounts—are frequently treated for this condition through Medicaid coverage.
In addition, reconstruction of breasts, testicles, penises, or other

tissues lost to illness or accident is routinely performed and covered. Further, treatments designed to help create genitals that meet social norms of appearance are frequently provided and covered for children born with intersex conditions (which has met increasing opposition in recent years).[16]

Much of the care provided to nontrans people but routinely denied to trans people by Medicaid programs has the sole purpose of confirming the social gender of nontrans patients. Reconstruction of breasts or testicles lost to cancer, hormone treatment to eliminate hair that is considered gender-inappropriate, chest surgery for gynecomastia, and other treatments are provided solely because of the social consequences and mental health impact faced by people who have physical attributes that do not comport with their self-identity and social gender. Thus, the distinction made in refusing this care to transgender people appears to be based solely on diagnosis. Denying care to a politically unpopular group that is provided to others in need of such care, advocates have argued, constitutes "diagnosis discrimination," a violation of federal Medicaid regulations. However, recent cases alleging these charges have not been won, and Medicaid policies regarding trans health care are actually worsening nationwide.[17]

For trans people who need this care, the health impact of this denial can have significant mental and physical health consequences. Depression, anxiety, and suicidality are conditions commonly tied to the unmet need for gender-confirming medical care.[18] According to the few studies that have been done on the issue, rates of HIV infection are also extremely high among transgender people.[19] One study found seroprevalence of 63 percent among African American trans women. A contributing factor to this may be the fact that many people seek treatments through the informal market and receive care without medical supervision because it is not available through other means. This avenue to care may result in inappropriate dosage, nerve damage, HIV, and/or hepatitis infection resulting from injecting without medical supervision or clean needles.[20]

Seeking gender-confirming care without coverage is also an avenue to harassment, profiling, and imprisonment for many trans youth and adults who engage in criminalized work to pay for the care, or who face criminalization due to the circumstances of their acquisition of the care. Further, because of the ways that medical requirements are used in gender reclassification policies of all kinds, the impact of being denied this gender-confirming care has ramifications in all other areas of life that relate to record-keeping and identity verification. Misclassification in all three of these realms—identity documentation, sex-segregated facilities, and health care access—combined with widespread family rejection and routinized stigmatization, produce conditions of exacerbated poverty, criminalization, and violence for trans populations. In each instance, the use of gender as a category of data for sorting populations—something that is taken as neutral and obvious to most administrators—operates as a potential vector of vulnerability. In the context of massive administrative systems mobilized to produce and manage targeted populations, such as public welfare systems, criminal punishment systems, and immigration enforcement systems, trans people face particular vulnerability to displacement, violence, and early death.

Gender Classification and Trans Vulnerability in the Context of Intensified Surveillance

The ongoing vulnerability of trans people stemming from administrative classifications of gender has become even more severe with the increase in identity verification procedures that have emerged since September 11, 2001. The declaration of the War on Terror ushered in a range of policy reforms and new government practices that have drastically increased surveillance and shifted the collection and use of identity data. One major element of this new surveillance is the increased sharing and comparison of different pools of data collected by different government agencies. Historically, the various state Departments of Motor Vehicles (DMVs), the Social Security Administration (SSA), the Internal Revenue Service (IRS), and other agencies that collect data about individuals mostly maintained their data for their own uses. Comparison of data between agencies about an individual only occurred during specific investigations.

The heightening of US security culture, inaugurated in the name of terrorism prevention, has drastically changed the deployment of this data. New practices have emerged and various agencies now compare their entire data sets and seek out mismatched information. The rationale for this activity is to track down people who have obtained identity documents or work authorization using false information. For example, when a DMV compares its records with the SSA, those people whose information is inconsistent between the two agencies will be contacted with a threat to revoke their driver's licenses. When the IRS compares its data with the SSA, employers are contacted and urged to take action to rectify the conflicting information or to terminate the employee. Undocumented immigrants are the primary targets of this new use of government data. These policies have drastically increased the vulnerability of immigrants to exploitation by employers, violence from the police and immigration enforcement, poverty, lack of access to vital basic services, and deportation.[21] These new rules have also increased the significance of the inconsistency of gender reclassification policies for immigrant and nonimmigrant trans people. The inability to have ID and records changed to reflect current gender—and the fact that some documents can be changed while others cannot—has dire ramifications: trans employees face being outed by the government to their employers, losing their driver's licenses, encountering new hurdles when seeking government benefits and services, and in general experiencing greater difficulty with all administrative systems.

The enhanced focus on identity surveillance is increasing the problems that emerge due to having an inconsistent administrative identity. The augmentation of US security culture

has raised the level of stability demanded of our identities and
has sharpened the tools that heighten the vulnerability of those
who are not "fully authorized" in any particular administrative
context. Data pool comparison practices are a significant problem
given the inconsistency of gender reclassification policies in the
United States. The War on Terror has prompted proposals for
an even wider variety of population-tracking databases along
with new uses of existing data sets collected by federal and
state agencies. These proposals are usually aimed at identifying
undocumented immigrants and bolstering military recruitment.
For instance, there have been proposals for a database that
would track information related to military recruitment for all
US residents under a certain age. An FBI database currently in
development would be the world's largest collection of biometric
data, compiling palm prints, facial images, and iris patterns.[22]
Purportedly banal and uncontroversial changes like the new
requirement that gender be listed on plane tickets are emerging
based on a cultural logic that gender is fixed and obvious and
therefore an easy classification tool for verifying identity.[23]

As with all such state care-taking programs, the aim of creating increased security for the nation hangs on the assumption of a
national subject that deserves and requires that protection: a subject for whom these identity classification and verification categories are uncontroversial. Because gender remains an ever-present
vector of identity verification, it is being put to use to achieve the
racialized nation-making goals of the War on Terror. These examples from the War on Terror are helpful not only in illustrating
how surveillance associated with military and immigration control
projects is implemented and operates, but also for illuminating
the dangers of projects commonly perceived as benign. Data collection and management-focused programs like driver's licensing,
Social Security benefits, and taxation are less often analyzed for
their racist and sexist impacts. In reality, these systems are part of
a national security project that constructs national norms to sort
populations for the distribution of life chances.

What Gender Classification Problems
Can Tell Us about Trans Politics and Law Reform

The moment of the War on Terror's bolstering of identity surveillance and increased exposure of poor people, immigrants, people of color, and gender outsiders to exploitation, imprisonment, and violence can help us comprehend the ways that racialized and gendered subjection and violence are presently operating, and can help us begin to examine approaches to intervention. First, this analysis points us to the realm of administrative, population-level intervention as an area of control and legal codification that may be more high-stakes for trans well-being even though it has been less visibly politicized than the symbolic realm of individual/intentional discrimination. The liberal rights-seeking strategy urges us to seek declarations from the state that trans lives are equal and worthy and that gender identity difference is not a formal barrier to citizenship. This model of inclusion and recognition, however, leaves in place the conditions that actually produce the disproportionate poverty, criminalization, imprisonment, deportation, and violence trans people face while papering it over with a veneer of fairness. Attention to the administration and distribution of life chances exposes the locations that generate that vulnerability, and that attention means we must refuse to use trans struggles to assert the neutrality of systems that reproduce racism, sexism, ableism, transphobia, xenophobia, and homophobia. Prioritizing analysis of and intervention in the distribution of life chances lets us get to what is really producing the harms trans people face, and to abandon law reform interventions that are primarily symbolic. Such an analysis can inform strategies that take up law reform campaigns tactically: when doing so provides immediate relief to harmful conditions, helps mobilize and build political momentum for more transformative change, provides an incremental step in dismantling a harmful system, and makes sense when weighed against dangers of legitimization and reification of violent systems.

Second, this inquiry gives us a vantage point for asking what a trans politics that is critical of surveillance might look like. It moves us away from an uncritical call to "be counted" by the administrative mechanisms of violent systems and instead allows us to strategize our interventions on these systems with an understanding of their operations and of their tendencies to add new categories of legibility as methods of expanding their control. This is particularly meaningful given that quests for recognition and inclusion tend to forgo such a politics in favor of being incorporated into harmful systems and institutions. The trend toward recognition and inclusion demands in the gay and lesbian legal rights context—the demands for inclusion in marriage, the military, the Census, and the police force—has created significant political division between people whose race, class, immigration, and gender positions and privileges give them the capacity to benefit from such inclusion, and those who will remain targets of systems of violence and control even if exclusion explicitly based on sexual orientation is legally prohibited. In the context of gender classification policies, a critical understanding of surveillance allows us to avoid making simplistic demands to have these policies "fixed" so that trans people can be more "accurately" classified. Rather, this analysis allows for the emergence of politics and resistance strategies that understand the expansion of identity verification as a key facet of racialized and gendered maldistribution of security and vulnerability. We can start to see how narrow demands to "fix" these policies for the least marginalized trans people—those who would have proper documentation if not for a gender classification problem—sharpens divisions between those who would benefit from inclusion and those who will remain locked out, or face worsened conditions, if new formal policies of inclusion or recognition are won. As we come to understand the broader context of racialized and gendered nation-making that population management is inherent to, we can comprehend how legal equality claims that fail to challenge the broader conditions of maldistribution can cause us to inadvertently produce a trans politics that supports and legitimizes those very systems and institutions that make trans people so vulnerable.

Third, these inquiries give us a new window for looking at the role of law and policy reform work in critical trans politics. As we critically examine law reform work that threatens to engender tools of legitimacy for harmful and dangerous social and political arrangements, and as we set our sights on developing strategies that actually impact trans people's survival, we need a new way of looking at the legal problems trans people face. A central element, which will be discussed more fully in the next chapter, is deemphasizing law reform more broadly, and ensuring that law reform is not the primary demand of our movements. Decentralizing legal strategies, however, does not mean abandoning them altogether. Trans people's lives are heavily mediated by a variety of legal barriers that create dire conditions, especially those related to the use of gender classification in a range of state care-taking/control programs. Legal work of various kinds can be a part of the arsenal of tools available for addressing those conditions. Using legal reform requires a careful, reflective analysis in each instance of the potential impact on the survival of trans populations. For example, we will have to ask ourselves, Is this change merely symbolic, or will it prevent trans poverty, criminalization, deportation, and death? Will this reform strengthen key systems of control or dismantle them? We must be acutely aware of the potential for dividing trans politics along lines of access and capacity to benefit from reforms, and we have to consciously work toward building shared analysis between and amongst trans and nontrans populations struggling against shared obstacles and mechanisms of control. These questions help us analyze what role legal work could play in mobilizing people for transformative change. Two examples will help illustrate how this kind of analysis can inform which law reform projects we do or do not take up.

A central question facing trans politics is if and how to use legal reform tools to intervene in the various problems trans people face in criminal punishment systems. As discussed in Chapter

Two, hate crime laws do not prevent violence against trans people but do add punishing power to a system that is a primary perpetrator of violence against trans people. Hate crime laws do not meet the criteria I am suggesting for law reform work because they create primarily symbolic change; hate crime laws co-opt the fear, grief, and rage of trans communities at the high levels of violence we face and the low worth our lives are given into the project of expanding a system that targets us. Instead of pursuing hate crime laws, we should turn toward legal work that relates directly to the criminalization of trans people and addresses issues like police harassment and violence, inadequate criminal defense, medical neglect, and the myriad violences facing imprisoned trans people. In the context of such work, our attention must stay focused on improving life chances for trans people and making sure that our work does not build up the criminal punishment system. When working to address conditions of imprisonment, then, we must avoid proposals that include constructing buildings or facilities to house trans prisoners, to hire new staff, or make any other changes that would expand the budget and/or imprisoning capacities of the punishment system. Alternatively, we should focus our efforts on decarceration tactics: increased access to adequate, safe drug treatment and other alternatives to imprisonment; access to competent/nontransphobic criminal defense counsel; access to resources for former prisoners to prevent the homelessness and poverty that often leads to additional criminalization; and direct support of prisoners who are experiencing medical neglect, violence, and retaliation. That direct support can include legal advocacy as well as emotional support and leadership development work. This approach, which uses direct individual legal services combined with mobilizing for systemic change that actually benefits the well-being of trans prisoners instead of expanding the criminal punishment system, requires continual reflection and evaluation to determine that each step considers the context of the work. This work needs to be based in a shared imagination of what ultimate transformative change we are pursuing, and what we think it will take to get there. For example, because this work seeks to mobilize a broad constituency to oppose criminalization and imprisonment, and sees trans prisoners and former prisoners as key leaders in that work because of their experience in and knowledge of criminal punishment systems, doing work to directly support their survival and political participation is an essential part of this strategy. Legal tools can be part of that struggle, but legal change is not its goal. Time and again, legal reforms of criminal punishment systems have resulted in expansions of those systems. Mindful of these dangers, we must ensure that legal work is always aimed at dismantling the prison industrial complex and supporting people entangled in it, knowing that the system is likely to try to co-opt our critiques to produce opportunities for expansion.

The matrix of the administrative programs that rely on gender classification is another location where we should apply this analysis in order to determine a path for legal reform. An understanding of the dire consequences of administrative gender classifications, especially given the expansion of identity surveillance in the wake of September 11th and the advent of the declaration of the War on Terror, points us to administrative law as a key site of the production of vulnerability for trans populations.[24] Turning away from the notion that declarations of nondiscrimination by local, state, and federal legislatures will somehow produce improved life chances for trans people and instead turning toward an examination of how the operations of DMVs, shelters, group homes, jails, prisons, schools, taxation systems, work authorization systems, and immigration enforcement rely on gender surveillance and forced classification allows us to intervene more meaningfully on the technologies of governance that are most harmful to trans people. When choosing targets within administrative systems, we again want to ensure that we are not building their capacity for control and violence. This has to include how we formulate arguments about these interventions. If, for example, we want to do work regarding identity documentation and how trans people

are being adversely impacted by new uses of government surveillance, we need to avoid neoliberal rhetoric about the "privacy
rights of hard-working, tax-paying trans Americans." Such arguments mobilize the same "us" versus "them" logic that fuels the
racist, anti-immigrant sentiments that support the growth of security culture and suggest that the main problem with the War on
Terror is how it accidentally creates problems for "law-abiding"
nonimmigrant trans people. Instead, we can be more effective
by joining forces with the many populations facing heightened
vulnerability to surveillance, and devise shared opposition to the
new practices and policies.

An example of this kind of work is the Sylvia Rivera Law
Project's participation in a coalition of immigrant rights organizations that formed in the mid-2000s in New York State to resist
changes that were being made by the state DMV with the aim of
eliminating driver's license access to undocumented immigrants.
The coalition opposed particular new policies and practices and
took a stand against the implementation of the REAL ID Act.
New York State had begun comparing its DMV records to the
federal Social Security Administration records and suspending
the driver's license of any person whose records had mismatching
information between the two sets of data. Trans and nontrans
immigrants were impacted, as were many trans nonimmigrant
people who had different genders on their driver's license than on
their Social Security records, differences resulting from different
administrative requirements. Social Security required evidence of
genital surgery to change gender on its records while the New
York DMV only required a doctor's letter stating that the person
was trans. The Sylvia Rivera Law Project (SRLP) joined the coalition and shared information with the coalition members about
how trans immigrants and nonimmigrants were being affected.
Building relationships with groups in the coalition expanded
understandings of trans policy issues of other coalition members and gave SRLP members (immigrants and nonimmigrants
alike) a political space in which to take up urgent local immigrant

justice work. SRLP spread the word about what was happening to its constituents, brought members to rallies and protests, and participated in the coalition's activities.[25] This collaboration provides a model for a trans political practice that refuses law and policy changes that would solely try to exempt trans nonimmigrants from the issue, thereby possibly further legitimizing these policies by refining their impact to those deliberately targeted during the racist, xenophobic uproar that produced these policy changes. Instead, SRLP's approach stands up for trans immigrants, nontrans immigrants, and trans nonimmigrants with a coalition of people targeted by these policies. It recognizes that anti-immigrant sentiment was the primary motivation for these policies, though some nonimmigrant vulnerable populations have been harmed as well, and demands change from a place of shared struggle and collective analysis. Working in coalitions of groups affected by immigration enforcement, poverty, criminalization, housing insecurity, and other key sites of the maldistribution of life chances, we can aim to have no one's messaging contribute to scapegoating another vulnerable population.

We can also approach administrative policies that govern gender classification with a strategy focused on demedicalization—for example, reducing and removing medical treatment requirements for gender reclassification. This work is important to reduce the racist and classist impacts of these policies. Reducing and eliminating medical evidence requirements for gender reclassification directly addresses trans people's survival issues, especially low-income people, youth, and people of color who are disproportionately deprived of health care access. These strategies are already being used effectively by activists around the country and have the additional benefit of building local leadership and relationships as people struggle with a range of local administrative systems (e.g., shelters, DMVs, foster care programs, drug treatment programs, jails, and prisons) that have harmful gender reclassification policies.[26] Many of these campaigns focus on the policies of various sex-segregated facilities and institutions to address the violence trans people face within them.[27] At all times, attention to how the work is being done, how it interacts with the broader context of neoliberal trends (surveillance, abandonment of the poor, criminalization, cooptation), and whether it can actually impact trans survival is required. Such an analysis necessitates contextualizing law reform in a set of broader understandings about power and control and with demands for transformation rather than inclusion and recognition.

This kind of contextualization moves us away from what critics have called the "single issue politics" that has produced much-lauded but illusory "success" in lesbian and gay politics. Further, this analysis illuminates neoliberal "victories" for what they truly are: betrayals of those most targeted by homophobia and transphobia, and successes for systems that want to be declared "fair" and "equal" while they worsen disparities in life chances with every passing year. The most popular law reform interventions imagine a world of white lesbians and gay men who face some kind of exclusion solely on the basis of sexual orientation and seek narrow changes that provide only formal inclusion. That narrow focus on sexual orientation means that the ways that race, class, immigration status, indigeneity, ability, gender, and other vectors of identity and experience interact with sexual orientation to create certain kinds of vulnerability are left unaddressed. The resultant legal reforms are so narrow in their understanding of the issues that they only provide access to the sought-after right for those who do not have other intervening vectors of marginality, if for anyone at all. For this reason, one might observe that the lesbian and gay rights agenda primarily operates to restore privileges of the dominant systems of meaning and control to those gender-conforming, white, wealthy gay and lesbian US citizens who are enraged at how homophobic laws and policies limit access to benefits to which they feel entitled. Advocates of single issue politics seek to restore the ability of wealthy gay and lesbian couples to inherit from each other with limited taxation, to share each other's private health benefits, to call on law enforcement to protect their property rights, and other such privileges of whiteness and wealth. In order to avoid a similar trajectory in the name of trans politics, our legal reform interventions need to do more than pick out the specific narrow ways that the law explicitly excludes trans people or that legal systems create obstacles for the most enfranchised trans people.

We need to conceptualize the ways that population-level interventions—the War on Drugs, the War on Terror, and the gutting of welfare and Medicaid programs—interact with regimes of gender classification and enforcement and utilize gender as a technology of control. We must examine how racism, sexism, capitalism, xenophobia, settler colonialism, and ableism combine to produce and sustain these violent systems of distribution while we simultaneously explore the specific vulnerabilities of trans populations in these systems. This analysis can facilitate strategies based in a broad understanding of how power and control operate and help us determine which interventions might yield the most redistribution of life chances with the least danger of legitimizing and reproducing the very conditions we oppose. Because individual rights-focused law reform operates as a cover for population-based practices of abandonment and imprisonment, we must resist logics that frame harm as primarily individual and that seek narrowly focused remedies accessible only to those already deemed "legitimate" bodies for claiming rights (white, noncriminalized, nonimmigrant, nondisabled, nonindigenous). Because reform projects always carry the danger of compromise and co-optation, and since law reform in particular tends to reproduce ideas of governmental fairness and justice, we have to employ an especially cautious analysis when using legal reform tools.

We must return for reflection frequently and look out for the common traps—building and legitimizing systems of control, dividing constituencies along the lines of access to legal rights, and advancing only symbolic change. We must not only refuse reforms that require dividing and leaving behind more vulnerable trans populations, but also try to assume that the most easily digestible invitations to be included are the very ones that bring us into greater collusion with systemic control and violence. It is not surprising that the first federal legislation formally to address harm against trans people was the Matthew Shepard and James Byrd, Jr. Act—a hate crime bill that would bring enormous resources to the criminal punishment system and do little or nothing to prevent trans death. To the extent that the mobilization of trans people and our allies begins to expose the crises of coercive and violent gender systems, those systems will respond, at least in part, with solicitation to join their projects and expand themselves in our names—and then tell us we have won victories, that enough has been done. In the face of that trend, we must think deeply and critically about how law reforms can be part of dismantling violent regimes of administering life and death and forgo them when they cannot.

NOTES

1.   I intentionally left xenophobia and settler colonialism off this list, because administrative law has been articulated as a primary vector of harm in these areas of struggle. Although some anti-discrimination laws include "national origin" as a protected category, the bulk of discussion about xenophobia is rightly and necessarily focused on immigration and criminal law enforcement, often specifically on the administration of those systems. The federal administrative agencies that receive perhaps the most attention from people involved in resistance movements focused on immigration and that more of those activists and organizations understand as harmful vectors of state violence are agencies that manage immigration under the Department of Homeland Security, such as US Citizen and Immigration Services, Immigration and Customs Enforcement (ICE), and Customs and Border Protection. Resistance to settler colonialism has often identified the range of policies that target indigenous people for erasure and elimination as including the work of various administrative agencies such the Bureau of Indian Affairs, the Bureau of Land Management, and the Fish and Wildlife Service. Many

scholars and activists opposing settler colonialism have highlighted how civil rights strategies, or strategies seeking inclusion in key institutions of US governance, fail to question the existence of the United States itself and its basis in land theft and genocide. Nandita Sharma and Cynthia Wright, "Decolonizing Resistance, Challenging Colonial States," *Social Justice* 35 (2008-2009): 120–138, 122. Of course, because immigrants and indigenous people are also people who are direct targets of homophobia, transphobia, racism, ableism, and sexism, their concerns are even further marginalized and less likely to be addressed when resistance is framed through narrow inclusion struggles focused on those vectors because such struggles fail to question, and even misguidedly embrace, the terms of citizenship and belonging that are established, defined and perpetuated through genocide and immigration exclusion policies. People struggling in the crosshairs, for example, of immigration enforcement and transphobia need both to be abolished—an anti-discrimination law that includes gender identity will not prevent them from being detained in a deadly immigration prison or deported. While saying all this, though, I also acknowledge that the greater focus on administrative systems in these struggles does not preclude them from the tensions this book identifies of separating impacted populations into more or less "deserving" groups through reforms that only reach a select few. Highly visible campaigns for various immigration campaigns going on right now seek policy changes for "good" immigrants and affirm the exclusion of all others, using factors like history of criminal conviction, military service, or access to college education as axes of division. These might be understood as falling into the neoliberal inclusion and recognition traps faced by social movements described in this book.

2. One widely discussed example is the differential punishment for possession and sale of crack versus powder cocaine. As many have described, a significant contribution to Black imprisonment in the United States stems from the policy decision to make the prison sentences for crack, which is more highly trafficked in Black communities, much harsher than sentences for powder cocaine, which is more frequently associated with white populations. Though the sentencing standards do not mention race or identify racist enforcement as a goal, the profoundly

racist framing of drug crime, especially in regard to crack, fueled the advent of the War on Drugs which produced a set of policy decisions with a decidedly racist outcome in terms of who spends how much time in prison for possession and sale of the same quantity of illegal drugs. Danielle Kurtzleben, "Data Show Racial Disparity in Crack Sentencing," *US News & World Report*, August 3, 2010, http://politics.usnews.com/news/articles/2010/08/03/data-show-racial-disparity-in-crack-sentencing.html; American Civil Liberties Union, "Interested Persons Memo on Crack/Cocaine Sentencing Policy" (May 2002). www.aclu.org/drug-law-reform/interested-persons-memo-crackpowder-cocaine-sentencing-policy; The Sentencing Project, "It's Not Fair. It's Not Working," www.sentencingproject.org/crackreform/.

3.   Mariana Valverde, "Genealogies of European States: Foucauldian Reflections," *Economy and Society* 36, no. 1 (February 2007): 176; Michel Foucault, *Society Must Be Defended: Lectures at the College de France, 1975–76*, Trans. David Macey (New York: Picador, 2009), 256.

4.   Mitchell Dean, *Governmentality: Power and Rule in Modern Society*, 2nd ed. (London: SAGE Publications, 2010), 20.

5.   In an article that examines the development of standardized patronyms, Scott and his co-authors write, "There is no State-making without State-naming. . . . To follow the progress of state-making is, among other things, to trace the elaboration and application of novel systems which name and classify places, roads, people, and, above all, property. These state projects of legibility overlay, and often supercede, local practices. Where local practices persist, they are typically relevant to a narrower and narrower range of interaction within the confines of a face-to-face community." Scott's work shows how the "pacification of a territory" that state-making requires involves replacing diverse local practices with national standards of naming and categorization that make people, places, and things legible to the state so that they can be counted, maintained, cultivated, and controlled. James C. Scott, John Tehranian, and Jeremy Mathias, "The Production of Legal Identities Proper to States: The Case of the Permanent Family Surname," *Comparative Studies in Society and History* 44, no. 1 (January 2002): 4–44.

6.   "On the one hand, we govern others and ourselves according

to what we take to be true about who we are, what aspects of our existence should be worked upon, how, and with what means and to what ends. . . . On the other hand, the ways in which we govern and conduct ourselves give rise to different ways of producing truth." Mitchell Dean, *Governmentality: Power and Rule in Modern Society*, 2nd ed. (London: SAGE Publications, 2010), 18. See also Geoffrey C. Bowker and Susan Leigh Star, *Sorting Things Out: Classification and Its Consequences* (Cambridge, MA: The MIT Press, 1999).

7. James C. Scott, *Seeing Like a State: How Certain Schemes to Improve the Human Condition Have Failed* (New Haven, CT: Yale University Press, 1998), 82–83.

8. Dean Spade, "Documenting Gender," *Hastings Law Journal* 59 (2008): 731; Christian Parenti, *The Soft Cage: Surveillance in America from Slavery to the War on Terror* (New York: Basic Books, 2003); and Christine B. Hickman, "The Devil and the One Drop Rule: Racial Categories, African Americans and the U.S. Census," *Michigan Law Review* 95 (1997): 1161.

9. Dean, *Governmentality*, 26, 27.

10. For a detailed listing of many of these policies in the United States and what each requires, see Spade, "Documenting Gender."

11. Jaime M. Grant, Lisa A. Mottet, and Justin Tanis with Jody L. Herman, Jack Harrison, and Mara Keisling, *National Transgender Discrimination Survey Report on Health and Health Care* (Washington: National Gay and Lesbian Task Force and National Center for Transgender Equality, October 13, 2010), www.thetaskforce.org/reports_and_research/trans_survey_health_heathcare.

12. Jamie M. Grant, Lisa A. Mottet, and Justin Tanis, *Injustice at Every Turn: A Report of the National Transgender Discrimination Survey* (Washington: National Gay and Lesbian Task Force and National Center for Transgender Equality, February 4, 2011), www.endtransdiscrimination.org/report.html. Another study estimated that the national unemployment rate for trans people is 70 percent. Patrick Letellier and Yoseñio V. Lewis, *Economic Empowerment for the Lesbian Gay Bisexual Transgender Communities: A Report by the Human Rights Commission City and County of San Francisco* (San Francisco: Human Rights Commission, 2000),

www.sf-hrc.org/ftp/uploadedfiles/sfhumanrights/docs/econ.pdf.

13. Jessica M. Xavier, *The Washington Transgender Needs Assessment Survey* Executive Summary (Washington, DC: Administration for HIV and AIDS, District of Columbia Department of Health, 2000), www.glaa.org/archive/2000/tgneedsassessment1112.shtml.

14. Chris Daley and Shannon Minter, *Trans Realities: A Legal Needs Assessment of San Francisco's Transgender Communities* (San Francisco: Transgender Law Center, 2003). A 2009 study found that 79 percent of transgender and gender nonconforming people had not been able to update their identity documents to reflect their current gender. Jamie M. Grant, Lisa A. Mottet, and Justin Tanis, *Injustice at Every Turn: A Report of the National Transgender Discrimination Survey* Executive Summary (Washington: National Gay and Lesbian Task Force and National Center for Transgender Equality, 2011), www.thetaskforce.org/downloads/reports/reports/ntds_summary.pdf.

15. D. Morgan Bassichis, "'It's War in Here': A Report on the Treatment of Transgender & Intersex People in New York State Men's Prisons" (New York: Sylvia Rivera Law Project, 2007), http://srlp.org/files/warinhere.pdf; Alexander L. Lee, *Gendered Crime & Punishment: Strategies to Protect Transgender, Gender Variant & Intersex People in America's Prisons* (pts 1 & 2), *GIC TIP Journal* (Summer 2004), *GIC TIP Journal* (Fall 2004). Christine Peek, "Breaking out of the Prison Hierarchy: Transgender Prisoners, Rape and the Eighth Amendment," *Santa Clara Law Review* 44 (October, 2004): 1211; Sydney Tarzwell, "The Gender Lines Are Marked with Razor Wire: Addressing State Prison Policies and Practices for the Management of Transgender Prisoners," *Columbia Human Rights Law Review* 38 (Fall 2006): 167.

16. For additional information, please visit the Intersex Society of North America website at www.isna.org. The struggle to end surgeries on children with intersex conditions has important political parallels with the struggles of trans people to obtain gender-confirming health care. Both point to the ways that medical authority polices gender categories by establishing and enforcing gender norms on bodies.

17. In recent years, Washington State and Minnesota have both undertaken changes in Medicaid policy to reduce coverage for

gender-confirming health care for trans people. New York State courts have denied claims of trans litigants seeking to challenge the state's regulation that bars coverage of this care to Medicaid recipients. Dean Spade with Gabriel Arkles, Phil Duran, Pooja Gehi, and Huy Nguyen, "Medicaid Policy and Gender-Confirming Health care for Trans People: An Interview with Advocates," *Seattle Journal for Social Justice* 8 (Spring/Summer 2010): 497.

18. One study found suicide attempts among 12 percent of trans women and 21 percent of trans men who had not begun treatment, and no suicide attempts among the same patients after having begun treatment. Friedemann Pfäfflin and Astrid Junge, "Sex Reassignment. Thirty Years of International Follow-up Studies after Sex Reassignment Surgery: A Comprehensive Review, 1961–1991," Trans. by Roberta B. Jacobson and Alf B. Meier (IJT Electronic Book Collection, Symposion Publishing, 1998), http://web.archive.org/web/20070807031128/http://www.symposion.com/ijt/pfaefflin/6003.htm.

19. A recent study of trans and gender nonconforming people found high rates of HIV in trans populations, especially among people of color and immigrants. "Respondents reported an HIV infection rate of 2.64%, over four times the rate of HIV infection in the general United States adult population. . . . People of color reported HIV infection at substantially higher rates: 24.90% of African-Americans, 10.92% of Latino/as, 7.04% of American Indians, and 3.70% of Asian-Americans in the study reported being HIV positive. This compares with national rates of 2.4% for African Americans, 0.8% Latino/as, and .01% Asian Americans. Non-US citizens in our sample reported more than twice the rate of HIV infection of US citizens." The study further found that those without high school diplomas, those with household income below $10,000/year, and those who had lost a job due to bias or were unemployed had substantially higher rates of HIV. Grant, Mottet, and Tanis, *Injustice at Every Turn*, 80.

20. *American Psychiatric Association, Diagnostic and Statistical Manual of Mental Disorders*, 4th ed. (2000), 576–582; Mario Martino, *Emergence: A Transexual Autobiography* (New York: Crown Publishers, 1977), 168–169, 190; Jan Morris, *Conundrum* (New York: Harcourt

Brace Jovanovich, 1974), 40–135; Karen M. Goulart, "Trans 101: Trans Communities Face Myriad Issues," *Philadelphia Gay News* (1999), www. queertheory.com/articles/articles_goulart_trans101.htm; Jamil Rehman et al., "The Reported Sex and Surgery Satisfactions of 28 Postoperative Male-to-Female Transsexual Patients," *Archives of Sexual Behavior* 28, no.1 (1999): 71–89; Pfäfflin and Junge, "Sex Reassignment"; Collier M. Cole et al., "Comorbidity of Gender Dysphoria and Other Major Psychiatric Diagnoses," *Archives of Sexual Behavior* 26, no. 1 (1997): 13, 18–19; Kristen Clements et al., "HIV Prevention and Health Service Needs of the Transgender Community in San Francisco," *International Journal of Transgenderism* (1999):3, 1&2; Kristen Clements-Nolle et al., "HIV Prevalence, Risk Behaviors, Health Care Use, and Mental Health Status of Transgender Persons: Implications for Public Health Intervention," *American Journal of Public Health* 91 (2001): 915, 917; HCH Clinicians' Network, "Crossing to Safety: Transgender Health and Homelessness," *Healing Hands* 6 (June 2002): 1, http://transhealth.transadvocacy. org/Newsletters/June2002HealingHands.pdf; Nina Kammerer et al., "Transgender Health and Social Science Needs in the Context of HIV Risk," in *Transgender and HIV: Risks, Prevention, and Care*, eds.Walter O. Bockting and Shelia Kirk (New York: Routledge, 2001) ,39, 41; Michael Rodger and Lindey King, "Drawing Up and Administering Intramuscular Injections: A Review of the Literature," *Journal of Advanced Nursing* 31 (2000): 574, 577; Joe Lunievicz, *Transgender Positive*, TheBody.com (November 1996), www.thebody.com/content/whatis/art30598.html, cited in Pooja Gehi and Gabriel Arkles, "Unravelling Injustice: Race and Class Impact of Medicaid Exclusions of Transition-Related Health Care for Transgender People," *Sexuality Research and Social Policy: Journal of NSRC* 5, no. 1 (March 2008): 7–35, 12–15. See also Brief for the Association of Gay and Lesbian Psychiatrists, as amicus curae in *In the Matter of the Review of Brian (a/k/a Maria) L.,* New York Supreme Court, Appellate Division, 1 Department, April 19, 2006.

21. Rates of deportation have continued to increase under the Obama administration. In July 2010 the *Washington Post* reported, "The Immigration and Customs Enforcement agency expects to deport about 400,000 people this fiscal year, nearly 10 percent above the Bush

administration's 2008 total and 25 percent more than were deported in 2007. The pace of company audits [seeking employment of undocumented workers] has roughly quadrupled since President George W. Bush's final year in office." Peter Slevin, "Deportation of illegal immigrants increases under Obama administration." *Washington Post* July 26, 2010, www.washingtonpost.com/wp-dyn/content/article/2010/07/25/AR2010072501790.html

22. Ellen Nakashima, "FBI Prepares Vast Database of Biometrics, $1 Billion Project to Include Images of Faces," *Washington Post*, December 22, 2007, A01.

23. Dean Spade, "Ma'am, um, I Mean, Sir, um, um, Ma'am?" *Cases and Controversies* (June 11, 2009), http://lawfacultyblog.seattleu.edu/2009/06/11/maam-um-i-mean-sir-um-um-maam/.

24. Toby Beauchamp, "Artful Concealment and Strategic Visability: Transgender Bodies and U.S. State Surveillance After 9/11," *Surveillance and Society* 6, n. 4 (2009): 356-366.

25. Sylvia Rivera Law Project, "Stop the Suspensions!" http://srlp.org/stop-suspensions; The REAL ID Act of 2005, Pub.L. 109–13, § 119 Stat. 302 (2005).

26. Activists in Colorado won a policy change in 2005 to remove surgery requirements from their state DMV gender designation change policy. In 2008, activists in Washington State successfully advocated for a birth certificate gender designation change policy that does not require any specific evidence of specific medical procedures. Activists in New York have been working since 2004 to win similar policy changes in New York City and New York State Departments of Health. Spade, "Documenting Gender."

27. Activists in San Francisco, New York City, Washington, DC, and Boston have won city policies that prevent the shelters systems of those cities from forcing trans people into homeless shelters correlated to birth-assigned gender. Spade, "Documenting Gender."

Chapter 5
Law Reform and Movement Building

SOCIAL MOVEMENTS AIMING TO MOBILIZE PEOPLE AROUND shared imaginations of transformation must contend with questions of infrastructure: how to devise methods of participation and decision-making, build and sustain leadership, create shared political analysis, and generate and manage resources to feed the work. If we are to focus on "bottom-up" mobilization for transformative change rather than top-down empty declarations of equality, we need to build social movement infrastructure that can support mobilization. This chapter begins with an analysis of why and how law reform–dominated agendas stem from professionalized, lawyer-overrun, foundation-funded organizational structures that have come to dominate social justice work in the context of neoliberalism. This chapter also introduces a useful tool, developed by the Miami Workers Center (MWC),[1] that considers social movement infrastructure in a way that helps us re-imagine the role of law reform tactics in resistance work focused on mobilization. Finally, this chapter provides several detailed examples of how organizations committed to trans liberation can and are creating movement infrastructure and critical trans political practice.

Having examined the limitations of traditional law reform strategies as well as some of the questions that emerge when using law reform tactics as part of trans resistance, this chapter now considers the broader question of how to place law reform projects in the context of trans movement building. The most visible lesbian and gay rights work has been criticized for its central focus on law reform goals, with critics arguing that such a narrow focus yields only formal legal equality gains that do not reach the most vulnerable targets of homophobia.[2] Further, the legalistic approach of that work has been linked to concerns about an unjust distribution of power and leadership, especially when the work is funded and directed largely by white, upper-class professionals who inevitably create an agenda that centralizes the concerns and experiences of people like themselves. Understanding the problems that this centering of legal demands has created in current lesbian and gay politics—a tendency nascent in emerging trans politics—requires an assessment of how the nonprofitization of social movements has changed the nature of political resistance work in the last four decades. Examining critiques of nonprofitization that are coming from activists opposing criminalization, immigration enforcement, and various other forms of state violence today, we can begin to think about how to find an appropriate role for legal work in trans resistance and as a means for building social movement infrastructures that are accountable to and centered in racial, economic, and gender justice.[3]

The rise of neoliberalism in the last forty years has presented social movements with two interconnected challenges to the political direction of queer and trans political resistance.[4] First, social movements have had to contend with the impact of neoliberalism on their constituencies. Dismantling of economic safety nets like welfare and public housing coupled with the growth of criminalization have devastated poor communities and communities of color. Increased immigration enforcement has greatly jeopardized already embattled immigrant communities, forcing them into crisis mode as they become increasingly exploitable by employers, less able to access social services, and entangled in prison and deportation systems. As Ruth Gilmore describes, the rise of neoliberalism from the 1970s to the present has caused the growth of a shadow state of volunteer-based and/or non-profit organizations that fill the gaps in social services created by the government abandonment.[5] The political, economic, and social conditions resulting from neoliberalism—including further imperiling poor communities by cutting survival services—have presented significant challenges to social movements trying to build resistance. At the same time, a second challenging dynamic has emerged: social welfare has increasingly become dependent on private businesses and foundations. Corporate funders have become the sponsors and benefactors of social services. The outcome is the privatization of social welfare programs. Not surprisingly, the increased need for survival services and decreased public resources for all social justice work has created troubling, often catastrophic results. This situation translates into overreliance by many organizations on income from corporations and accumulated wealth stored in foundations. This often leads to a disconnect from the driving forces behind the organizations' work: the transformative change being demanded by directly impacted communities.

Critical Ethnic Studies scholar Dylan Rodríguez has described this trend of nonprofitization of social movements in the context of the explosive liberation movements of the 1960s and 70s. In response to the significant challenges those movements raised to white supremacy, heteropatriarchy, capitalism, and colonialism, and to their success in generating widespread support and solidarity and shifting essential paradigms, US law enforcement infiltrated and attempted to destroy those movements, often through criminal prosecution and violence.[6] Rodríguez argues that the emergence of the nonprofit industrial complex represents the carrot that corresponds to the stick of criminalization of social movements. Together, these two forces established narrow parameters in which social movement work could occur—solely in forms that do not threaten the white supremacist political and economic status quo of the United States. Thus, work that fills in gaps in services and provides limited survival support while simultaneously stabilizing and advancing existing inequities is funded, and work that exposes and challenges those root causes and conditions of harm and subjection is targeted for destruction. As Rodríguez writes,

> [T]he structural and political limitations of current grass-roots and progressive organizing in the United States has become stunningly evident in light of the veritable explosion of private foundations as primary institutions through which to harness and restrict the potentials of US-based progressive activisms. . . . [T]he very existence of many social justice organizations has often come to rest more on the effectiveness of professional (and amateur) grant writers than on skilled—much less "radical"—political educators and organizers. . . . [T]he assimilation of political resistance projects into quasi-entrepreneurial, corporate-style ventures occurs under the threat of unruliness and antisocial "deviance.". . . [F]orms of sustained grassroots social movement that do not rely on the material assets of institutionalized legitimacy . . . have become largely unimaginable within the political culture of the current US Left.[7]

Key Concerns with the Emerging Model of Nonprofits

In recent years, the critique of nonprofitization has grown and scholars and activists have outlined how this trend impacts the development of resistance politics.[8] A key observation of this analysis is that, along with the rise of nonprofitization and philanthropic control, there has been a shift away from the traditionally central strategy of social movement work: building change by mobilizing the participation of a mass base of directly impacted people who share an experience of harm and a demand for transforming it. These critics have identified some key ways that nonprofitization has dangerously modified social movements and moved them away from being participatory and mass-based.

One critique of the effect of the emergence of the nonprofit sector as the single location for social justice work is that it has separated the provision of direct, survival-based services from organizing. Social services operating on a charity model—disconnected from any political mobilization aimed at getting to the root causes of the need for these services—receives funding while social justice organizing that engages people in need toward a shared goal of transforming conditions tends to be either under-funded or completely unfunded. Nonprofits using particular single strategies (e.g. services alone, or law and policy reform without services or organizing, or media monitoring and response without organizing or services) tend to be siloed, further contributing to the de-politicization of survival services. Consequently, services organizations offer little opportunity for vulnerable communities facing poverty, homelessness, unemployment, deportation, and criminalization to build networking relationships for analysis and resistance. Instead of deploying survival services as a point of politicization, a locus from which people can connect their immediate needs to community-wide issues of maldistribution and harm, services are provided through a charity or social work model which individualizes issues to each specific client and too often includes an element of moralizing that casts social service "clients" as blameworthy. People are treated as if their homelessness or joblessness is a result of their personal failure to be sufficiently industrious, rather than a result of structural conditions produced by capitalism, white supremacy, and settler colonialism. By buffering some of the worst effects of capitalist maldistribution, then, these services become part of maintaining the social order; they both naturalize systemic inequity and preclude sustained engagement with the political and economic conditions that produce that inequity by focusing on its symptoms instead of root causes.[9]

Critics have also pointed out that the increase in the quantity of nonprofit organizations has been accompanied by a greater prevalence of service-based and policy reform work, rather than the base-building organizing that produces the mass mobilization required for effective social justice movements.[10] This means that the nonprofit structure undermines the transformative potential of social justice work. Because social justice nonprofits are funded through foundations—frequently directed by corporations and wealthy individuals—the strategies of this work have become more conservative, focusing on small reforms that stabilize systems of maldistribution that benefit those funders. Base-building, mobilizing organizing that emerges from communities facing a daily onslaught of poverty and violence and demands massive redistribution has been replaced by policy work that tinkers with harmful systems or produces merely symbolic change and service work that alleviates suffering for very few and legitimizes the status quo. Service and policy reform organizations typically engage in change directed by educated elites (e.g., lawyers, administrators, social workers, public health experts), and produce narrow political demands that maintain the status quo.

The governance structures of most nonprofits, characterized by boards consisting of donors and elite professionals (sometimes with tokenistic membership for the community members who are directly affected by the organization's mission) perpetuate dynamics of white supremacy, capitalism, patriarchy, ableism, and xenophobia. Racism, educational privilege, and classism within nonprofits mirrors colonialism in the way that the direction of the work and decisions about its implementation are made by elites rather than by the people directly affected by the issues at hand. Nonprofits serving primarily poor and disproportionately people of color populations are frequently governed almost entirely by wealthy white people with college and graduate degrees. Staffing follows this pattern as well, with most nonprofits requiring formal education as a prerequisite to working in administrative or management-level positions. Thus, the nature of the infrastructure in many social justice nonprofits often leads to concentrated decision-making power and pay in the hands of people with education, race, gender, and class privilege rather than in the hands of those bearing the brunt of the systems of maldistribution. Consequently, the priorities and implementation methods of such organizations frequently do not reflect the perspective or approach that might be taken by the people in whose name the organization operates. This dynamic leads to the reproduction of the very same systems of maldistribution that organizations are purportedly targeting. Inside those organizations, white elites determine the fates of the vulnerable and get paid to make decisions about their lives while people directly impacted are kept out of leadership.

Part of the reason that decision-making power in nonprofits becomes concentrated in the hands of elites is because of the way organizations secure funding. The foundation funding of nonprofits takes the direction of the work out of the hands of the people affected by it and concentrates it on the agendas and time lines of funders, discouraging long-term self-sustaining movements from emerging. The process of successfully applying for funding, including having 501(c)(3) status (the IRS code for nonprofit organizations that are exempt from federal taxes) or a fiscal sponsor, researching applicable grants, writing formal funding requests using specialized language, having an awareness of current trends in funding, and having personal relationships with funders requires skills, relationships, and networks that are concentrated among people with wealth and white privilege. Being able to direct work and spin it to a funder's values is, more often than not, the key to successful fundraising. Furthermore, as political strategist and author Suzanne Pharr has pointed out, the use of short-term funding cycles (often 1–5 years) and the focus on producing deliverables that demonstrate quantifiable impact in measures that funders believe to be significant has meant that nonprofit organizations have been encouraged to operate on short-term goals rather than being supported in building long-term sustainable structures to achieve transformative demands.[11] Under this model, funders seek to see concrete returns (e.g., statistics about numbers of clients served or clear evidence of policy change) on their investment within a limited grant period. Base-building work that involves less concretely tangible returns or changes that work on a longer time horizon—such as the growth of shared political analysis within a community or relationship building—is undervalued and discouraged. This model encourages organizations to identify goals that can be achieved quickly, not to implement the long-term strategies necessary for more transformative changes to politics and culture.

Another problem with the dominance of the nonprofit sector has been the creation of a cultural shift in social justice activism toward professionalization, corporatization, and competition between groups for scarce resources.

Funder-driven elitism led to a professionalization of social justice organizations where corporate business models are increasingly used to manage organizations. This trend is evidenced by a rise in nonprofits' use of such terms as CEO (chief executive officer) and CFO (chief financial officer) for top-level staff,[12] the prevalence of hierarchical pay scales in which people are compensated at very different rates based on valuations that are similar to those used in the private sector, and other white supremacist, classist, and often heterosexist labor practices that reflect capitalist business values rather than social justice values. Many critics have lamented that young activists are increasingly looking at social movement work as a career track and a paycheck; the expectation of being paid has become central to decisions about what kinds of activism and organizing these activists pursue.[13] Business models of management that focus on top-down decision-making coupled with organizational structures in which educational, race, and class privilege often correspond to high positions in the hierarchy result in decision-making, compensation, and quality of life at work concentrated in the hands of white people with graduate educations (e.g., lawyers, social workers, people with degrees in nonprofit management).

The increasing centrality of the nonprofit model is also a concern because of its role in the maldistribution of wealth in the United States. Nonprofits are one way that wealthy people and corporations avoid tax liability. Most of the money that gets redirected out of the tax system by philanthropy does not go to social justice. Christine Ahn has provided an analysis that encourages taxpayers to recognize that money funneled into nonprofits by wealthy philanthropists is actually tax money diverted out of the government and into focused causes.[14] Even those of us who are critical of how the government spends tax money at present (primarily on war, immigration enforcement, and criminalization) can recognize that giving wealthy people a way out of being taxed and a way to support their pet projects is unjust. Wealthy people can put their money into foundations that bear their name, invest it where they choose, and are required to pay out very little of the money in the foundations each year—only 5 percent. This means that wealthy people get to keep control of their pile of money, shelter it from taxation, and sprinkle small amounts of it on whatever they like. According to Ahn,

> The fact that most private foundations are governed by wealthy white men may partially explain why only 1.9 percent of all grant dollars in 2002 were designated for Black/African Americans; 1.1 percent for Latina/os; 2.9 percent for the disabled; 1 percent for the homeless; 0.1 percent for single parents; and 0.1 percent for gays and lesbians. The majority of grants go to universities, hospitals, research, and the arts, while barely 1.7 percent goes to fund civil rights and social action.[15]

Even the tiny portion of philanthropic money that ends up in social justice organizations comes with strings attached that allow wealthy philanthropists to have a hand in directing the work. Ahn's analysis instructs social justice activists to remain critical of the trend of nonprofitization—even, or especially, while making use of nonprofit structures in our work—because of its role in reducing tax liability of the rich and placing decisions about wealth redistribution in the hands of the wealthy.[16] Ahn encourages social justice activists to view redirected tax money as their money. While rich people keep large amounts of money out of the tax system by funneling money through foundations that allow them to spend it on their own interests, everyone else has their income and necessities taxed to pay for wars. Meanwhile, city, state, and federal governments are complaining of deficits and pulling support from education, health care, transportation, and other vital infrastructure necessities. Ahn's work points out how philanthropy and nonprofitization permits further theft of resources by the rich and increased loss of essentials to poor people.

Building Transformative Resistance: Tools and Strategies

Drawing on previous social movements that used a variety of strategies to build community resistance, the Miami Workers Center (MWC) developed a useful tool for analyzing the roles of various tactics in the project of mobilization: the Four Pillars of Social Justice Infrastructure. This model is helpful for understanding how multiple strategies can fit together to build participatory, mass-based movements. The model also illustrates how the dynamics of nonprofitization and foundation control have created important obstacles to movement building. The Four Pillars that MWC describe are the Pillar of Policy, the Pillar of Consciousness, the Pillar of Service, and the Pillar of Power. The Pillar of Policy includes work that changes policies and institutions using legislative and institutional strategies, with concrete gains and benchmarks for progress. The Pillar of Consciousness includes work that aims to shift political paradigms and alter public opinion and consciousness, including media advocacy work, the creation of independent media, and public education work. The Pillar of Service encompasses work that directly serves vulnerable people and helps stabilize their lives and promote their survival, including work that provides critical services like food, legal help, medical care, and mental health support. Finally, the Pillar of Power is about achieving autonomous community power by building a base and developing leadership: building membership organizations of a large scale and influence (quantity) and developing the depth and capacity of grassroots leadership (quality).

The Four Pillars model is aimed at assisting social justice movements to understand how these seemingly different kinds of work—which often are located in disparate nonprofit organizations that do not collaborate extensively and sometimes cling narrowly to one or two strategies—are in fact intertwined, complementary, and essential. The Four Pillars model focuses on helping movements and organizations understand that the Pillar of Power—perhaps the most neglected area in the current nonprofit industrial complex–dominated social justice context—is the most essential pillar for change and that, to be effective and avoid just stabilizing the status quo, the other pillars must be engaged to support the Pillar of Power.

The Four Pillars model is useful for evaluating an organization's overall role in movement building, identifying areas of needed collaboration, and formulating a theory of change. If, for example, we acknowledge that depoliticized, stigmatizing direct service work that is disconnected from the Pillar of Power is the norm as part of the shadow state, we can develop ideas about what direct services that support base-building, leadership development, and mass mobilization might look like.

If survival services (food, shelter, legal services, and physical and mental health services) were part of a mobilization strategy, they would look very different from the social services models we see in nonprofit organizations today.

First, nonprofit organizations would have a goal of assisting vulnerable people to connect with others experiencing similar harms. Such connections help individuals build shared analysis about the conditions they are facing and gain leadership skills to contribute to resistance struggles. This might include making sure

people are receiving services from others in the affected population rather than from outsider elites. Such a strategy would also
include aiding people who receive services to learn how to take
part in providing those services, which often means having their
provision governed by former and current recipients of those
services. It would mean seeing services as part of the project of
bringing more directly impacted people into organizational and
movement leadership, and as vital to building opportunities to
form relationships and connections between people coming in
for services and people already working in the organization. This
model moves people from a "client" role to a "member" role, creating space for members of vulnerable communities to acquire
skills that will expand their participation and leadership in the
struggles that concern them. Under the current social service
model, people seeking services are often stigmatized for "dependency," treated disrespectfully by professional service providers
who have race, education, class, ability, and gender privileges others do not have, and provided help only for individual problems,
if at all. Service work that operates to support the Pillar of Power
understands services as immediately urgent but also as only one
part of a much larger strategy to address the underlying and root
causes that produce such urgent need.

The Four Pillars model allows for recognition of the vital need
for all four pillars: direct services are not simply a Band-Aid, as
is sometimes argued, but instead can be understood as an essential part of building mass mobilization. Additionally, providing
direct services not only allows the base of people most adversely
affected to survive and politically participate, but also can serve
as a road to participation in resistance work if those services are
provided in a politicized context. People often come to political
work through their own experiences and intimate knowledge of
harm and need. Ensuring that direct services are locations for
deepening the political understanding produced by interaction
with systems of control, and mobilizing direct services as opportunities to join with others facing similar harms, are essential to

producing resistance strategies led and directed by those directly impacted by harmful systems.

Similarly, media justice work aimed at changing hearts and minds is not the single key strategy for change, as is sometimes presumed by those who are deeply invested in the idea that current political conditions are primarily the result of ignorance or misunderstanding on the part of voters or the public. However, critical media analysis and political education are important components of increasing political awareness and changing paradigms. This understanding can help us resist the belief that just getting that one "good" article about an issue in the *New York Times* will produce the change we want. The conditions under which we live do not result solely from ignorance or consent, and convincing elites to think about those conditions in a certain way is not the path to building meaningful transformation. The privileging of elite media strategies at the expense of other tactics can actually undermine the transformative potential of organizations. This view also reminds those of us committed to transformative change that elite strategies mired in a particular type of expertise, such as policy reform and work with the mainstream media, must always be engaged in service to the larger struggle to transform the underlying conditions that produce maldistribution. All strategies must work to build up the leadership of the most vulnerable people in the struggle. Realizing the interconnectedness of different strategies for change and their various roles in building mass movements allows organizations to resist the pressures created by competition for funding to operate competitively and separately from others engaging in different strategies.

We can engage a range of tactics in the Pillar of Consciousness in conjunction with work in the other pillars. Our paradigm-shifting work comes not only (if at all) through engaging with mainstream media, but also through making our own media, creating political education programs that simultaneously build the leadership abilities of our constituencies, and a variety of other mobilization tactics. We lose an enormous amount of capacity for change when media work is limited to specific organizations that operate separately from other parts of the movement and that do not use membership models or engage directly impacted populations. Those organizations tend to be willing to water down messages to be palatable for conservative media outlets, or to use talking points that divide us by relying on tropes that assert norms of deservingness and undeservingness. Analyzing social justice movement infrastructure through the Four Pillars model helps integrate disparate, often competing strategies, and offers a chance to reframe the emphasis on elite media work, policy reform, and services created by the nonprofit industrial complex. It helps us recognize that power does not only reside in the boardrooms of the television networks or the offices of elected officials, but rather that transformation worth winning is accomplished through bottom-up mobilization.

The Four Pillars model and the critique of nonprofitization are useful for situating the role of legal work in trans resistance. Examining how nonprofitization concentrates agenda-setting and strategic decision-making power can reveal how and why law reform demands have reached such prominence in organizations run by lawyers and other people with privileges that make them more invested in formal legal equality. These interventions also help us identify what roles legal work should have in a critical trans politics focused on developing and mobilizing a base to create transformative change. These roles include[17]

Providing legal services to the most vulnerable trans people. Providing free legal assistance to trans people experiencing violence at the hands of administrative and legal systems (immigrants, prisoners, people entangled in the child welfare system, people with disabilities, people receiving public benefits) can be an important Pillar of Service activity if it is tied into a mobilization strategy. Services can be an entry point into political organizing if the services are part of a strategy of enabling people to build relationships with others experiencing similar harm, building leadership skills, and developing the shared political analysis that allows people to participate and lead in governing the provision of the services themselves.

Demystifying legal systems. Because legal and administrative systems cause enormous harm in the lives of trans people, lawyers and others with knowledge of and experience in legal systems can play a role in demystifying legal systems and collaborating with resistance organizations to build a shared analysis about how the law operates. Redistributing legal "expertise" is essential, since part of what legal systems aim to do is deskill and silence those most targeted by them, anointing only certain privileged people to operate as recognized actors within them. Lawyers in particular need to be careful of how we wield our expertise. We tend to take up disproportionate space in decision-making processes, and are trained in a professional culture that tends to enhance internalized domination behaviors. We are also some of the people most likely to be paid for social movement work. Sometimes lawyers can help movement leaders strategize around who the targets of various campaigns could be, or help locate the weak points in certain legal systems. However, this role is easily overstated; people targeted by violent legal systems usually know more about how those systems actually work, and lawyers often only know how they work on paper (and sometimes mistakenly believe that to be how they actually work). Legal training can often make people less rather than more adept at strategizing change because we get overly invested in how systems purport to work. In general, law school teaches people how to stop thinking outside of legal solutions to problems, which often means we can only think of ways to slightly tinker with harmful systems, thereby strengthening, stabilizing, and legitimizing them. The focus of legal education is working inside the existing legal system. Even the small part of legal education that addresses poor people's struggles is concerned with narrow reforms and courtroom strategies, not supporting rent strikes or squatting or prison abolition or indigenous land struggles. Essentially, legal education is not about actually challenging the root causes of maldistribution.[18]

Developing law and policy reform targets as campaign issues. Because administrative systems cause enormous harm to trans people every day, issues related to how these systems operate tend to be deeply felt and broadly applicable to our constituencies. For that reason, law and policy reform targets can sometimes be a good place to direct our organizing. This organizing can provide opportunities to reframe an issue, bring directly impacted people who have not previously been part of political organizing into leadership, build shared political analysis about important forms of systemic harm, and establish and advance relationships within and between constituencies. When these law/policy reform campaigns are chosen, they can build momentum and membership in a movement organization. Winning certain reforms may even provide some relief to members experiencing harm. The limited effect of law and policy reform victories can also often build shared analysis among organizers about how empty legal equality can be, and can generate enhanced demands for transformation as organizing continues. Taking up law and policy targets can make sense when deployed as a tactic in service to a larger strategy of mass mobilization. If law and policy changes are won solely through the work of a few white lawyers meeting with bureaucrats or elected officials behind closed doors, this does not achieve the mobilization goals that require building a demand (and momentum behind that demand) across a broad spectrum of directly impacted people and winning it through collective efforts of a large group. The goals of this work should not be merely about changing what laws and policies say. Instead, the work should build the capacity of directly impacted people to work together and push for change that will significantly improve their lives. Ideally, those who are propelled into political action by involvement in a campaign stay with the work, continue to develop skills and analysis, and bring others to organizing. Together, people can construct increasingly broad imaginations of transformative change. Even after small victories, enormous harms must still be addressed as newly won policies are often not followed or implemented, and important lessons are learned about sustained struggle and the effectiveness of collective action.

Providing technical assistance. A final important role for legal workers is to provide technical assistance to movements. Movement organizations run into many legal questions that lawyers can use their training to answer. Sometimes it is about filling out forms to create a collective or cooperative business that employs members and raises money for our struggles. Sometimes it is about defending against government attacks that include illegal surveillance and criminal prosecution. Movement organizations are often targets of local and state governments, either in carefully planned offensives or sudden police attacks on organizational events, and the legal assistance that organizations can end up needing can be costly or difficult to procure. Having lawyers engaged with resistance organizations in ways that are focused on being of service to those organizations and their constituents instead of dominating their political agendas with legal expertise can be useful to forwarding transformative work.

The analysis provided by the Four Pillars model helps us think about the ways that so much social change work has become separated from mobilization in the context of nonprofitization. The model helps us re-evaluate our work, including our legal strategies, in order to re-center participatory movement building focused on leadership by and for those directly impacted. This analysis can also help us evaluate organizational and movement structures to ensure they produce space for political demands to emerge from the bottom up. As we let go of elite, liberal notions like the conviction that getting the right article placed in the *New York Times* or winning the right lawsuit will create equality, we can create broader social movement infrastructure that leads to transformation of the root causes of maldistribution of life chances. Rather than concentrate our limited resources on narrow demands for inclusion that imagine that people experience transphobia separate from other systems of meaning and control, demands for deeper transformation emerge when we build participatory movements based in racial and economic justice values, and centralize the leadership of those most vulnerable to multiple vectors of control.

In trans political spaces led by low-income people and people of color, demands are emerging that far exceed the possibilities of legal reform. Racial and economic justice struggles that call for prison abolition, health care and housing for all, an end to immigration enforcement, and the end of poverty and wealth are significantly different goals than the inclusion and recognition-focused demands that typify litigation and legislation strategies. These emerging broader demands focus on the deep transformations required to improve the life chances of those facing multiple intersecting vulnerabilities and violences. These demands are shaped by a commitment to refuse compromises that divide constituencies with reforms that offer increased access to people with certain privileges while leaving others without access—or even more marginalized than before. This critical trans politics is emerging from membership-based organizations, including Southerners on New Ground (SONG), The Audre Lorde Project (ALP), Fabulous Independent Educated Radicals for Community Empowerment (FIERCE!), the Sylvia Rivera Law Project (SRLP), and Communities United Against Violence (CUAV). These organizations have developed shared values about building participatory movements, and are innovating and building on structures modeled in various historical and contemporary movements in the United States and abroad, especially women of color feminism. These organizations share certain key principles for structuring their work to be participatory and centered in racial and economic justice, and to resist some of the tropes of nonprofitization.

Some of the key principles that underlie and shape this work include

- Ensuring that work is led by those most directly impacted;
- Using an intersectional framework for understanding the multiple vectors of vulnerability converging in the harms

members face (such as racism, sexism, xenophobia, trans-phobia, homophobia, ableism);

• Striving to model the transformative change that an organization imagines for the world in the day-to-day operations of the organization itself, also known as practicing what we preach;

• Remaining process-oriented rather than end-oriented, practicing ongoing critical reflection rather than assuming there is a moment of finishing or arriving;

• Continually developing new leaders, ever-expanding participation, and focusing on building the leadership skills of those who face the greatest barriers to participation and leadership;

• Rooting work in the understanding that meaningful change comes from below, deep change is not top-down or granted by elites;

• Striving for accountability and transparency within and between organizations, so that an organization's constituency knows how decisions are made and where money is spent so that allied organizations and movements know what to expect from each other and can challenge each other to work according to shared principles of social justice and collaboration;

• Recognizing relationships as the underlying support system of the work and the change we seek and need and focusing resources on strengthening and building relationships.[19]

Several key strategies are being taken up by the various organizations that are shaping their work through these shared values. First, the use of nonhierarchical governance models, including collective structures, is valued as a way of addressing the problematic concentration of decision-making power in a small number of elite leaders, such as executive directors and boards.[20] Consensus decision-making is often a feature of such structures because it focuses on maximum participation and rejects the majority-rules

approach that so often permeates nonprofit organizations and social movements, creating greater barriers to participation in governance for people experiencing intersecting vectors of vulnerability. Consensus decision-making also assists groups in focusing
their process on building shared understandings and ensuring no
important concerns are ignored simply because they are held by
a minority of people.[21]

Second, many organizations are experimenting with ways to
make the social movement organization workplace more fair to
workers. This includes flattening pay scales, ensuring that all positions come with benefits such as health insurance, and working to
guarantee that the workplace and benefits are accessible to people
who frequently face barriers to participation and leadership in
social justice–related employment, particularly people without
formal education, people with criminal convictions, people with
disabilities, indigenous people, people of color, trans people, and
immigrants. This also includes making sure that trans health care,
reproductive health care, and mental health care are covered by
insurance plans; creating flexible work schedules for people with
disabilities and/or dependents; eliminating higher education requirements wherever possible; and providing extensive job training rather than requiring applicants to already have developed
professional skills. The aim of these initiatives is to avoid replicating and entrenching disparities in educational, health care, and
other systems within the organization.

Third, many of these organizations have implemented highly
structured leadership development models and programs aimed
at increasing the leadership and governance capacity of their
constituents. For example, FIERCE!, an organization dedicated
to building "the leadership and power of lesbian, gay, bisexual,
transgender, and queer (LGBTQ) youth of color," has created
and implemented the Education for Liberation Project (ELP).
This program offers stipends to trans and queer youth of color
to enable them to participate in political workshops and internships aimed at skill-sharing, analysis-building, and leadership

development.[22] Participants work through semester-long ELP program levels, starting with ELP 1, where they learn basic political history and basic organizing theory such as how campaigns are developed and implemented. Participants then move on to increased leadership and governance power in the organization as they move through additional ELP program levels. The goal is to develop ELP members into leader-organizers who then work to develop the leadership of other trans and queer youth of color. Leadership development programs like ELP work to identify potential leaders from the constituency, focusing on members whose experiences of intersectional vulnerability give them particular insight into the operation of systems of control and power, and providing development training to deepen their capacity to lead. Some organizations stipend freedom school programs and internships[23] to ensure that low-income and youth members can afford to come and learn political history, analysis, and organizing strategies.[24] Many such leadership development programs are tiered, providing low-commitment entry points to encourage new members to become involved and eventually move into deeper, more committed leadership roles as their knowledge of the issues and connection with the organization grows. These models focus on maximizing the participation of the most directly impacted people, deepening their leadership skills by helping them participate in every aspect of the organization's work.

Many of these organizations aim to be staffed entirely by members of the organization who come directly from the constituency impacted by its work, often proceeding through internal leadership development programs and into staff roles. Many also aim to have staffing consistently turn over as new members develop leadership capacities. In this way, the organization itself becomes a vehicle for developing skilled leaders while simultaneously undertaking organizing campaigns, providing services, and/or advancing advocacy. These organizations also often create and maintain explicit criteria to ensure governance by the most directly affected people. Many implement guidelines regarding race, ability, gender, gender identity, immigration status, or other quotas to guide hiring and membership growth.[25] These guidelines help concretize organizational commitments about governance and leadership that can often erode as organizations are flooded with volunteers with race and educational privilege who want to help but who also often end up taking over due to their increased access to skills and professional development, their quantity of free time, and the dominating habits and attitudes that are often developed in people with such privileges. These organizations also often maintain a critique of "founders' syndrome," the dynamic that occurs when an organization's founder stays in a paid leadership position too long, becoming a repository of organizational knowledge and control regardless of what the organization's structure says about the democratic participation of all members. Keeping an eye on that dynamic, openly dialoguing about decision-making and leadership development, and encouraging staff turnover can ensure that the leadership and ownership of the organization do not become concentrated.

Grassroots fundraising is also highly valued by these organizations as an alternative and/or supplement to foundation funding.[26] Raising money in small amounts from the directly impacted populations, from individual allies, and through revenue generating activities and events can increase the autonomy of organizations, releasing them from the limitations created by reliance on corporate funders and foundations. Some organizations use membership dues, often available on a sliding scale, as a fundraising tool that also contributes to organizational accountability as members have ownership of their work and a commitment to govern.[27]

These strategies reflect an awareness of the ways that nonprofitization, foundation control, and the replication of racist, sexist, ableist, transphobic, and classist models of organization and governance restrict and contain social justice work. As trans politics continues institutionalizing in various ways, these models provide a way to avoid replicating the pitfalls of lesbian and gay rights and other political formations that have centralized the leadership of people with privilege and formulated strategies and demands that fail to improve the life chances of those most vulnerable to poverty, imprisonment, and violence. Political work rooted in broad participation, committed to centering the experiences of the most vulnerable, and focused on practicing resistance values at all levels is less likely to be co-opted by legal reform agendas that strengthen and legitimate systems of control and derail demands for meaningful transformation.

The critiques of nonprofitization and the innovative methods of building movement infrastructure that many resistance organizations are engaged in developing are particularly important given an analysis of neoliberalism and the central role of the population-management mode of power in producing political and economic arrangements. The context of neoliberalism has shifted and constrained resistance in many ways, including co-opting social movement work as a source of ideas and justifications for harmful state/corporate projects (e.g., the expansion of increasingly privatized prison and punishment systems). Social justice work has been shaped into shadow state work that stabilizes and legitimizes the maldistribution of life chances. As Paul Kivel points out, nonprofit work often operates as a "buffer zone." This work provides very minimal services to those most disserved by the enormous wealth divide, "mask[ing] the inequitable distribution of jobs, food, housing and other valuable resources . . . shift[ing] attention from the redistribution of wealth to the temporary provision of social services to keep people alive." It also "keeps people in their place in the hierarchy" by directing dissatisfaction with or resistance to unfair conditions into narrow channels that do not fundamentally disrupt the status quo.[28] For these reasons, there is an urgent necessity to create movement infrastructure that has critical capacities to examine sites of co-optation, interrogate impact rather than simply intent, and avoid siloed and divisive methods and strategies.

At the same time, it is evident that the very operations of power we critique in the broader world also need to be constantly examined within movement organizations and other resistance formations. Building institutions of any kind includes confronting the dangers of stagnation of leadership, ideas, ways of knowing, and mechanisms of distribution. As we create social movement infrastructure, we constantly risk falling into the very modes of population-management power that we critique in state and corporate formations. Many resistant and self-declared "revolutionary" movements and formations have demonstrated that the capacity to create an imagined population in need of protection and imagined "threats" and "drains" is not solely an activity of nation-states and governments. Resistance organizations and movements also frame deserving and undeserving populations, frequently collect standardized data that makes certain populations inconceivable or impossible, and establish modes of distribution that make some people more secure at the expense of others. Foucault warned that socialists have not dealt with the problem that the kind of population-focused power their models of governance wield has an inherent "state racism"—his term for illuminating the ways that power, when mobilized to cultivate the life of the population, always includes a process identifying "threats" and "drains" who must be killed through abandonment, massacre, or other means in order to protect that population.[29] Anarchist formations also face these dangers. We must remember that whenever we propose new systems of distribution and imagine a better world, we also—often unknowingly—establish disciplinary and population-management norms that marginalize and/or vilify. Even if we reject certain existing state forms, process-oriented and relentlessly self-reflective practice must attend all of our work if we are to resist the dangers of new norms that we invariably produce.

Women of color feminism is a political tradition that has confronted this danger head-on by analyzing the challenges that differences of all kinds present when politics is based on universalizing experiences. In Chela Sandoval's study of "oppositional consciousness," she describes how women of color have resisted and critiqued white feminist thought, pointing to how it has tended to make the gender binary the central axis of critique while ignoring the impact that race, class, culture, and other vectors of subjection have on experiences of gendered control.[30] By talking about gender and sexism without examining and accounting for how race and other attributes mediate experiences of gender and sexism, white feminists constructed a purportedly universal category of women's experience that actually hides and erases the experiences of women of color. Sandoval looks to the divides that emerged in feminist politics in the 1970s as a place to understand how social movements are commonly split amongst various groups who gravitate toward and rigidly cling to certain truth claims. These particular frames of "oppositional consciousness" become mutually exclusive, producing significant struggle between various wings of the movement. Sandoval argues that US feminists of color have created a different form of oppositional consciousness, which she calls "the differential form," that resists the absolutism that often produces rigidity and stagnation in social movements. The differential form of oppositional consciousness utilizes various articulations of truths as tactics practiced through a commitment to resisting violence and subordination, allowing practitioners to switch between them as necessary.[31]

This attention to resisting absolutism and practicing a flexible, thoughtful, reflective, tactical approach to resistance is an enormously useful model for resisting the dangers of institution-building and "state racism" outlined earlier. Women of color feminists have developed resistance practices focused on process, evaluation, consensus, transparency, and a healthy suspicion of universal claims about what constitutes liberation. These values and practices have heavily influenced much contemporary people of color–led queer and trans activism. These organizations often aim to operate with the assumption that their work is imperfect, that they are likely to have unintentionally overlooked or

excluded highly vulnerable groups, and that their strategies and
structures require perpetual re-evaluation and adjustment. Self-
critique and nondefensiveness are highly valued in these settings.
A critique of institutionalization has become a central feature of
the women of color–led analysis of nonprofitization.[32]

Many scholars and activists have asserted that we need to examine whether we are working to keep an organization going or
whether we are working toward the transformative changes we
seek, in order to recognize and re-strategize when those two goals
are at odds. This work has illustrated how and why resistance
movements must be careful not to replicate business model approaches to organizational growth that encourage us to chase any
and all opportunities for funding in order to sustain and grow the
organization by any means, even if we lose sight of our missions.
This critical contribution also reminds us that the ultimate aim
of social service organizations in particular is to put themselves
out of business; ideally, their work aspires to reach and resolve the
root causes of the need for services.

Prison abolition activists, many of whom ground their work
in women of color feminism, offer an important analysis of how
the societal norms and values that uphold and bolster practices
of mass imprisonment in the United States also directly impact
interpersonal and activist realms. Organizations like Critical
Resistance, the Audre Lorde Project, INCITE!, Communities
United Against Violence, and generationFIVE have been leading
national and local work that includes an analysis of how the racist, classist, patriarchal, and ableist frameworks that undergird the
idea of imprisonment are also part of the consciousness of people
who live in a culture based on imprisonment and criminalization.
These frameworks have to be transformed in our bodies, minds,
and lives, as well as in government structures. The framing of
harm as a problem of bad individuals who need to be exiled is
one that appears again and again, not just in our criminal punishment systems, but in schools, employment settings, organizations, activist formations, neighborhoods, groups of friends, and

families. Abolitionists are trying to build models for dealing with harm that do not rely on exile, expulsion, or caging, but instead examine the root causes of harm and seek healing and transformation for both people experiencing and people responsible for harm. This strategy is visible in "transformative justice" work that seeks alternative processes that do not use policing or criminal courts to address harm. GenerationFIVE, an organization whose mission was to "end child sexual abuse in five generations" has developed an approach to transformative justice based in their recognition that "state and systemic responses to violence, including the criminal legal system and child welfare agencies, not only fail to advance individual and collective justice but also condone and perpetuate cycles of violence."[33] They worked to develop responses to violence, including intimate violence, that "transform inequity and power abuses . . . [provide] survivor[s] safety, healing and agency, [create] community response and accountability . . . [and] transform[] . . . community and societal conditions that create and perpetuate violence."[34] Many scholars and organizers are working to develop these principles and practices in a variety of settings, including in social and activist communities and networks. The "no exile" principle is challenging to implement in a context where everyone has been socialized through the perpetrator-perspective to believe that the caging of people classified as "dangerous" and targeted for banishment is a cornerstone of societal organization. Building practices to address harm while resisting exile as a solution is the kind of seemingly impossible political project that is not only attainable but has deeply transformative potential.

Racial, gender, disability, and economic justice activists around the United States and the globe are working on innovative organizational structures and practices that resist many of the worst dangers and obstacles presented to people struggling against the harms and violences of neoliberalism. These methods of analysis and models of organizing offer important, thought-provoking critiques of disciplinary and population-management power, illustrating the possibility of developing practices that can help build transformative change while avoiding the traps that have caught and destroyed many large-scale resistance projects. Focusing our critical political analysis on our own daily work and lives just as rigorously as we focus it on the large-scale operations of government and corporate systems is essential to building resistance work with the potential to meaningfully transform the existing distribution of life chances. As Foucault suggests,

> the real political task in a society such as ours is to criticize the workings of institutions that appear to be both neutral and independent; to criticize and attack them in such a manner that political violence that has always exercised itself through them will be unmasked so that one can fight against them. If we want right away to define the profile and the formula of our future society without criticizing all the forms of political power that are exerted in our society, there is a risk that they reconstitute themselves.[35]

An emerging critical trans politics must take up these calls for innovation and creative engagement and offer our particular experiences with and perspectives on the operations of power and normalization to the resistant imaginations that are emerging.

NOTES

1. According to their mission statement, the Miami Workers Center "helps working class people build grassroots organizations and develop their leadership capacity through aggressive community organizing campaigns and education programs [and] also actively builds coalitions and enters alliances to amplify progressive power and win racial, community, social, and economic justice. [T]he Center has taken on issues around welfare reform, affordable housing, tenants and voter rights, racial justice, gentrification and economic development, and fair trade. We have spoken out against war and empire, greed, racist policies, and discriminatory initiatives against immigrants and gay and lesbian people."

www.miamiworkerscenter.org.

2.   Lisa Duggan, *The Twilight of Equality? Neoliberalism, Cultural Politics, and the Attack on Democracy* (Boston: Beacon Press: 2004).

3.   INCITE! Women of Color Against Violence, ed., *The Revolution Will Not Be Funded: Beyond the Non-Profit Industrial Complex* (Cambridge, MA: South End Press, 2007).

4.   Some of the text in the sections that immediately follow this note is adapted from "The NPIC and Trans Resistance," Dean Spade and Rickke Mananzala, *Sexuality Research and Social Policy: Journal of NSRC* 5, no. 1 (March 2008): 53–71.

5.   Ruth Wilson Gilmore, "In the Shadow of the Shadow State," in *The Revolution Will Not Be Funded: Beyond the Non-Profit Industrial Complex,* ed. INCITE! Women of Color Against Violence (Cambridge, MA: South End Press, 2007), 41–52.

6.   Dylan Rodríguez, "The Political Logic of the Non-Profit Industrial Complex" in *The Revolution Will Not Be Funded: Beyond the Non-Profit Industrial Complex,* ed. INCITE! Women of Color Against Violence (Cambridge, MA: South End Press, 2007), 21–40; Ward Churchill and Jim Vander Wall, *The COINTELPRO Papers: Documents from the FBI's Secret Wars against Dissent in the United States* (Cambridge, MA: South End Press, 2002), 1–20.

7.   Rodríguez, "The Political Logic of the Non-Profit Industrial Complex," 27.

8.   See Rodríguez, "The Political Logic of the Non-Profit Industrial Complex"; Andrea Smith, "Heteropatriarchy and the Three Pillars of White Supremacy: Rethinking Women of Color Organizing," in *Color of Violence: The INCITE! Anthology,* ed. INCITE! Women of Color Against Violence (Cambridge, MA: South End Press, 2006), 66–73; Robert L. Allen, "Black Awakening in Capitalist America," in *The Revolution Will Not Be Funded: Beyond the Non-Profit Industrial Complex,* ed. INCITE! Women of Color Against Violence (Cambridge, MA: South End Press, 2007), 53–62; Gilmore, "In the Shadow of the Shadow State"; Spade and Mananzala, "The NPIC and Trans Resistance," *Sexuality Research and Social Policy: Journal of NSRC* 5, no. 1 (March 2008): 53–71; Madonna Thunder Hawk, "Native Organizing Before the Non-Profit Industrial

Complex" in *The Revolution Will Not Be Funded: Beyond the Non-Profit Industrial Complex*, ed. INCITE! Women of Color Against Violence (Cambridge, MA: South End Press, 2007), 101–106.

9.   Paul Kivel, "Social Service or Social Change?" in *The Revolution Will Not Be Funded: Beyond the Non-Profit Industrial Complex*, ed. INCITE! Women of Color Against Violence (Cambridge, MA: South End Press, 2007), 129–150. It is important to note that only a small percentage of people seeking services generally receive them. A study in Washington State found that 88 percent of low-income people cannot get the help of an attorney for their civil legal problems. Poverty legal services are constantly severely underfunded and overrun with clients whose needs they cannot meet. Task Force on Civil Equal Justice Funding, Washington Supreme Court, *The Washington State Civil Legal Needs Assessment* Executive Summary (Seattle: Task Force on Civil Equal Justice Funding, 2003). Another study showed that for every person who seeks poverty legal services, another is turned away—which is significant considering that many people in need never seek services because they do not know they are available or they face other obstacles related to language, ability, transportation, or imprisonment. Other research has shown that 99 percent of defendants in eviction cases in Washington, DC, and New Jersey go to court without a lawyer. Legal Services Corporation, *Documenting the Justice Gap in America: The Current Unmet Civil Legal Needs of Low-Income Americans*, 2nd ed. (Washington, DC: Legal Services Corporation, 2007), www.lsc.gov/justicegap.pdf. Again, considering how many people never even make it to housing court to try to fight an eviction, these numbers are particularly concerning. The existence of poverty legal services legitimizes legal systems that target poor people and people of color by suggesting that legal help is available, while the reality is that they provide help to only a few of those few who meet their criteria (i.e., you cannot get immigration help if you have no legal avenues to immigrate or eviction help if you will not have the money for rent). Wealthy funders of poverty legal services can rely on good public relations for their contributions to this work while resting assured that these inadequate resources will never significantly threaten business as usual.

10. Christine Ahn, "Democratizing American Philanthropy," in *The Revolution Will Not Be Funded: Beyond the Non-Profit Industrial Complex*, ed. INCITE! Women of Color Against Violence (Cambridge, MA: South End Press, 2007), 63–76; Suzanne Pharr, "Social Justice Movements and Non-Profits: Historical Contexts," address presented at INCITE! and the University of California Santa Barbara Women's Studies Department, *The Revolution Will Not Be Funded: Beyond the Non-Profit Industrial Complex,* University of California Santa Barbara, April 30–May 1, 2004. Conference proceedings, CD-ROM, disk one, www.incite-national.org/index.php?s=101.

11. Suzanne Pharr, *The Revolution Will Not Be Funded conference,* 2004.

12. Suzanne Pharr, *The Revolution Will Not Be Funded conference,* 2004.

13. Thunder Hawk, "Native Organizing Before the Non-Profit Industrial Complex."

14. Ahn, "Democratizing American Philanthropy."

15. Ahn, "Democratizing American Philanthropy," 68.

16. Ahn also points out how gender and race coincide with foundation decision-making. A 2000 study found that 66 percent of foundation board members were male and 90 percent were white. Ahn, "Democratizing American Philanthropy," 66, citing US Senate Committee on Finance, *Recommendations for Reform of the United States Philanthropic Sector* (statement by the National Committee for Responsive Philanthropy), June 22, 2004, 12, www.senate.gov/~finance/hearings/testimony/2004test/062204rctest.pdf.

17. Some of the text below is adapted from an essay I wrote, "For Those Considering Law School," *Unbound: Harvard Journal of the Legal Left* (2010), http://www.legalleft.org/category/2010-issue/.

18. Dean Spade, "Be Professional!" *Harvard Journal of Law & Gender* 33 (2010): 71–86.

19. These points are based on an analysis of data gathered by a research group that I participated in. The research group interviewed membership-based organizations during 2008–2009 to learn more about their membership models and the reasons why these organizations used

those particular models. A community report that captures key findings of this research is forthcoming from the Sylvia Rivera Law Project in 2011. Some of the text in this section is adapted from the portions of that report that I authored.

20. The Sylvia Rivera Law Project is an example of a racial and economic justice–focused organization using a collective governance model developed and based on other collectively run organizations such as Sista II Sista (www.sistaiisista.org), Manavi (www.manavi.org), the Asian Women's Shelter (www.sfaws.org), and the May First Technology Collective (operational from 1999–2005).

21. *On Conflict and Consensus*, a tool often used by organizations to learn consensus decision-making and to train members on how to participate in it. C. T. Lawrence Butler and Ann Rothstein, *On Conflict and Consensus: A Handbook on Formal Consensus Decisionmaking* (Takoma Park, MD: Foods Not Bombs Publishing, 1987).

22. FIERCE!, www.fiercenyc.org.

23. Freedom Schools were first established by the Student Non-Violent Coordinating Committee (SNCC) during the civil rights movement in the 1960s. These institutions were aimed at providing free education for African American students in the southern United States and promoting socio-political and socio-economic racial justice. Perhaps the most prominent examples of Freedom Schools were established in Mississippi in 1964.

24. Other organizations that explicitly stipend members and provide access to education, analysis, and organizing through their programs include Queers for Economic Justice, http://q4ej.org/; the School of Unity and Liberation (SOUL), http://www.schoolofunityandliberation.org/; and FIERCE!, www.fiercenyc.org/index.php?s=102.

25. For example, the Sylvia Rivera Law Project *Collective Member Handbook* requires the organization to have the staff, the collective, and each specific team within the organization be at least 50 percent plus one person of color and at least 50 percent plus one trans, intersex, or gender nonconforming person.

26. Tyrone Boucher and Tiny aka Lisa Gray-Garcia, "Community Reparations Now! Tyrone Boucher and Tiny aka Lisa Gray-Garcia Talk

Revolutionary Giving, Class, Privilege, and More," *Enough,* http://
www.enoughenough.org/2010/05/community-reparations-now-tyrone-
boucher-and-tiny-aka-lisa-gray-garcia-talk-revolutionary-giving-class-
privilege-and-more/; Dean Spade, "Getting It Right from the Start:
Building a Grassroots Fundraising Program," *Grassroots Fundraising
Journal* (January/February 2005): 10–12.

27. Two examples of grassroots organizations using a membership
dues model to generate revenue are the Ontario Coalition Against Poverty
(OCAP), who "mount campaigns against regressive government policies as they affect poor and working people [and] provide direct-action
advocacy for individuals against welfare and ODSP [Ontario Disability
Support Program], public housing and others who deny poor people
what they are entitled to; believ[ing] in the power of people to organize
themselves," www.ocap.ca; and Desis Rising Up and Moving (DRUM), a
"multigenerational, membership led organization of working class South
Asian immigrants" founded to "build power of South Asian low wage immigrant workers, families fighting deportation and profiling as Muslims,
and youth in New York City," www.drumnation.org.

28. Kivel, "Social Service or Social Change?" 134–135.

29. Michel Foucault, *Society Must Be Defended: Lectures at the
College de France, 1975-76,* Trans. David Macey (New York: Picador,
2003), 256, 262-263.

30. Chela Sandoval, *Methodology of the Oppressed* (Minneapolis:
University of Minnesota Press, 2000), 45–47.

31. Sandoval, *Methodology of the Oppressed,* 59, 60.

32. It is no surprise, then, that the anthology that has brought
this critique to the fore of grassroots organizing in the United States in
the last several years was edited by INCITE! Women of Color Against
Violence and came out of their 2004 conference, *The Revolution Will Not
Be Funded.* See also INCITE! Women of Color Against Violence, ed. *The
Revolution Will Not Be Funded: Beyond the Non-Profit Industrial Complex*
(Cambridge, MA: South End Press, 2007).

33. "generationFIVE's mission is to end the sexual abuse of children
within five generations. Through survivor leadership, community organizing, and public action, generationFIVE works to interrupt and mend

the intergenerational impact of child sexual abuse on individuals, families, and communities. We integrate child sexual abuse prevention into social movements and community organizing targeting family violence, economic oppression, and gender, age-based and cultural discrimination, rather than continuing to perpetuate the isolation of the issue. It is our belief that meaningful community response is the key to effective prevention." From www.generationfive.org.

34. generationFIVE, "Towards Transformative Justice: Why a Liberatory Response to Violence Is Necessary for a Just World," *RESIST* 17, no. 5 (September/October 2008), www.resistinc.org/newsletters/articles/towards-transformative-justice.

35. Noam Chomsky and Michel Foucault, *Human Nature: Justice vs. Power* (Dutch television, 1971), online video, http://video.google.com/videoplay?docid=-1634494870703391080#; see also Noam Chomsky and Michel Foucault, *The Chomsky-Foucault Debate: On Human Nature* (New York: The New Press, 2006).

Conclusion
"This Is a Protest, Not a Parade!"[1]

IN 2005, TRANSJUSTICE, A PEOPLE OF COLOR TRANS organizing initiative at the Audre Lorde Project, organized and led the first annual New York City (NYC) Trans Day of Action for Social and Economic Justice.[2] Since its inception, the event has taken place on every Friday before New York City's Pride weekend in June, with the Dyke March following on Saturday and the Pride Parade on Sunday. The Trans Day of Action brings together organizations and individuals from across the New York City area who are unified around a set of demands centered in racial, economic, and gender justice. The statement announcing the first Trans Day of Action provided a stark analysis of racialized-gendered state violence in the United States:

> Gender policing has always been a part of the United States' bloody history. State-sanctioned gender policing targets Trans and Gender Non-Conforming [TGNC] people first by dehumanizing our identities. It denies our basic rights to gender self-determination, and considers our bodies to be property of the state. Gender policing isolates TGNC people from our communities, many of which have been socialized with these oppressive definitions of gender. As a result, we all too often fall victim to verbal and physical violence. This transphobic violence is justified using medical

theories and religious beliefs, and is perpetuated in order to
preserve US heterosexist values.[3]

The statement goes on to identify many areas of concern, including the high unemployment rate of people of color, increased
targeting of immigrants through Social Security and DMV policies, the failure of New York City's anti-discrimination law to be
implemented or enforced by the Commission on Human Rights,
police brutality, and state-sanctioned mass murder of communities of color, as illustrated by the "blatant governmental negli-
gence in the Gulf region during Hurricane Katrina."

The Trans Day of Action for Social and Economic Justice
in New York City stands in profound contrast to many aspects
of Pride celebrations around the United States and around the
world. Such celebrations have been heavily critiqued over the
last two decades for their consumerist and patriotic themes; their
marginalization of queer and trans people of color, low income
people, immigrants, and people with disabilities; and their drift
away from political resistance and toward entertainment and corporate sponsorship. Major corporate brands like Budweiser, TD
Bank, Delta Airlines, Walgreens, and even oil companies sponsor
pride celebrations around the world. In Edmonton, Alberta, protests arose in 2009 when the Edmonton Pride Parade was officially renamed the "TD Canada Trust Pride Parade and Celebration
on the Square."[4]

In San Francisco, an annual San Francisco Trans March was
initiated in 1999, first as a party in the Tenderloin neighborhood
and later as an organized march that occurs on the Friday night of
Pride Weekend preceding Saturday's Dyke March and Sunday's
Pride Parade. A comparison of the San Francisco Trans March
and the NYC Trans Day of Action can be helpful in illustrating the questions currently facing trans politics about whether
to proceed in the model of lesbian and gay rights work or choose
a more critical path. Some controversy has surrounded the San
Francisco Trans March. In 2006, racial- and economic-justice focused trans activists criticized the march's organizers for inviting

a representative of the District Attorney's office and Bevan Dufty, a member of the San Francisco Board of Supervisors, to speak at the pre-march rally. A letter of protest by the Trans/Gender Variant In Prison committee (TIP) about the speaker invitations demonstrated the concerns. First, the letter highlighted the role of the District Attorney's office in targeting trans people, people of color, people with disabilities, youth, and poor people. It outlined specific stories of trans people facing violence in San Francisco's jails for criminalized behavior resulting from poverty against whom the District Attorney's office pursued harsh punishments and long sentences. It juxtaposed the targeting and violence faced by trans people at the hands of the city's criminal punishment system with the commitment of the District Attorney's office to prosecute anti-trans hate crimes, describing how such efforts, if anything, worsened violence against trans people in the city. It further noted that although statistics suggested that law enforcement personnel were responsible for a significant portion of hate violence against trans people in San Francisco, none had been prosecuted for hate crimes by the District Attorney's office. The letter further objected to the inclusion of Supervisor Dufty, noting his membership in the conservative block of the Board of Supervisors and his work to block legislation that would help poor and working class people by preventing evictions and create low-income housing. The letter also described how having a police escort for the march and inviting the District Attorney negatively impacted participation by people on probation or parole. Finally, it argued that these invited public officials were not real allies of trans San Franciscans, but were instead exploiting the event to gain votes and continue work that harms trans people.[5]

The contrast between the San Francisco Trans March, a gathering organized primarily around a concern for increasing trans visibility, and the New York City Trans Day of Action for Social and Economic Justice, a protest march focused on key issues in the racialized-gendered distribution of life chances impacting trans people of color in NYC, is sharp. TransJustice's work in organizing the Trans Day of Action raises demands that exceed visibility, inclusion, and recognition. Their work directly resists collusion with criminal punishment systems and other sites of racial, economic, and gender violence. The organizing methods employed by TransJustice, including governance and leadership by people of color and a focus on membership development, produce conditions for formulating a more transformative agenda. Critiques of the speakers invited to the 2006 San Francisco Trans March by TIP demonstrate the kind of critical trans politics that small, people of color-led trans organizations are practicing around the United States, aiming to push racial and economic justice to the center of trans resistance.[6]

Trans resistance is emerging in a context of neoliberalism, where the most obvious option is to struggle for nothing more than incorporation into the existing social order. The contrast between these two marches provides a useful illustration of the tensions emerging in trans politics that center on questions of wealth distribution, race, gender, ability, and immigration. As we are continually invited to participate in building and growing the systems of control that shorten trans lives, we must remember that the inclusion and recognition offered by these invitations is not only disappointingly solely symbolic, but actually legitimates and expands harmful conditions. We can translate our pain and grief about the violence we face into a demand to expand the punishing power of the criminal system that targets us. We can watch as more jurisdictions pass anti-discrimination laws meanwhile trans people remain unemployed, incapable of getting ID, denied social services and health care, and imprisoned. Structured abandonment and imprisonment remain the reality of neoliberalism for the majority of trans people, yet law reform strategies beckon us to seek legitimation and protection from neoliberal legal regimes. The paths to equality laid out by the "successful" lesbian and gay rights model to which we are assumed to aspire have little to offer us in terms of concrete change to our life chances.

Our inclusion in that model legitimizes systems that harm us and further obscures the causes and consequences of that harm.

The political conditions created by neoliberalism terrorize and shorten the lives of trans people, and threaten to subsume trans resistance. Trans people are told by legal systems, state agencies, employers, schools, and our families that we are impossible people who are not who we say we are, cannot exist, cannot be classified, and cannot fit anywhere. We have been told by lesbian and gay rights organizations, as they continually choose to leave us aside, that we are not politically viable and that our lives are not a political possibility that can be conceived. At the same time, the nonprofit industrial complex tells us that we have to run our resistance organizations like businesses, that participatory or collective models of governance are inefficient and idealistic, that we must tailor our messages to what the corporate media can understand, and that our demands need to fit within the existing goals of the institutions that are killing us. The demands that are emerging from the most vulnerable trans communities for the abolition of prisons, police, and borders, and for full trans-inclusive health care and food, housing, and education for everyone are the kinds of demands that are incomprehensible to reform movements focused on rights claims. These broader, transformative demands cannot be won in courts, and they emerge from those for whom narrow legal reform demands have little to offer. White-led, lawyer-dominated lesbian and gay rights organizations—even those that have added a "T" to their mission statements—cannot comprehend these demands and cannot win them using narrow elite media and law reform strategies focused on inclusion. The perceived impossibility of the very lives of trans people, especially those who are simultaneously targets of racism, colonialism, xenophobia, ableism, and/or ageism of which trans identity is only a part, and the perceived impossibility of the demands and methods of resistance emerging from the most targeted and impacted populations, are symptomatic of the inherent conflicts and divides produced (and often hidden) by neoliberalism.

Some emergent projects, in addition to those already discussed throughout this book, stand out as examples of a developing trans politics that demands more than what is offered by the narrow space of neoliberal cooptation. I have chosen to discuss in detail several of these projects in the next section: diverse community solutions to violence that do not rely on policing or criminal courts; Transforming Justice, a national alliance of organizations and individuals focused on trans imprisonment in the United States; the advocacy strategies targeting transphobic practices in New York City's welfare system; and prison letter-writing projects. Through the following examples, we can see the necessary disruption offered by substantive demands and by particular processes of mobilization. These projects are also instructive because they confront significant challenges and obstacles: lack of resources to support the work; overwhelming need from vulnerable community members; lack of developed leadership in community members; and the vulnerability of leaders to harms associated with racism, sexism, poverty, imprisonment, disability, and transphobia. These challenges point us in the direction of the problems that need to be addressed as we continue to strategize resistance.

Community Solutions to Violence
That Do Not Rely on Police

Across the country, racial and economic justice centered feminist, queer, and trans organizations are working on methods of addressing violence that do not involve the police or criminal courts.[7] This work has been taken up in different forms and with different areas of focus. Groups working on these strategies include Safe OUTside the System (SOS) Collective of the Audre Lorde Project in New York City;[8] For Crying Out Loud! and Communities Against Rape and Abuse (CARA) in Seattle;[9] Creative Interventions in Oakland,[10] Community United Against Violence (CUAV) in San Francisco,[11] and the national organization generationFIVE, among many others. These organizations contend that policing and criminal punishment exacerbates racist, sexist, homophobic, ableist, transphobic, and anti-immigrant violence in their communities, and are experimenting with transformative approaches to dealing with harms such as intimate partner violence, child abuse, and bashing. They understand that the root causes of violence are the abusive and exploitative power relations produced through systemic racism, sexism, transphobia, settler colonialism, ableism, poverty, and criminalization, and actively refute the idea that violence comes from bad people who need to be locked up. These organizations are developing a range of strategies aimed at addressing violence without feeding the criminal punishment system. These strategies include providing support and resources to survivors of violence in order to expand choices in and around dangerous situations as well as avenues to healing; creating opportunities for people who have been harmful, people who have been harmed, and their communities to transform, heal, and change behavior; responding to harm by developing solutions that center the wellness of the survivor and the prevention of future harm (neither of which the criminal punishment system provides); providing training to build the capacity of individuals and communities to form healthy relationships, nonviolently resolve conflict, support vulnerable members, and identify and break patterns of intimate and family violence; and establishing safe havens in neighborhoods that enable people to flee harassment and/or violence without calling the police.

This work combines at least three of the four pillars of social justice infrastructure outlined by the Miami Workers' Center. These organizations directly assist people in need, create new paradigms for understanding violence, and share these paradigms through various political education programs. They build participation in collective action while developing leadership by those most directly impacted by systemic, institutional, and interpersonal harm. The work explicitly avoids using the criminal punishment system.

Some of these organizations also lead campaigns that include law and policy reform demands such as decriminalization of sex work or drug use, stopping police–ICE collaboration, increasing poverty alleviation programs, and other reforms. These campaigns aim to reach the root causes of violence rather than relying on the state's capacity for punishment. All of these formations are also working through organizational structures that aim to resist the harmful aspects of nonprofitization and build infrastructure centered in racial, gender, and economic justice. All of this work is experimental, and in the early stages of development, and all requires consistent self-reflection and critique. Nonetheless, it illustrates how a critical queer, feminist, and trans politics is currently taking shape on the ground across the United States.

Transforming Justice

Transforming Justice is a national alliance of organizations and individuals focused on trans imprisonment in the United States. The project emerged in 2005 from the staff of the Sylvia Rivera Law Project (SRLP), who identified a need to build shared analysis about trans imprisonment. SRLP saw that after years of agitation by itself and by other organizations, more attention (albeit very little) was beginning to be paid to the dire circumstances facing trans prisoners. However, there was not a base of shared political understanding among the organizations who were beginning to do law and policy work on the issues regarding the nature of imprisonment, the dangers of prison reform as a possible vector of prison expansion, and the alternative politics of prison abolition. As some of the larger LGBT organizations began to minimally take up the issue, it became clear that they were not connected to prison-related movements that had developed an analysis about the ways reform efforts have repeatedly been co-opted by forces interested in expanding imprisonment.

In the 2000s, prison-focused activists were witnessing a disturbing new manifestation of this trend. New proposals were emerging for "gender-responsive prisons." Purportedly in the name of making prisons better for women prisoners, proposals were emerging to build more women's prisons—which would of course result in more women being imprisoned.

Organizations concerned about gender and criminalization were recognizing and resisting this moment of co-optation of critiques of the treatment of women prisoners to imprison more women, and trans organizations saw potential danger in trans people's experiences of violence being used to foster "reform" projects that would also expand imprisonment. SRLP reached out to other organizations—both people of color-led small trans organizations like the Transgender, Gender Variant/Genderqueer, and Intersex Justice Project (TGIJP) and larger organizations with LGBT projects such as the American Friends Service Committee—to talk about the possibility of a national gathering where people could share their analyses and possibly come to some consensus about refusing to take up prison-expanding tactics. As the idea emerged, organizers from TGIJP and TIP[12] in the San Francisco Bay Area introduced models and ideas for centering the experiences and leadership of formerly imprisoned trans people in the organizing of the event. The group discussed how this event could be a leadership development opportunity for trans people caught in the cycle of poverty and imprisonment, ways to include currently imprisoned trans people in the planning and in the event itself, and how to utilize the support of lawyers and other professionals at national organizations without centralizing their leadership.

Eventually, the group created a two-level planning method—local and national. A local weekly meeting called "Marvelous Mondays" was initiated, offering food and support to those who wanted to show up and get involved. As the word spread, the Monday meetings became an important gathering place for many formerly imprisoned trans women coping with addiction, poverty, discrimination, homelessness, and ongoing criminalization. The local group worked on numerous projects, including

creating a survey aimed at acquiring the perspective and input
of imprisoned trans people on the project that involved visiting
currently imprisoned trans people in California with the survey
and distributing it by mail. The group also designed a website
for the event and developed a popular education curriculum to
use with attendees. Members of the local group also joined in
conference calls with the national planning group, which worked
on fundraising for the event, crafting and sending out invitations
to people around the country, and other aspects of programming.
The national group included many attorneys and other allies to
imprisoned trans people who aimed to provide support to the
process while centering leadership development and governance
of the process by directly impacted people.

Ultimately, the planning process resulted in Transforming
Justice, a two-day conference focused on the experiences of imprisoned trans people. It was an invite-only event. The invited
organizations were asked to send members who were trans people, formerly imprisoned people, people of color, or otherwise
part of highly criminalized populations. This was an important
strategy to disrupt cycles of leadership development in nonprofits
that tend to offer white people, people with educational privilege,
and nontrans people opportunities to travel, build analysis, and
network. It was also aimed to prevent the event from being overrun by students, researchers, professionals, and others who might
drown out the presence and leadership of trans former prisoners.
The result was a conference at which the attendance, participation, and leadership of trans women of color and formerly imprisoned trans people were centered, and where attorneys and
other allied professionals with educational privilege were in the
minority. The conference included opportunities for attendees
to write to currently imprisoned trans people, discussions led by
former prisoners about criminal punishment and immigration
enforcement systems as well as priorities for change, interactive
sessions that encouraged attendees to meet one another and learn
about each other's work, and discussions of the politics of prison

abolition. The event also included a focus on sustainability in the work with health workers offering massage, quiet spaces, counseling, and other support for attendees. By the end of the weekend, the attendees had crafted and agreed to five points of unity:

> 1. We recognize cycles of poverty, criminalization, and imprisonment as urgent human rights issues for transgender and gender non-conforming people.
> 2. We agree to promote, centralize, and support the leadership of transgender and gender non-conforming people most impacted by prisons, policing, and poverty in this work.
> 3. We plan to organize to build on and expand a national movement to liberate our communities and specifically transgender and gender non-conforming people from poverty, homelessness, drug addiction, racism, ageism, transphobia, classism, sexism, ableism, immigration discrimination, violence, and the brutality of the prison industrial complex.
> 4. We commit to ending the abuse and discrimination against transgender and gender non-conforming people in all aspects of society, with the long-term goal of ending the prison industrial complex.
> 5. We agree to continue discussing with each other what it means to work towards ending the prison industrial complex while addressing immediate human rights crises.[13]

After the event, the organizers conducted in-depth evaluations with attendees about their experiences and began the process of determining what role the Transforming Justice formation might continue to play as a national alliance or coalition. The evaluation and planning process again focused on questions of how Transforming Justice could be governed by those most directly impacted, how to further develop the leadership skills of people living in criminalized trans communities, how to avoid compromising the mission of the work due to pressure from funders, how to balance the benefits of maintaining paid staff positions for developing leaders in communities that need employment opportunities against the costs of entering the competitive dynamics of nonprofit fundraising, and how to create a sustainable structure that supports local grassroots organizing and does not consolidate power in a national body.

The Transforming Justice national coalition and resulting conference models a trans politics committed to prioritizing the experiences, knowledge, and leadership of the most vulnerable. Transforming Justice suggests ways of de-professionalizing social movement work while building participatory, perpetually self-reflective structures. This work is confronted with ongoing challenges. Throughout the organizing of the conference, issues related to criminalization consistently came to the fore as members continued to face obstacles to their well-being. Several members struggled with addiction, and relapses of individual organizing members impacted the group. The housing insecurity of some members prevented them from consistently attending and participating in meetings or following through with commitments. Some key organizers found the stress of working on the event impacted their mental health. Other organizers were imprisoned during the event planning and were no longer able to participate in the same way. Essentially, the very conditions that prompt the need for this work continue to threaten and harm it. The organizing itself can sometimes be a source of support for members during hard times, bringing people together who can offer understanding and share resources. Yet, doing under-resourced work to dismantle massively violent systems can also cause stress and undermine the health of people doing the work, as many people who have been burned out in nonprofits are well aware. Organizing in a context where most members are impacted by addiction and other health issues—problems often created by exposure to continued violence and trauma—can mean that significant conflict is a part of the environment. Resource scarcity can exacerbate the stress of the work in ways that worsen conflict. Participants in the planning process who were in the role of allies, such as white lawyers and other nonprofit staffers with educational privilege, had to continually work on internalized dominance behaviors that can become obstacles to building leadership of directly impacted people.

The structural barriers to that leadership were many, and allies struggled to participate in ways that were truly supportive of that leadership and did not overtake the space necessary for growth and cultivation. The Transforming Justice coalition planning and organizing experiences are instructive in describing the kinds of challenges that create persistent obstacles to these processes, as well as for articulating strategies for how to do work under such conditions. As the group continues to develop its structure as a national alliance, it is devising innovative methods for addressing the challenges that come with doing work based in prioritizing the leadership of those most directly impacted. In 2010, the national alliance sent a delegation to the US Social Forum and conducted a workshop aimed at helping people from around the country who are active on issues related to the criminalization of trans people assess next steps for the national work. Transforming Justice is currently considering a proposal to plan its next national gathering, hoping to continue to build relationships between regions and further develop the capacity of local leaders to participate in resistance. Moving forward, Transforming Justice has increasingly focused on ensuring that its framework for thinking about trans imprisonment fully includes criminal imprisonment, immigration imprisonment, and psychiatric/medical imprisonment, and is forming key partnerships to center this broad frame in its emerging work.

Human Resources Administration Advocacy, New York City

In 2010, TransJustice, the Sylvia Rivera Law Project, FIERCE!, Housing Works,[14] Queers for Economic Justice (QEJ),[15] and others won a significant victory in a struggle with the Human

Resources Administration (HRA) of New York City, the division of the city's Department of Social Services that administers welfare and other poverty-related programs. These groups, which formed a coalition they called the HRA Review Committee, won a policy that aims to address the discrimination and abuse trans people face in HRA programs. Their 2009–2010 campaign built off earlier work taken up by the New York City Lesbian, Gay, Bisexual, and Transgender Community Center (the Center),[16] the Sylvia Rivera Law Project, and the Transgender Law and Policy Institute (TLPI).[17]

In 2005, the Center, SRLP, and the TLPI worked with an HRA advisory committee to draft a set of "best practices" that would address a range of issues faced by trans people seeking benefits and services through HRA. The recommendations aimed to confront problems trans people have with HRA's gender classification procedures, discrimination in welfare offices, discrimination in workfare programs, placement in gender-segregated shelters, and more. The recommendations sought to create procedures to address these issues. After the Best Practices document was finished, HRA and the municipal Law Department stalled; the document never became HRA policy.

In 2009, the HRA Review Committee took up these issues again, this time creating a grassroots organizing campaign that used open meetings, the participatory membership structures of the organizations in the coalition, public petitions, and online social networking tools to raise awareness and build public pressure demanding that HRA change its policies and practices. This work had emerged through organizations that center the participation of low-income, homeless people, and people of color in trans communities, and that foster the leadership and organizing capacities of these populations through campaign work focused on issues identified as the most urgent. The methods used to fuel this campaign departed significantly from the established model of lesbian and gay rights work. Rather than behind-closed-doors meetings between elites and government officials, or in lawsuits with the least marginalized people headlining as plaintiffs, the work focused on collective action by low-income trans people of color. It prioritized change that impacts the daily lives of highly vulnerable trans people rather than advancing symbolic change. It centered politically stigmatized populations—public assistance recipients and trans people—and reframed their experiences and their relation to the state. While there is no doubt that this was a policy reform project, its relationship to the Pillar of Power significantly departed from the law and policy reform methods typically centered in lesbian and gay rights work. The specific demands brought to the table by the HRA Review Committee will not end homelessness or poverty—they are incremental and reform-oriented—but they are part of a broader strategy and power analysis rooted in and generated by the experiences of people facing multiple vectors of marginality that demands change to the specific harms they face.

The process of developing the campaign and bringing directly impacted people into its work was aimed at building the leadership of trans public benefits recipients, expanding the membership of racial and economic justice–centered queer and trans organizations, and creating capacity for future campaigns. When the new policy was won, it was a watered down, thin version of the initially proposed "Best Practices" document drafted by the 2005 committee. However, this new policy was more effective, I would argue, than if the original document—drafted by white movement professionals (including myself) without a community-based campaign behind it—had been immediately codified by HRA. The HRA, and all similar and related poverty-focused government agencies, do not follow their own policies, do not train their workers about their policies, and are unaccountable for their mistreatment of poor people. The process of winning the policy in 2010, even with its weakened language, is a more significant victory because the communities impacted by the policy are aware of it, consistently demand its enforcement, and continue to build relationships with other impacted people by distributing the policy (as a palm card) in welfare offices and trans gathering spaces citywide. The members of the coalition are aware of the policy's inadequacies just as they are aware that HRA is unlikely to follow its own policies. After all, they have witnessed and been subject to HRA's egregious behavior as public benefits recipients. However, their win is a significant moment in their mobilization efforts, which will not stop with this singular achievement. This organizing produced a new set of community leaders who understand the inner workings of HRA, who have deep relationships with one another and with organizations focused on their concerns, and who know that HRA is a target they can force to make change. This policy reform target was but one tactic in the broader work of these organizations to mobilize queer and trans people for racial, economic, and gender justice. These events demonstrate how law and policy reform can operate as a useful tactic when taken up in a long-term mobilization strategy and when focused on the immediate needs of highly vulnerable populations. These features ensured that the win was not merely symbolic, was a moment of increased politicization of impacted people rather that pacification of resistance and legitimization of harmful conditions, and actually built resistance capacity for continued struggle.

Prison Letter-Writing Projects

Around the United States and beyond, organizations focused on providing penpals to imprisoned trans people are emerging and increasingly collaborating with one another. Some of these projects are student-run and affiliated with colleges and universities, some are part of nonprofit organizations that also do other work, and others are autonomous groups not affiliated with larger institutions. These penpal programs connect trans people and allies who are not imprisoned with imprisoned trans people to create supportive relationships and networks. Directly supporting individual prisoners is something trans prison abolitionist organizations like TGIJP and SRLP have identified as a key part of their work, especially given their awareness of the ways population-wide prison reform programs almost always lead to prison expansion, both in the realm of punishing power and in the construction of new facilities. Combating the isolation and exile logic of imprisonment by building relationships between individuals and communities on both sides of prison walls is an important part of decarceration. Many trans prisoners lack family support and often have few or no connections to people on the outside. Having a relationship with a nonprisoner increases the prisoner's access to advocacy tools and resources and can help with isolation and mental health. Penpal programs can also provide mutual opportunities for political education and involvement, and can provide key support in planning for life after release. The penpal relationship can also help expose the violences of imprisonment that often remain hidden when their targets are isolated from contact with the outside.

These projects are also important to legal organizations like SRLP and TGIJP because many imprisoned trans people cannot be helped by lawyers—many of the horrors they live through have been dismissed by courts and lawmakers—so these organizations must find other ways to support their survival and political engagement. These projects utilize a variety of strategies to match prisoners with penpals, and to support the nonprisoner penpals in providing useful resources, coping with difficulties that come up, and in remaining committed and consistent in their communication. Recently, some of these projects, including Hearts on a Wire in Philadelphia, Black and Pink in Boston, SRLP in New York, Bent Bars in London, and the Prisoner Correspondence Project in Montreal have created a quarterly conference call where they share resources, challenges, and ideas for the continuation and advancement of the work.[18] This is vital service work in the sense that it provides direct support to people whose lives are extremely vulnerable and may help with issues such as brutality, food deprivation, and lack of access to health care. This work also helps establish support upon release to prevent re-imprisonment. At the same time, these projects are part of movement building: they foster the leadership skills of penpals on both sides of the prison walls through the exchange of political analysis and personal experience. For queer and trans students and young people, these projects often provide a means of connecting to a queer and trans politics that centers questions of racism, poverty, and criminalization, an important alternative to the marriage/consumption-centered lesbian and gay politics that is most widely visible to emerging activists.

These projects are also centered in a practice of building non-professional relationships that ground political practice and understanding in mutual care and trust. They are about connecting two penpals on shared ground for a mutual relationship, rather than creating a client-service provider dynamic. The groups working on these projects center a critical analysis of power dynamics that exist whenever prisoners and nonprisoners communicate, and they work to provide support to penpals to confront and examine those dynamics. This provides an opportunity for the development of a social justice analysis very different from what happens when nonimprisoned people come to relationships with imprisoned people only in professional service-provision settings. These penpal projects move beyond a depoliticized services model that turns marginalized people in need into "clients" or "recipients." These projects instead create conditions for supporting vulnerable people that are holistic and based in demands for transformative change rather than structures of system stabilization.

The projects I have briefly described above—community solutions to violence that do not rely on the police, the HRA policy reform campaign, Transforming Justice, and trans penpal projects—offer just a few examples of the kinds of work being taken up by activists and organizations struggling to address conditions faced by trans and gender nonconforming people in ways that are part of a broad politics of racial and economic justice and that recognizes the central role of criminalization, immigration enforcement, and poverty in trans subjection. This work prioritizes building leadership and membership on a "most vulnerable first" basis, centering the belief that social justice trickles up, not down. These projects are emerging in the same moment when many are challenging the structures of LGBT rights frameworks and formations that are reproducing harmful conditions. Challenges to the prioritization and resource concentration in marriage reform work are growing louder. Many are questioning the hate crime law strategy as a way to address violence and are opposing hate crime laws inclusion campaigns. Organizations like the Sylvia Rivera Law Project and the Peter Cicchino Youth Project[19] have challenged the lawyers-only, behind-closed-doors agenda setting and decision-making that has been typical of lesbian and gay rights approaches and that, sadly, are being emulated in emerging transgender legal circles.[20] Additionally, in the United States and around the world, people are creating innovative mobilization models focused on trans politics that are deeply rooted in and connected to social movements for racial and gender justice, wealth redistribution, and opposition to imperialism.

The fruitlessness of "victories" in which trans identity is called upon to legitimate the exile logic of criminalization and the "equal opportunity" logic of anti-discrimination opens many key strategy questions for our resistance. The call to seek out formal legal equality through demands for inclusion in hate crime legislation and employment-focused anti-discrimination laws beckons trans populations to claim and embrace a kind of recognition that not only fails to offer respite from the brutalities of poverty and criminalization, but also threatens to reduce our struggle to another justification for and site of expansion of the structures that produce the very conditions that shorten our lives.

We are invited to demand that trans people are "human" when "human" is still defined through norms of race, indigeneity, gender, ability, and immigration status that actually limit the invitation to a very small part of the trans population.[21] We must build a critical trans politics that refuses these invitations and that boldly resists the regimes of abandonment and imprisonment that neoliberalism requires. These other trans politics often appear impossible, incomprehensible, and nonviable in the context of recognition and inclusion focused nonprofitized social movements. But such a trans politics is possible, and happening right now. Many trans activists and organizations are taking up critical engagements with the infrastructure of social change. By rejecting elite strategies centering law reform and mainstream media messaging, these locations of resistance offer models of participatory, mobilization-focused struggle led by those living on the sharpest intersecting edges of multiple systems of control. Such a politics is unrecognizable as "LGBT politics" in the current moment. Lesbian and gay rights politics has articulated an agenda centered in formal legal equality and single-issue politics embracing divisive framings of "family" and "law and order" in white supremacist, nationalist, homonormative terms. The existence of critical practices that resist the pulls of recognition despite the enormous pressures to be legible in neoliberal terms demonstrate the collective desire for trans political practices that actually address trans survival. It is this space, where questions of survival and distribution are centered, where the well-being of the most vulnerable will not be compromised for promises of legal and media recognition, where the difficult work of building participatory resistance led from the bottom up is undertaken, where we can seek the emergence of deeply transformative trans resistance.

NOTES

1.   Overheard at the Trans Day of Action march in New York City, June 2007.

2.   TransJustice is a "project of the Audre Lorde Project, a community organizing center for Lesbian, Gay, Bisexual, Two-Spirit, and Transgender People of Color in the New York City area" that, according to their mission statement, "works to mobilize its communities and allies into action on the pressing political issues they face, including gaining

access to jobs, housing, and education; the need for Trans-sensitive health care, HIV-related services, and job-training programs; resisting police, government and anti-immigrant violence." http://alp.org/tj and www.myspace.com/transjusticenyc.

3.   Statements issued by TransJustice in 2005. See also TransJustice, "Trans Day of Action for Economic and Social Justice," in *Color of Violence: The Incite! Anthology*, ed. INCITE! Women of Color Against Violence (Cambridge, MA: South End Press, 2006), 227–330.

4.   Saturday Submissions, "The Commercialization of Gay Pride," HomoRazzi.com, July 30, 2009, www.homorazzi.com/article/gay-pride-parade-commercialization-sponsorship-corporate-queer-recruitment-army-td-bank-stonewall/.

5.   Trans/Gender Variant In Prison committee (TIP), June 19, 2006, on file with the author. According to their mission statement, the goal of TIP "is to challenge and end the human rights abuses committed against transgender, gender variant/genderqueer and intersex (TGI) people in California prisons and beyond [though] recognizing that poverty borne from profound and pervasive discrimination and marginalization of TGI people is a major underlying cause of why TGI people end up in prison." http://tgijp.org.

6.   In 2010, racial and economic justice–focused trans activists deepened their dialogue with San Francisco Trans March organizers in an attempt to shift the focus of the San Francisco event to reflect a politics centered in the most urgent political issues facing trans populations in the Bay Area. It will be interesting to see how the event continues to evolve as constituents struggle over these very different approaches.

7.   Ching-In Chen, Jai Dulani & Leah Lakshmi Piepzna-Samarasinha, Eds., *The Revolution Starts at Home: Confronting Intimate Violence Within Activist Communities* (Brooklyn, NY: South End Press, 2011).

8.   "The Safe OUTSide the System (SOS) Collective works to challenge violence that affects LGBTSTGNC people of color. We are guided by the belief that strategies that increase the police presence and the criminalization of our communities do not create safety. Therefore we utilize strategies of community accountability to challenge violence."

http://alp.org/community/sos.

9. The Survivor Support Team of For Crying Out Loud! "seek[s] to facilitate the healing and empowerment of survivors of sexual trauma. We are here *for survivors* to help them meet their unique needs, to listen, to provide alternatives to mainstream responses to sexual assault. As survivors and allies we do this to restore and create joy within our communities." For Crying Out Loud!'s Aggressor Accountability Team works "to create survivor-defined, community-supported plans for accountability without the cops." http://forcryingoutloud206.wordpress. com. Communities Against Rape and Abuse (CARA) "promotes a broad agenda for liberation and social justice while prioritizing anti-rape work as the center of our organizing. We use community organizing, critical dialogue, artistic expression, and collective action as tools to build safe, peaceful, and sustainable communities. Our blog provides a Black feminist analysis of contemporary politics, debates & local Seattle issues." http://cara-seattle.blogspot.com/.

10. The vision of Creative Interventions "is based upon liberation— the positive, life-affirming, transformative potential within communities. All activities and projects . . . are meant to unearth and build upon the often hidden and devalued knowledge and skills expressed by generations of people who have courageously defied violence and created new spaces for safety and self-determination." www.creative-interventions.org.

11. Community United Against Violence (CUAV) "works to build the power of LGBTQQ communities to transform violence and oppression. We support the healing and leadership of people impacted by abuse and mobilize our broader communities to replace cycles of trauma with cycles of safety and liberation. As part of the larger social justice movement, CUAV works to create truly safe communities where everyone can thrive." www.cuav.org.

12. "TGIJP addresses human rights abuses against TGI prisoners through strategies that effect systemic change." http://tgijp.org.

13. *Transforming Justice* Conference, San Francisco, City College of San Francisco, October 13–14, 2007, http://srlp.org/transformingjustice.

14. Housing Works is "the largest community-based AIDS service organization in the United States, as well as the nation's largest

minority-controlled AIDS service organization [offering] lifesaving services, such as housing, medical and mental health care, meals, job training, drug treatment, HIV prevention education, and social support to more than 20,000 homeless and low-income New Yorkers living with HIV and AIDS." www.housingworks.org.

15. Queers for Economic Justice is "a progressive non-profit organization committed to promoting economic justice in a context of sexual and gender liberation. Our goal is to challenge and change the systems that create poverty and economic injustice in our communities, and to promote an economic system that embraces sexual and gender diversity. We are committed to the principle that access to social and economic resources is a fundamental right, and we work to create social and economic equity through grassroots organizing, public education, advocacy, and research. We do this work because although poor queers have always been a part of both the gay rights and economic justice movements, they have been, and continue to be, largely invisible in both movements. This work will always be informed by the lived experiences and expressed needs of queer people in poverty." http://q4ej.org.

16. "Established in 1983, the Lesbian, Gay, Bisexual & Transgender Community Center has grown to become the largest LGBT multi-service organization on the East Coast and second largest LGBT community center in the world. [The Center] provides a home for the birth, nurture and celebration of our organizations, institutions and culture; cares for our individuals and groups in need; educates the public and our community; and empowers our individuals and groups to achieve their fullest potential." www.gaycenter.org.

17. The Transgender Law and Policy Institute works to "bring experts and advocates together to work on law and policy initiatives designed to advance transgender equality." www.transgenderlaw.org.

18. Hearts on a Wire (PO Box 36831, Philadelphia, PA 19107), http://community-justice.org/projects/phn/sneakpeaks/hearts-on-a-wire/; Black and Pink (Community Church of Boston, 565 Boylston Street, Boston, MA 02116), www.blackandpink.org; Bent Bars Project (Bent Bars Project, PO Box 66754, London WC1A 9BF), www.co-re.org/joomla/index.php/bent-bars; and Prisoner

Correspondence Project (QPIRG Concordia c/o Concordia University, 1455 de Maisonneuve O, Montreal, QC H3G 1M8), www.prisonercorrespondenceproject.com.

19. The Peter Cicchino Youth Project "conduct[s] legal clinics at drop-in centers for runaways and LGBT youth . . . [and] engage[s] in systemic advocacy and impact litigation around issues such as the mistreatment of LGBT youth in New York City's foster care and juvenile detention systems. Finally, we work with LGBT young adults who are "aging" out of foster care, to ensure that they receive legally required discharge planning, and to give them the skills they need to successfully transition into independent, adult lives." www.urbanjustice.org/ujc/projects/peter.html.

20. Gabriel Arkles, Pooja Gehi, and Elana Redfield, "The Role of Lawyers in Trans Liberation: Building a Transformative Movement for Social Change," *Seattle Journal for Social Justice* 8 (Spring/Summer 2010): 579.

21. "Aspiring to humanity is always a racial project." Andrea Smith, "Queer Theory and Native Studies: The Heteronormativity of Settler Colonialism," *GLQ: A Journal of Lesbian and Gay Studies* 16, no.1–2, (2010): 42.

Acknowledgments

THE IDEAS IN THIS BOOK WERE DEVELOPED IN CONVERSATION and collaboration with many people, and I am deeply grateful for all who seek to bring a collaborative, generous approach to queer and trans politics, to academia, and to legal advocacy in the face of pressures to do otherwise.

Thank you to my editors at South End Press, Alex Straaik, Kenyon Farrow, Jocelyn Burrell, Alexander Dwinell, and Asha Tall. Thank you for your work on this book and for publishing so many of my favorite books. Thank you to Josh MacPhee for designing this book and for all the inspiration your work provides.

Many thanks to people who provided feedback on drafts of chapters of this book along the way, including Grace Hong, Chandan Reddy, Craig Willse, Jane Anderson, Rolan Gregg, Bob Chang, Morgan Bassichis, Calvin Burnap, Cybele, Soniya Munshi, Emily Thuma, Erica Meiners, and Angela Harris. Emily Drabinski deserves special thanks for reading the full draft in only three days at the end of the process and providing very valuable feedback.

I am grateful for the mentorship and support provided at various stages during which the ideas in this book were developing by Paisley Currah, Janet Halley, Kendall Thomas, Katherine Franke, Ruthie Wilson Gilmore, Andrea Smith, Bob Chang, Kara Keeling, Andrea Ritchie, Eric Stanley, Jack Halberstam, Tayyab Mahmud, Urvashi Vaid, Eli Clare, Leslie Feinberg, Lisa Duggan, Susan Stryker, Gabriel Arkles, Carmen Gonzalez, Nick Gorton, Pooja Gehi, Elana Redfield, Imani Henry, Carrie Davis, Lily

Kahng, Angela Harris, Shannon Minter, Maggie Chon, and Alex Lee. I am particularly grateful to the Critical Race Studies faculty at UCLA Law School whose teaching shaped so many of the ideas in this book, including Cheryl Harris, Devon Carbado, Kimberlé Crenshaw, and Jerry Kang.

Thank you to several people and places that hosted me in various capacities while writing, including the Blue Mountain Center, The Centre for Law, Gender and Sexuality at Kent Law School, Julie Shapiro, Dori Midnight, the Mogielnicki's Bittersweet, the Williams Institute at UCLA, and CUNY Law School.

Special thanks to three collaborators whose constant engagement has been responsible for so much of my political and intellectual development, Craig Willse, Morgan Bassichis, and Rickke Mananzala.

Many people provided love and friendship that sustained me during the writing of this book, some of whom are Bridge Joyce, Chris Boots Hanssmann, Dori Midnight, Craig Willse, Sandy Heider, Morgan Bassichis, Daniel McGee, Jolie Harris, Rania Spade, Katrina Spade, Ellen O'Grady, Emily Thuma, Aren Aizura, Nick Gorton, Lawe Mohtadi, Emma Hedditch, Riley Spade, Kale Spade, Ahovra Steinhaus, Wynne Greenwood, Kaycee Wimbish, Liz Little, Wu Tsang, E. E. Miller, Bernadine Mellis, Xylor Jane, Leila P., Andrea Lawlor, Ida Smith, Asha Greer, Rolan Gregg, Thomas Morgan, Phil Thomes, Paisley Currah, Emmett Ramstad, T. C. Tolbert, Tennessee Jones, Dallas Maynor, Sarah Lamble, Emily Grabham, Soniya Munshi, Belkys Garcia, Chandan Reddy, Colby Lenz, Cybele, Calvin Burnap, Sonja Sivesind, Angélica Cházaro, Devon Knowles, Gabriel Arkles, Pooja Gehi, Travis Sands, Catherine Sameh, Erin Small, Emily Roysdon, Tara Mateik, Allison Palmer, Lara Comstock, and Albert, Josh, Janie, Finley, Tanner, Ann-Riley, and Mikey Goldschmidt. My sister, Lis Goldschmidt, requires special acknowledgment for clothing, feeding, sheltering, witnessing, and caring for me for my entire life. I will never finish being grateful for whatever forces put us here together. I am also grateful to my mom, who modeled cursing and raising hell and community building and deep friendship and trying to heal and questioning authority during the short time we had together and who succeeded in giving her kids so much more space than she was given.

Thanks to my colleagues and students at Seattle University School of Law for much inspiration and support. Thanks to Tina Ching, Alex West, Terri Nilliasca, and Robyn Mellen for research assistance.

Enormous thanks to all the brilliant people doing the various kinds of innovative trans advocacy, research, and organizing that this work discusses and relies on, and to those who did all the work that came before and made today's articulations of trans politics possible. I am especially grateful to all the past and present collective members of the Sylvia Rivera Law Project whose relentless dedication to practicing transformative politics against all odds is my greatest source of optimism, including Alisha Williams, Alvin Starks, Andrea Delmagro, Bali White, Belkys Garcia, Bran Fenner, Carrie Davis, Catherine Granum, Chase Strangio, D. Horowitz, Daniel McGee, Dee Perez, Diana Oliva, Doyin Ola, Edgar "Chaco" Rivera Colon, Elana Redfield, Eli Dueker, Emily Nepon, Franklin Romeo, Gabriel Arkles, Gabriel Foster, Gael Guevara, Isaac Kwock, Jack Aponte, Jamie Stafford-Hill, Jorge Irizzary, Julienne Brown, Kim Watson, Ksen Pallegedara, Margarita Guzman, Michelle O'Brien, Mickey Lambert, Mila Khan, Nadia Qurashi, Naomi Clark, Pooja Gehi, Rachel Peters Qadir, Reina Gossett, Rickke Mananzala, Riley Snorton, Ryder Diaz, Soniya Munshi, Sonja Sivesind, Stefanie Rivera, Stella Atzlan, and Taila Thomas.

I am inspired by many teachers, leaders, and trouble makers who were lost too soon, including Sylvia Rivera, Amanda Milan, Dana Turner, Ruby Ordenana, Victoria Arellano, Tyra Hunter, Isaac Kwock, Regina Shavers, Mary Parlee Goldschmidt, Karen Shea Silverman, Bob Kohler, Jean Geldart, Frank Parlee, Chloe Dzubilo, Sanesha Stewart, and most recently, Tracy Bumpus. I hope this work can make a small contribution to building the worlds they imagined and hoped for when they were here.

Index

About the Author

DEAN SPADE IS AN ASSISTANT PROFESSOR AT THE SEATTLE University School of Law, where he teaches Administrative Law, Poverty Law, Law and Social Movements, and Critical Perspectives on Transgender Law. In 2002, Dean founded the Sylvia Rivera Law Project, a nonprofit law collective that provides free legal services to transgender, intersex and gender non-conforming people who are low-income and/or people of color works to build trans resistance rooted in racial and economic justice. SRLP operates on a consensus-based collective governance model, prioritizing the governance and leadership of trans, intersex, and gender non-conforming people of color. From 1998 to 2006, Dean co-edited the paper and online zine *Make* (archived at http://makezine. enoughenough.org). Dean is co-editor, with Tyrone Boucher, of the online journal *Enough* (http://enoughenough.org), which focuses on the personal politics of wealth redistribution. *Normal Life: Administrative Violence, Critical Trans Politics and the Limits of Law* is Dean's first book. For more writing by Dean Spade, see http://www.deanspade.net.

About South End Press

South End Press is an independent, collectively-run publisher with more than 250 titles in print. Since our founding in 1977, we have met the needs of readers who are exploring, or are already committed to, the politics of radical social change. Our goal is to publish books that encourage critical thinking and constructive action on the key political, cultural, social, economic, and ecological issues shaping life in the United States and in the world. In this way, we provide a forum for a wide variety of democratic social movements, and an alternative to the products and practices of corporate publishing. For current information on our books, please visit our website, www.southendpress. org; to request a free catalog or make a donation, mail us at South End Press, PO Box 24773, Brooklyn, NY 11202, or email southend@southendpress.org.

Community Supported Publishing

Celebrate the bounty of the harvest! Community Supported Agriculture (CSA) is helping to make independent, healthy farming sustainable. Now there is Community Supported Publishing (CSP)! By joining the South End Press CSP you ensure a steady crop of books guaranteed to change your world. As a member you receive new titles or a choice heirloom selection free each month and a 10% discount on everything else. Subscriptions start at $20/month. To join the movement please visit: www.southendpress.org/2006/items/80129.

RELATED TITLES FROM SOUTH END PRESS

The Revolution Starts at Home: Confronting Intimate Violence Within Activist Communities
Edited by Ching-In Chen, Jai Dulani & Leah Lakshmi Piepzna-Samarasinha

Exile & Pride: Disability, Queerness, and Liberation
by Eli Clare, afterword by Dean Spade

Queerly Classed: Gay Men and Lesbians Write About Class
Edited by Susan Raffo

In Kashmir: Gender, Militarization, and the Modern Nation-State
by Seema Kazi

Black Geographies and the Politics of Place
Edited by Katherine McKittrick and Clyde B. Woods

Our Enemies in Blue: Police and Power in America
by Kristian Williams

When the Prisoners Ran Walpole: A True Story in the Movement for Prison Abolition
by Jamie Bissonette

Incognegro: A Memoir of Exile and Apartheid
by Frank B. Wilderson, III